PLANNING
A Wedding
TO REMEMBER

BEVERLY CLARK

WILSHIRE PUBLICATIONS

To my husband,
After all these years together
I am humbled by the incredible gift we've been given,
a true soulmate and beloved traveling companion on Life's Journey.
Here's to a road which has no end.

Published by Wilshire Publications

Copyright ©1986, 2002 by Beverly Clark

Revised Editions © 1989, 1992, 1995, 1999, 2002 by Beverly Clark

Editorial Director: Robin La Fevers

Book Design: Victoria Torf

Front and Back Cover Photography: Schaf Photo

Black and White Illustrations: Victoria Torf

Copy Editor: Gail Kearns

10 9 8 7 6 5 4 3 2 1

ISBN 0-934081-23-9

Published by Wilshire Publications

A division of Beverly Clark Collection

Distributor to gift and bridal trade

1705 South Waukegan Road • Waukegan, IL 60085

Tel.: (800) 888-6866 • Fax: (866) 238-6331 • www.beverlyclark.com

Distributor to the book trade:

Publishers Group West

1700 Fourth St. • Berkeley, California 94710

Tel.: (510) 528-1444 • Fax: (510) 528-9555

Printed in Hong Kong

the *Wedding*
of

_____

&

_____

who *were*
married

on _____

at _____

by _____

WHAT people *have* SAID *about* PREVIOUS editions *of*

PLANNING
A Wedding
TO REMEMBER

"Beverly Clark is recognized as an authority in the area of wedding planning and wedding necessities. Ms. Clark has done a superb job of leading the bride from the time she says, 'I will,' until after she says, 'I do.' This book will help you through the trauma as well as the pleasure of planning a wedding."

Doris Nixon, National Bridal Service

"Everything you ever wanted to know about weddings and special touches too..."

Los Angeles Times

"Beverly Clark has taken the wedding planning process to a new plane... she covers all of the nuts and bolts and teaches you to plan with class and elegance."

Gerard J. Monagham, President
Association of Bridal Consultants

"Planning a Wedding to Remember offers a thorough look at wedding preparations...its suggestions are...practical and useful...will answer just about any wedding question you'll have."

Leonard Maltin on Video Entertainment Tonight

"An absolute bonanza...author Beverly Clark hasn't left out any detail."

Arthur Stern, Wedding Photographers International

"...one of the most thorough planning tools I've ever seen."

Hallmark Retail Services

"A definite must for anyone planning a wedding."

NBC Network

OTHER *books* BY the *Author*

table of contents

chapter twenty-two

PARTY ON!

chapter twenty-three

THE BUSINESS SIDE OF MARRIAGE

chapter twenty-four

THE SECOND TIME AROUND

chapter twenty-five

PRACTICE MAKES PERFECT

chapter twenty-six

YOUR HONEYMOON

chapter twenty-seven

YOUR WEDDING DAY

WEDDING *calendar* checklist

RULES OF ENGAGEMENT

	12 months	9 to 11 months	6 to 8 months	4 to 5 months	3 months	2 months	1 months	2 weeks	1 week	Wedding Day	After Wedding
Announce your engagement to friends and family ...	❑										
Arrange for an engagement photograph	❑										
Attend any engagement parties		❑									
Announce your engagement in newspaper		❑									

SOLID AS A ROCK

	12 months	9 to 11 months	6 to 8 months	4 to 5 months	3 months	2 months	1 months	2 weeks	1 week	Wedding Day	After Wedding
Shop for an engagement ring	❑										
Shop for wedding rings				❑							
Pick up wedding rings						❑					

PICK A STYLE, ANY STYLE

	12 months	9 to 11 months	6 to 8 months	4 to 5 months	3 months	2 months	1 months	2 weeks	1 week	Wedding Day	After Wedding
Determine your wedding style and formality	❑										
Prioritizing your Minimum Wedding Requirements...	❑										

PLANNING 101

	12 months	9 to 11 months	6 to 8 months	4 to 5 months	3 months	2 months	1 months	2 weeks	1 week	Wedding Day	After Wedding
Hire a bridal consultant if you plan to use one	❑										
Select a date and time for your wedding	❑										
Discuss size of guest list	❑										
Begin compiling guest list	❑										
Begin planning reception		❑									
Research primary wedding vendors		❑									
Send "Save the Date" cards, if using		❑									
Complete guest list				❑							
Coordinate accommodations for out of town guests ...					❑						
Contact guests who have not responded								❑			
Confirm that all vendors received necessary payments...								❑			

ASSET MANAGEMENT

	12 months	9 to 11 months	6 to 8 months	4 to 5 months	3 months	2 months	1 months	2 weeks	1 week	Wedding Day	After Wedding
Come up with a budget you can live with	❑										
Decide who is contributing what financially	❑										

THE HEART AND SOUL OF YOUR WEDDING

	12 months	9 to 11 months	6 to 8 months	4 to 5 months	3 months	2 months	1 months	2 weeks	1 week	Wedding Day	After Wedding
Discuss who will officiate at your ceremony		❑									
Begin discussions with your officiant			❑								
Begin any required pre-marital counseling			❑								
Discuss wedding vows			❑								
Plan ceremony decorations				❑							
Finalize decisions for ceremony, including readings, vocals, etc				❑							
Review ceremony with officiant					❑						
Select ceremony music					❑						

WEDDING *calendar* checklist

THE HEART AND SOUL OF YOUR WEDDING *continued*

	12 months	9 to 11 months	6 to 8 months	4 to 5 months	3 months	2 months	1 months	2 weeks	1 week	Wedding Day	After Wedding
If using personalized wedding vows, begin writing them now					❏						
Finalize ceremony details with officiant						❏					
Finalize ceremony music						❏					
Go over special seating arrangements with ushers									❏		

SETTING YOUR SITES

	12 months	9 to 11 months	6 to 8 months	4 to 5 months	3 months	2 months	1 months	2 weeks	1 week	Wedding Day	After Wedding
Research and reserve your ceremony and reception location	❏										
Discuss on-site catering, if available		❏									

YOUR SUPPORTING CAST

	12 months	9 to 11 months	6 to 8 months	4 to 5 months	3 months	2 months	1 months	2 weeks	1 week	Wedding Day	After Wedding
Select bridal attendants		❏									
Select groom's attendants		❏									
Select responsible person to handle guest book						❏					
Buy thank you gifts for your attendants							❏				

THE COUTURE CONNECTION

	12 months	9 to 11 months	6 to 8 months	4 to 5 months	3 months	2 months	1 months	2 weeks	1 week	Wedding Day	After Wedding
Begin shopping for your wedding gown		❏									
Begin shopping for bridesmaids dresses		❏									
Order your bridal gown. Confirm delivery date.			❏								
Order headpiece and other accessories			❏								
Order bridesmaids' dresses and accessories			❏								
Have the mothers coordinate and select their dresses				❏							
Reserve men's formal wear				❏							
Schedule first bridal gown fitting					❏						
Schedule first bridesmaid gown fitting					❏						
Shop for bridal lingerie					❏						
Experiment with makeup and hairstyles					❏						
Make all hair, nail, and makeup appointments					❏						
Make sure attire for flower girl or ring bearer has been ordered					❏						
Schedule dress fittings						❏					
Final dress fittings							❏				
Begin breaking in bridal footwear							❏				
Pick up wedding gown									❏		
Pick up bridesmaids' dresses									❏		
Pick up groom's attire									❏		
Make sure you have all wedding attire and it fits									❏		

WEDDING *calendar* checklist

THE WRITE STUFF

	12 months	9 to 11 months	6 to 8 months	4 to 5 months	3 months	2 months	1 months	2 weeks	1 week	Wedding Day	After Wedding
Research invitation styles			☑								
Finalize invitation wording (make sure to proofread!)			☑								
Decide on necessary invitation inserts			☑								
Order invitations, inserts, announcements, and thank you notes			☑								
Pick up printed invitations (proof read again upon receipt!)				☑							
Address invitations and announcements				☑							
Put together directions and accommodation cards for out of town guests						☑					
Mail invitations						☑					
Design and print wedding programs, if using						☑					
Designate someone to mail announcements							☑				
Mail announcements											☑
Send wedding picture and announcement to newspaper											☑

A GRAND AFFAIR

	12 months	9 to 11 months	6 to 8 months	4 to 5 months	3 months	2 months	1 months	2 weeks	1 week	Wedding Day	After Wedding
Begin planning your reception		☑									
Compile a list of all rentals needed: tent, tables, chairs, linens, china, cutlery		☑									
Reserve all rental equipment			☑								
Decide on reception decorations			☑								
Make or buy favors for guests				☑							
Arrange for guest parking at ceremony and reception site				☑							
Discuss reception traditions you plan on using					☑						
Order placecards, table numbers, and menu cards for reception					☑						
Confirm final reception details						☑					
Have all accessories, toasting goblets, ring pillow, garter, candles, etc.						☑					
Prepare any wedding toasts								☑			
Plan the seating arrangements for the reception								☑			
Arrange for someone to be in charge of gifts brought to reception								☑			

FEEDING THE MASSES

	12 months	9 to 11 months	6 to 8 months	4 to 5 months	3 months	2 months	1 months	2 weeks	1 week	Wedding Day	After Wedding
Research catering options for reception		☑									
Select a caterer		☑									
Finalize menu				☑							

WEDDING *calendar* checklist

	12 months	9 to 11 months	6 to 8 months	4 to 5 months	3 months	2 months	1 months	2 weeks	1 week	Wedding Day	After Wedding
FEEDING THE MASSES continued											
Confirm all details with caterer	☐	☐	☐	☑	☐	☐	☐	☐	☐	☐	☐
Give head count to caterer and review details	☐	☐	☐	☐	☐	☑	☐	☐	☐	☐	☐
Confirm final guest count	☐	☐	☐	☐	☐	☐	☐	☑	☐	☐	☐
LET THEM EAT CAKE!											
Begin researching wedding cake designers	☐	☐	☑	☐	☐	☐	☐	☐	☐	☐	☐
Order cake	☐	☐	☐	☑	☐	☐	☐	☐	☐	☐	☐
Confirm delivery arrangements with baker	☐	☐	☐	☐	☐	☐	☐	☐	☑	☐	☐
A ROSE BY ANY OTHER NAME											
Research and reserve a florist	☐	☑	☐	☐	☐	☐	☐	☐	☐	☐	☐
Select flowers for the bridal party	☐	☐	☐	☑	☐	☐	☐	☐	☐	☐	☐
Select flowers for the ceremony	☐	☐	☐	☑	☐	☐	☐	☐	☐	☐	☐
Select flowers for the reception	☐	☐	☐	☑	☐	☐	☐	☐	☐	☐	☐
Confirm final details with florist	☐	☐	☐	☐	☐	☑	☐	☐	☐	☐	☐
RHAPSODY IN B MAJOR											
Research bands and DJs	☐	☑	☐	☐	☐	☐	☐	☐	☐	☐	☐
Book the band or DJ	☐	☑	☐	☐	☐	☐	☐	☐	☐	☐	☐
Consider taking dancing lessons, if desired	☐	☐	☐	☐	☑	☐	☐	☐	☐	☐	☐
Confirm all details with musicians	☐	☐	☐	☐	☐	☑	☐	☐	☐	☐	☐
Finalize music selections	☐	☐	☐	☐	☐	☑	☐	☐	☐	☐	☐
Give all musicians the list of music to be played	☐	☐	☐	☐	☐	☐	☑	☐	☐	☐	☐
PRETTY AS A PICTURE											
Research and book a photographer	☐	☑	☐	☐	☐	☐	☐	☐	☐	☐	☐
Confirm final details with photographer	☐	☐	☐	☐	☐	☑	☐	☐	☐	☐	☐
Have a formal bridal portrait taken	☐	☐	☐	☐	☐	☐	☑	☐	☐	☐	☐
Give photographer a list of pictures you want	☐	☐	☐	☐	☐	☐	☑	☐	☐	☐	☐
LIGHTS, CAMERA, ACTION!											
Research and book videographer	☐	☑	☐	☐	☐	☐	☐	☐	☐	☐	☐
Confirm details with videographer	☐	☐	☐	☐	☐	☑	☐	☐	☐	☐	☐
Give videographer list of desired shots	☐	☐	☐	☐	☐	☐	☑	☐	☐	☐	☐
THE LONG AND WINDING ROAD											
Discuss your wedding transportation needs	☐	☐	☑	☐	☐	☐	☐	☐	☐	☐	☐
Reserve your wedding transportation	☐	☐	☑	☐	☐	☐	☐	☐	☐	☐	☐
Distribute transportation provider a schedule (with addresses) for wedding day	☐	☐	☐	☐	☐	☐	☐	☐	☑	☐	☐

Never Look A Gift Horse In The Mouth

	12 months	9 to 11 months	6 to 8 months	4 to 5 months	3 months	2 months	1 months	2 weeks	1 week	Wedding Day	After Wedding
Register for wedding gifts			❏								
Keep a careful record of all gifts received			❏								
Write thank-you notes immediately			❏	❏	❏	❏	❏	❏	❏	❏	❏

Party On!

	12 months	9 to 11 months	6 to 8 months	4 to 5 months	3 months	2 months	1 months	2 weeks	1 week	Wedding Day	After Wedding
Plan bridesmaid's party						❏					
Host bridesmaid's party							❏				
Attend the bachelor/ bachelorette party								❏			
A Wedding Breakfast or Brunch											❏

The Business Side Of Marriage

	12 months	9 to 11 months	6 to 8 months	4 to 5 months	3 months	2 months	1 months	2 weeks	1 week	Wedding Day	After Wedding
Check blood test and marriage license requirements in your state				❏							
Decide where you'll live after the wedding				❏							
Discuss whether or not to have a prenuptial agreement				❏							
Draw up any prenuptial agreement						❏					
Complete all physical and dental appointments							❏				
Get blood test and marriage license							❏				
Get necessary forms to change your name							❏				
Arrange for gifts brought to the reception to be taken to your new home									❏		
Make sure you have your marriage license									❏		

Practice Makes Perfect

	12 months	9 to 11 months	6 to 8 months	4 to 5 months	3 months	2 months	1 months	2 weeks	1 week	Wedding Day	After Wedding
Plan rehearsal dinner				❏							
Finalize plans for wedding rehearsal					❏						
Finalize plans for rehearsal dinner					❏						
Make rehearsal arrangements						❏					
Write detailed minute-by-minute wedding day schedule								❏			
Hand out wedding day schedule									❏		
Have wedding rehearsal									❏		
Have rehearsal dinner									❏		

Your Honeymoon

	12 months	9 to 11 months	6 to 8 months	4 to 5 months	3 months	2 months	1 months	2 weeks	1 week	Wedding Day	After Wedding
Begin researching your honeymoon		❏									
Finalize all honeymoon plans and make any deposits			❏								
Research passport and Visa requirements				❏							

WEDDING *calendar* checklist

YOUR HONEYMOON *continued*

	12 months	9 to 11 months	6 to 8 months	4 to 5 months	3 months	2 months	1 months	2 weeks	1 week	Wedding Day	After Wedding
Shop for any honeymoon clothes	❏	❏	❏	❏	☑	❏	❏	❏	❏	❏	❏
Obtain all passport and visa requirements	❏	❏	❏	❏	☑	❏	❏	❏	❏	❏	❏
Reconfirm all honeymoon reservations	❏	❏	❏	❏	❏	❏	❏	❏	☑	❏	❏
Make sure you have plane tickets	❏	❏	❏	❏	❏	❏	❏	❏	☑	❏	❏
Pack your suitcase	❏	❏	❏	❏	❏	❏	❏	❏	☑	❏	❏

YOUR WEDDING DAY

	12 months	9 to 11 months	6 to 8 months	4 to 5 months	3 months	2 months	1 months	2 weeks	1 week	Wedding Day	After Wedding
Be sure to eat something — you have a big day ahead	❏	❏	❏	❏	❏	❏	❏	❏	❏	❏	☑
Groom should make sure he has the wedding rings and the officiant's fee	❏	❏	❏	❏	❏	❏	❏	❏	❏	❏	☑
Fix hair at least 3 hours before ceremony	❏	❏	❏	❏	❏	❏	❏	❏	❏	❏	☑
Make sure nails are done	❏	❏	❏	❏	❏	❏	❏	❏	❏	❏	☑
Allow plenty of time to apply make-up	❏	❏	❏	❏	❏	❏	❏	❏	❏	❏	☑
Have all accessories together	❏	❏	❏	❏	❏	❏	❏	❏	❏	❏	☑
Start dressing about one-and-a-half hours before ceremony	❏	❏	❏	❏	❏	❏	❏	❏	❏	❏	☑
Get to ceremony location on time	❏	❏	❏	❏	❏	❏	❏	❏	❏	❏	☑
Make sure luggage is in the car or the hotel where you will stay your first night	❏	❏	❏	❏	❏	❏	❏	❏	❏	❏	☑
Give best man and maid of honor the wedding rings	❏	❏	❏	❏	❏	❏	❏	❏	❏	❏	☑
Give officiant's fee to best man	❏	❏	❏	❏	❏	❏	❏	❏	❏	❏	☑
Don't forget to take the marriage license to the ceremony	❏	❏	❏	❏	❏	❏	❏	❏	❏	❏	☑
Have best man and maid of honor sign wedding certificate as witnesses	❏	❏	❏	❏	❏	❏	❏	❏	❏	❏	☑

Start dressing about one-and-a-half hours before ceremony — If pictures are being taken before the ceremony, then have yourself and attendants ready about two hours before the ceremony (photographer and bridal attendants should arrive forty-five minutes to an hour before the ceremony for pictures)

Introduction

*Y*ou've died and gone to heaven. He, you know — the one — finally popped the question and you said (no surprise here) YES! Your feet haven't touched the ground since. Well, soon you'll have to come back down to earth and begin planning the most romantic, exciting, and demanding day of your life.

Weddings carry an enormous weight in that they are a celebration that reflects the full emotional intensity of our decision of who we marry — possibly the most important decision we'll ever make. Toss in the fairy tale dreams of your youth, parent's dreams of a family reunion, and friends' expectation of an extravaganza on par with a Hollywood production, and it's no wonder planning a wedding can cause some people to question their sanity, or at the very least, their grasp on reality.

Rest assured that it can be done, gracefully no less. All it takes is excellent planning, good organizational skills, and the willingness to communicate with all of those involved. In fact, the skills you acquire and use in the planning of your wedding will come in quite handy as you begin your marriage; the ability to listen, compromise, respect each other's needs and boundaries, and still stay passionate and committed to the task at hand. That just about sums up the state of marriage, as well as the way to plan a wedding that celebrates your uniqueness as a couple and the very real commitment you've made to each other.

If you toss in some good grace, a sense of humor, and good old-fashioned fun, well then, that's a sure recipe for success.

In this new and completely updated and revised edition of *Planning a Wedding to Remember*, we've included planning tools and ideas that will help engaged couples remember to have fun and enjoy the planning process. Engaging new tips and ideas, quizzes to help you identify your own personal wedding style, suggestions on how to delegate and compromise, and an entire chapter devoted to the myriad wedding planning tools available on the World Wide Web, are all new to this edition. Of course we've kept all the planning and etiquette advice, checklists, planning calendars, worksheets, gifts, and guest lists that have helped over two million brides plan their weddings so far. But we've jazzed it up some. Made it more fun. We want to help brides and grooms-to-be remember to enjoy the journey, as well as the destination.

Planning your wedding, like your marriage, will be the best of times, and occasionally it will seem like the worst of times. But, if you take the time to do it right, you will successfully set the stage for a beautiful and love-filled life together. ✳

Rules of *Engagement*

SPREADING the *good* news

So you're in love. And this time, it's the Real Thing. Not only do you feel a little thrill every time he walks through the door, but there's that one thing that only he can do, that makes your toes curl and your knees go weak. And most importantly, you feel as if your heart has finally come home. CONGRATULATIONS!!

Finding someone you want to spend the rest of your life with is the emotional equivalent of winning the lottery. (Especially if you've been dating awhile!) It's a time of pure magic, when the anticipation of your life together is exhilarating and full of possibilities. Let yourself linger and enjoy the moment. After all, you will never be newly engaged again, so make the most of it and revel in all the experiences it will bring.

But of course, who wants to linger when you have so many people you can't wait to tell! Actually, for some of you, *tell* might be putting it a bit too mildly. What you really want to do is shout it from the rooftops. It's such a happy secret, how can you possibly keep it under your hat!

→ While you may be tempted to schedule a local parade, hold fast. There is some etiquette and tradition that surrounds the sharing of this good news.

→ The couple should inform the bride's parents first. If the bride's parents have never met the groom, or have voiced some concerns over him in the past, it might be wiser for the bride to tell them privately. In person is always best, but if distance presents an obstacle, then the phone will do quite nicely, thank you. It's certainly much better than to risk having them hear through the grapevine.

→ Often the groom has already discussed his decision with his parents, but if not, they would be next in line for the impending nuptial announcement.

→ You should then try to make arrangements for everyone in both the families to meet as soon as possible.

→ If one of you has children, they need to be the first to know. Have the parent tell them — alone! Even when you anticipate your children's reaction to be positive, there will be many questions. They will feel much safer discussing those questions and concerns openly with you if there's no one else present. Remember that the situation has the potential to be stressful for children, even if they are excited about their new stepparent. They will need lots of reassurances, and it will help if you include them in the process as much as possible.

→ If either of you have an ex-spouse, then you should tell them yourself. Don't let them find out by accident, especially not through one of your children. Also keep in mind that there may be legal issues such as child support, or alimony, that will need to be discussed.

→ Now that you've gotten all the requisite etiquette out of the way, you will also want to phone or write all of your close friends and relatives as soon as possible and let them in on the exciting news. Or, you may decide to surprise them all at once, and announce the wonderful news at a family gathering or party.

ENGAGEMENT PARTIES

Traditionally, it is the bride's parents who claim this honor first, but anyone who wants to throw an engagement party can — including you and your fiancé.

If you are going with tradition and the bride's parents are hosting the party, the engagement announcement is generally made during a toast given by the bride's father or her fiancé. A toast is the perfect way to officially fill the guests in on the exciting news, especially when the news may be a surprise to them. The groom's father or other friends may also want to join in on the fun and toast the happy couple.

Any type of party is perfectly appropriate for an engagement party — a brunch, luncheon, dinner, or cocktail party. Guests can be invited by phone or written invitation, depending on the time and formality of the event. Be sure to avoid hurt feelings by only inviting guests that you also plan on inviting to the wedding.

Often, engagement parties are surprises, where the guests are invited to a party but have no idea regarding the engagement. In that case, the invitations should be a general party invitation. If you want guests to know about the engagement beforehand, you can mention it in the body of the invitation.

"Please join us in celebrating the engagement of . . ."

If you are throwing an engagement party yourself, there are lots of fun ways to celebrate this thrilling occasion. From casual get-togethers to high-style affairs, here are some fun ideas to get you started.

ENGAGEMENT
party
tips

You both must attend all engagement parties.

Gifts are generally not given and should not be expected.

If you do receive gifts, make sure to open them later so you don't risk embarrassing those who didn't bring one.

Make sure to send a thank you note to anyone who did bring a gift.

Thank the hosts of your engagement party with a note and a small gift of flowers, wine, or a dinner invitation.

A beach party, pool party, or barbecue

Nothing beats a relaxed get together with friends and family enjoying the great outdoors. This is a great way to announce your engagement if you've been dating for a long time and your friends have just been waiting for you to get around to becoming engaged.

A wine tasting or microbrewery party

This is a fun, slightly more formal type of gathering where you can let your personality shine through. Serve lots of tasty appetizers with the wine or beer. You might consider printing up cocktail napkins announcing your engagement to use for the evening.

A cocktail party

A cocktail party featuring a new, personalized cocktail named after yourselves — the James and Kara Royale perhaps, or the Mike and Maddy Martini — is a fun way to announce your engagement. Cocktails are making a huge comeback, and a cocktail party is the ultimate in sophisticated entertaining. Pull out all the stops and use fun cocktail glasses. Set up a bar area and consider renting a bartender for the event. A few elegant hors d'oeuvres provide the perfect accompaniment.

A Tex Mex party

Somehow Tex Mex food feels more casual than other dinner parties. It is also a good, easy way to feed lots of people without too much last-minute fuss. Add some ice-cold margaritas and possibly a piñata, and you'll be all set.

An intimate sit-down dinner

The traditional dinner party is an elegant way to announce your engagement. This type of party lends itself particularly well to the engagement announcement being made by a formal toast.

An elegant open house

This is a good way to invite lots of people but avoid overtaxing your entertaining skills. By their very nature, open houses are "drop-in" affairs and you can accommodate a large number of people spread out over a whole afternoon or evening.

A champagne and hors d'oeuvres party

Nothing says celebrate like champagne! Try featuring a wide selection of champagnes that celebrate the bubbly's diversity. If you're feeling very extravagant, you might consider announcing your engagement via a personalized "vintage" of champagne. There are many wineries that offer personalized labels for their wines, and this would certainly be a unique way to let your guests know your good news.

NEWSPAPER ANNOUNCEMENTS

You've personally told everyone you can think of and are now ready to announce your engagement to the world at large. Or at least your hometown.

You can place a formal announcement in both your and your fiancé's local newspapers. You will need to check with your newspaper to see what their policy is. Most often, they will provide forms for you to fill out. Ask whether or not the newspaper will allow you to include an engagement picture. Specify the date on which you want the announcement to appear, and provide your name, address, and "please return" on the back of the picture, as well as a self-addressed stamped envelope to have the picture returned. It is also smart to check if there's a fee for publication of the announcement.

If the parents of the bride are divorced, either parent may announce the engagement, but typically the parent with whom the bride has lived places the announcement. However, both parents should be mentioned in the article. If one parent is deceased, the surviving parent makes the announcement. If both parents are deceased, the engagement may be announced by a relative, a

The Internet is also a great way to announce your engagement, whether you e-mail an announcement or design your own wedding website.

friend, or by the bride herself. As an example, the announcement would read "Susan Elizabeth Petty will be married in September to Robert Lee Townsend." Even when the article appears in the groom's parents' local newspaper, they should not be the ones to make the announcement. The word "late" should precede any reference made to a deceased parent.

The engagement should not be announced prior to one year before the wedding and not later than six weeks ahead of the date.

ENGAGEMENT ANNOUNCEMENT EXAMPLE

To Appear: _____ _____
      (Date) *(Your parents' names)*

                                _____
                                  (Street Address)

                                _____
                                  (City, State, Zip)

                                _____
                                (Area code, telephone number)

Mr. and Mrs. _____ of _____
                 (your parents' names)   *(their city, if out of town)*

announce the engagement of their daughter _____
                                              (your first and middle names)

to _____ the son of
            (your fiancé's first and last names),

Mr. and Mrs._____ of _____
              (your fiancé's parents names)   *(fiancé's parents' city).*

No date has been set for the wedding. (Or, The wedding will take place in _____.)
                                                        (month of wedding).

BROKEN ENGAGEMENTS

Occasionally it happens. And while it is never pleasant, surely it is better to live with a broken engagement than an unhappy marriage. Consider it an important life lesson and move on. But, before you move on, make sure to let family and friends know of your change in plans.

Start by calling or sending a brief note to family and close friends. Remember, no explanation is necessary, just a simple statement of the facts. You'll want to notify your caterer, florist, photographer, and officiator as soon as possible. Once this is done, inform the newspapers that carried your formal announcement by sending them a notice similar to this:

> Mr. and Mrs. Richard Frye announce the engagement of their daughter, Laura, has ended by mutual consent.

Of course, the ring should be given back to your fiancé. Also, any gifts received should be immediately returned to family and friends, even the monogrammed ones. ✳

CHANGE in *plans*

If the invitations have already been sent and time permits, send the guests a printed announcement as follows:

> Mr. and Mrs. Richard Frye announce that the marriage of their daughter, Laura, to Mr. Charles Wiss will not take place.

Solid as a Rock

FINDING *the* perfect ENGAGEMENT *ring*

The first, and possibly largest, dilemma surrounding the engagement ring is whether or not the groom-to-be should surprise his beloved with a ring he's selected himself when he proposes, or should he wait so they can shop together.

Well I can unequivocally say that it depends on the woman involved. Some women (bless them!) will be truly thrilled with anything their fiancé picks out, precisely because it was what he picked out for her. Then there are the rest of us. For better or for worse, many women (bless them!) can't help but want to have some input on the life-changing, with-them-forever-till-the-day-they-die piece of jewelry.

To put it in simpler terms for puzzled fiancés-to-be, how would you feel if she bought you jockey shorts for the rest of your married life when you really preferred boxers? You'd wear them (maybe), but there'd always be that little pinch, that constant reminder that what you were wearing was really not your preference. Keep in mind that the selection of a ring involves much more than mere aesthetics. There are also issues of how comfortable the ring will feel on her finger, and how the style of it will stack up against her lifestyle. Would you want her to select your wedding band with no input from you?

If you really want to surprise her, there are some ways to get at least an idea of her more basic preferences. When you're out together, try noticing someone wearing an especially noteworthy ring. Nudge your future fiancé and whisper, "Take a look at that rock, will you!" There's a chance you can then gracefully segue the conversation into a general discussion of ring styles.

You can also pay attention to her other jewelry. Does she always wear yellow gold? Silver? Is her taste classic and conservative? Does she work a lot with her hands, possibly ruling out any setting that sticks out too far? Does she have sensitive skin prone to allergies that would perhaps require her to consider 18K gold vs. 14K. The biggest risk here is that sometimes women have much different taste and fantasies regarding their engagement ring when compared to their everyday type of jewelry.

SELECTING THE RING

There are an unbelievable variety of styles out there to choose from, and if you can't find what you like, many jewelers will be happy to design one to your precise specifications. Most brides tend to gravitate toward a diamond for their engagement ring, although it's certainly not required. You can choose any stone you like. However, before you even begin shopping, whether together or alone, you will need to determine your budget.

HOW MUCH TO SPEND?

An important mantra to chant as you begin your shopping together is, *A bigger diamond does not guarantee a better marriage.* Keep this in mind at all times since you may be tempted (or urged) to overspend.

Talk with your fiancé. This might be a good time to bring up a general discussion of financial goals and priorities. Admittedly, this can be an awkward conversation, so it's a good time to trot out those two golden bastions of engaged and married life — communicate and compromise. Listening to each other is critical, as is making a sincere effort to refrain from reading more into the situation than is there. Just because he isn't thrilled with the idea of spending a great sum of money on an engagement ring, doesn't mean he doesn't love you. Maybe it's always been a dream of his to own a house for his bride to live in. That is equally romantic, though not as easy to wear on your finger and flash in front of your admiring friends, saying, "Check this out."

Whatever your budget, rest assured that the perfect ring is out there, just waiting for you – whether it's an extravagant $10,000 showpiece, or a more delicate ring, still big on style but with a more manageable price tag in the $1,000 and under range.

If you can't spend as much as you'd like on an engagement ring, here are some suggestions that may help:

- 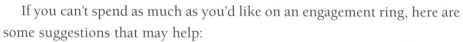 Consider a slender, plain gold or platinum wedding band without additional diamonds on it.

- 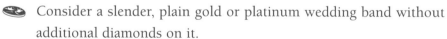 Consider a ring that is styled in such a way that you can have it altered or restyled later when finances might not be as tight.

- White or yellow gold is much less costly than the trendier platinum.

- Decide on a smaller ring now with the intention of rewarding yourself with an anniversary band later.

- Consider a stone other than a diamond. Rubies, sapphires, emeralds, peridots, aquamarines, tourmalines, or perhaps your birthstone, all make spectacular rings.

- Look for a delicate ring that still has strong elements of style in the workmanship: elaborate metalworking, the smallest wink of a diamond, etc.

SHOPPING FOR THE RING

When shopping for a ring that most clearly illustrates the depth of your love for each other (how's that for a tall order for a measly little ring to fill?), make sure you deal with a reliable, reputable jeweler. Choose one who has been in business for a long time or ask friends and relatives for recommendations. Look for a jeweler (or a store with a gemologist on staff) who has a diploma or certificate from the Gemological Institute of America. This indicates the jeweler has had formal training in his or her field. Shop around and compare several rings from different jewelers and avoid shops that pressure you to buy on the spot. Shop with a note pad to record GIA's designation of the various stones. Ask to see samples of diamonds in various colors and clarity grades. You can probably find a stone in the middle of the scale and avoid paying for status you — or anyone else — can't discern. Once the size and the GIA color and clarity grade have been determined, then you can compare similar stones for the best price.

DIAMONDS

If you are going with the traditional choice of a diamond, here are the essential Four C's you need to keep in mind when selecting one. Color — along with cut and clarity — determine the price per carat.

Color – The clearer the diamond, the greater its value. Diamonds are graded on a scale with the greater amount of color in the stone, the lower the stone's value. The only exception is for very rare colored diamonds, which are extremely valuable. Clear or colorless stones are referred to as perfect.

Cut – (Not to be confused with Shape) Accuracy in cutting is essential to the beauty and sparkle of the diamond and determines its brilliance and flash. The stones are proportioned and faceted to maximize the brilliance through their crowns. Imperfect stones, cut by a skilled jeweler, can still sparkle and shine like there's no tomorrow (and when you're in love, there isn't).

Clarity – This is the term that refers to the internal flaws contained within a stone (also known as inclusions). The fewer flaws within a diamond, the more light is reflected. If they are large and visible to the naked eye, they will also affect the beauty of the stone; otherwise, they will only affect the value. Flawless or perfect stones are stones with no imperfections, and obviously the most valuable and expensive. However, if the inclusions are not visible, it's possible to find an imperfect stone that is more brilliant (see Cut) and contains less color, therefore appearing more "perfect" than a flawless stone.

GEMOLOGICAL *institute* *of* america

The GIA assigns letters of the alphabet to colors, beginning with the letter D as the clearest color and down to the letter L classification (except AD, which is reserved for the very finest jewels).

The GIA also grades the inclusions or imperfections of a stone, which is also important to know in order to comparison shop effectively. Their grading system begins with FL, for flawless diamond, a stone which contains no imperfections that can be seen with a 10x jeweler's loupe. It goes down from there to VVS (very, very small spots), VS (very small spots), all the way to a I3 diamond, which has obvious imperfections. The average person usually can't find any flaws with the naked eye down to a VS2 designation.

Ask your jeweler to show you similar size stones in varying color and clarity, to enable you to select the one that fits both your taste and budget. Once you've determined the size and quality stone you like (for example a .60 carat, K color, VS1 brilliant cut), then you can compare other similar stones to find the best price.

WHAT to *do if a jeweler has misrepresented a stone?*

Contact the Jewelers Vigilance Committee, 25 West 45th St., New York, New York 10036. Their phone number is 212-997-2002. This group can investigate your complaint and take action against fraudulent firms in the jewelry business.

CONSIDER *this*

A trend emerging in the diamond industry is brand name diamonds. Some companies such as Di3tar and Lazare, have patented technology that allows them to create innovative ways of cutting diamonds, enhancing their brilliance in unique ways. You might consider one of these exclusive cuts, but be forewarned. They are usually more costly.

Another style trend

is the resurgence of interest in heirloom rings. These diamonds were cut in accordance with older technology and can be less brilliant than modern rings. Because of that, it is possible to get a larger diamond for less money due to the older style cut. If this vintage look appeals to you, be sure to research this option. The estate sections of jewelry stores or old estate sales are great places to start.

Carats – Diamonds, just like cereal and crackers, are sold by weight, not volume. Their weight is referred to as carats. This is the size of the diamond and, along with color, cut and clarity, will determine its price. A higher-quality, smaller diamond may be worth more than a lower-quality, larger stone. As the size increases from one carat to over two or three, the price per carat increases tremendously.

Shape – The brilliant or round cut is the most common. Other shapes include oval, pear, marquise, emerald cut, and heart-shaped. Look at a variety of shapes so that you can see how the cut of the different shapes affects its sparkle.

| Brilliant | Oval | Pear | Marquis | Emerald Cut | Heart Shape |

Once you've decided on the diamond, have an independent appraiser appraise it before you finalize the purchase. Most jewelers in America either use or recognize the classifications of the Gemological Institute of America. Ask your jeweler for the GIA's rating of color and clarity on each stone you're considering. Once the appraiser has confirmed what the jeweler has claimed, it's safe to buy.

SETTINGS

After you've decided on a diamond that is forever in your eyes, you will need to consider settings. Metal choices consist of gold, either white or yellow, and platinum. Right now, the platinum trend is on the upswing, but at nearly twice the cost of gold per ounce, it will swing that price tag right on up there, too.

INSURANCE

The Gemological Institute of America, 580 5th Avenue, New York, New York 10036, 212-944-5900, will grade your stone and provide a certificate with unquestionable proof of your diamond's identity as well as its grade. Make sure to get a written guarantee and permanent registration for the diamond when you purchase it. Then get a written appraisal of the replacement value for insurance purposes. You should list the diamond separately on your personal property insurance policy. In the event that you don't have such a policy, see about adding the diamond to your parents' policy temporarily. Have your ring re-appraised every few years and increase your insurance policy accordingly. ✳

ENGAGEMENT *ring* worksheet

Stone	store #1	store #2	store #3	store #4	store #5
Jewelry Store					
Size (number of carats)					
Cut (shape of stone)					
Color (grade D-L)					
Setting (14ᴋ, 18ᴋ yellow gold, white gold, platinum)					
Price per carat					
Total Price					

Final Choice

Stone Description _____ Price _____

Setting Description _____ Price _____

Total Price _____

Jewelry Store _____

Address _____

Phone Number _____

Sales Representative _____

Other _____

JEWELRY *shopping* worksheet

Store Information	Engagement Ring	Bride's Wedding Ring	Groom's Wedding Ring	Other Jewelry	Total Cost
Name, phone, salesperson	*Description & Cost*	*Description & Cost*	*Description & Cost*	*Description & Cost*	

Jeweler Final Choice

Address Information: _____

Final Selection: _____

Deposit Paid: _____

Balance Due: _____

Delivery Date: _____

Pick a Style, Any Style

DEFINING your *wedding* VISION

Some of you may have been planning your wedding since you were three years old. Others, perhaps, vowed never to walk down the aisle, having found that perfect someone merely the icing on the cake of your well planned life, so planning a wedding is a mere afterthought. Add to that the fact that many of us plan our weddings with different goals in mind. For some, it is the ultimate in romantic statements as to who you are as a couple. For others, it's the perfect chance to throw the party of a lifetime, and for yet others, it's a superb opportunity to have everyone you love under one roof. Then there are those of us who are just dying to star in our own Hollywood production or Cinderella fantasy. Whatever your goal, if you have one, weddings can be as unique as the brides and grooms who plan them.

Traditionally, wedding style has primarily been the degree of formality that you choose for your celebration. However, just as personal style is much more than the clothes you buy or the way you wear your hair, so too is wedding style much more than the degree of formality you decide upon. Style is that indefinable something that sets your look apart from the rest of the world; the subtle little details as well as the sweeping grand gesture. The colors you choose, yes, but more importantly, how you apply them. True style is an extension of who you are, as much a part of your personality as your sense of humor or whether you are shy or outgoing.

Some of you know exactly what your style is, and how to interpret it for any event that comes up. Others are less sure, so now is a perfect time to sit down and try to define your personal wedding style. You can use the following quiz to get you thinking in the right direction.

WHAT'S your Wedding STYLE?

1. *You love shopping for clothes at:*
   A. Stores that carry unstructured clothes with clean simple lines in luscious neutral tones.
   B. Department stores that carry a good variety and selection as well as the chance for a great sale.
   C. Small boutiques whose signature style reflects your own.
   D. Eclectic describes your shopping haunts as well as your style. Vintage clothing stores to the Army/Navy Surplus and everything in between so you can pull together your own personal look.
   E. High-end department stores where the personal shoppers all know you by name.
   F. Straight off the runways, if you can afford it, and designer outlets if you can't.

2. *Which words would you like to describe your wedding?*
   A. Creative, elemental, spiritual, simple, contemporary
   B. Traditional, lovely, romantic, festive
   C. Delicate, ethereal, fantasy, romantic, magical, sentimental
   D. Avante garde, hip, urban, unique, lively
   E. Sophisticated, elegant, chic, luxurious, polished
   F. Lavish, dramatic, glamorous, theatrical, grand, elaborate

3. *You have been dreaming of your wedding:*
   A. You've never really thought about it.
   B. The day you discovered you were head over heels in love.
   C. Since you were a little girl, planning and fantasizing the whole time.
   D. Wedding? Oh, gosh. I guess if we're getting married we're going to need to have a wedding!
   E. Occasionally, thinking how fabulous it would be, when you met the right man.
   F. Since the day you were born.

4. *Your favorite flowers are:*
   A. Peonies
   B. Roses
   C. Lilies of the Valley or Sweet Peas
   D. Orchids
   E. Tulips
   F. Narcissus

5. *What do you consider the most important function of your wedding ceremony?*
   A. To express the intimate, spiritual connection between the two of you.
   B. Pledging your love and devotion to one another while maintaining cultural and family traditions.
   C. Experiencing the most romantic day of your entire life.
   D. Exchanging vows that are as unique and complex as your love for each other.
   E. Creating a tasteful celebration of your mutual love and commitment.
   F. Proclaiming your love for one another for the whole world to see.

6. *Your favorite drink is:*
   A. Pure mineral water
   B. Chardonnay — smooth and classic
   C. Strawberry Daiquiris — sweet and frothy
   D. Cosmopolitans
   E. Dry Martini
   F. Champagne — preferably Dom Perignon

7. *When dressing for a night out on the town you wear:*
   A. A slim column of textured raw silk.
   B. A special dress you bought just for the occasion.
   C. Something flirty and feminine.
   D. A funky combination of retro chic with designer accents.
   E. Basic blacks with a plunging back and incredible earrings.
   F. A red dress that shows your curves to their best advantage.

8. *It was the size of your fiancé's [fill in the blank] that attracted you to him in the first place.*

   A. Soul

   B. Brain

   C. Heart

   D. Sense of humor

   E. Resume

   F. Private jet

9. *Your favorite workout is:*

   A. Yoga, swimming

   B. Aerobics, running, golf

   C. Horseback riding, ballet

   D. Kick boxing, tae bo, rock climbing

   E. Sailing, tennis

   F. Running to catch a taxi in your stiletto heels

10. *Your favorite romantic movie is:*

   A. *Sense and Sensibility, Crouching Dragon, Hidden Tiger*

   B. *Emma, You've Got Mail*

   C. *Runaway Bride, Shakespeare in Love*

   D. *Nurse Betty, As Good As It Gets*

   E. *Sabrina, What Women Want*

   F. *Pretty Woman, Breakfast at Tiffany's*

11. *Your wedding budget is:*

   A. Sufficient for the simple celebration you have in mind.

   B. Comfortable, since all of you are contributing.

   C. So tight it squeaks.

   D. Hip, funky and creative doesn't necessarily translate into lots of $$$.

   E. Coming up with the funds is no problem.

   F. The sky's the limit.

12. *You spend time outdoors:*

   A. Often — you have a deep appreciation for all the elements of nature and love to walk in the rain as well as enjoy a sunny day.

   B. Frequently — while pursuing the many outdoor activities you enjoy.

   C. Whenever the mood strikes.

   D. Any time you are pursuing your latest adventure: scuba diving, rock climbing, parachuting, etc.

   E. For an occasional walk, game of tennis, or to sit at a sidewalk café.

   F. Long enough to dash from one building to the next.

WHAT is your STYLE? Here are the answers!
(Don't peek until you've completed the test!)

If you answered mostly A's, you are the Zen Bride.

You are a minimalist in all things. You prefer to allow a simple and quiet beauty to shine through. For you, it's all about a simple presentation of the elements involved — elements that you have painstakingly chosen for their unique individual, understated elegance. Your style could be summed up as: A whisper that shouts.

For your bridal gown, as well as other facets of your wedding and reception, you'll be drawn to clean lines and fabrics that underscore your beauty as opposed to overwhelm it. You are drawn to natural fabrics and elements of nature as part of your style.

Celebrate the simple beauty of life. Unfussy, with an easygoing spirit.

If you answered mostly B's,
then you are the Classic Traditionalist.

You love the classics. White shirts, blue jeans, khaki chinos, and little black cocktail dresses with pearls are the staples of your life. And you wear them with flair, allowing your fresh clean beauty to shine through. You cherish the traditions that have been a part of your life because, well, they're tradition. You look forward to incorporating all of that into your own wedding. Nothing too out of the ordinary, certainly nothing too trendy, you embrace tradition in all its forms. You love the solid strength of traditional choices along with the sense of being a part of a larger community of brides who have followed these same traditions for years.

If your answers were mostly C's,
then you are Hopelessly Romantic.

This is not just a great party, it's a celebration of your love for one another. More than the other styles, you seek to infuse every aspect of your wedding with emotional significance. Your romantic nature can take a playful, whimsical approach, or can be of the epic proportions of Victorian or Medieval eras. You are the bride most likely to drive away in a horse-drawn carriage amid a flock of perfectly timed doves.

If you answered mostly D's,
then you are the Adventurous Trendsetter.

Never one to sit back and let others take the lead, you are out there in the forefront of fashion and lifestyle trends. You've already put yourself on the list of potential Space Shuttle passengers and you were the first one in your state to get a tattoo (tongue piercing, belly ring). If there are more than three other people doing it, then to you it's passé. Not only do you march to the tune of a different drummer, you are the drummer! Daring does not even begin to describe you. You might consider exchanging your vows in a hot air balloon, or from some tropical spot no one you know can even pronounce. If you do have a more traditional celebration, then you'll infuse it with your own eclectic taste — perhaps one of the softly colored wedding gowns instead of the traditional white or ivory. Or saying vows the two of you have written yourselves to uniquely describe your feelings for each other, and incorporating unusual elements at the reception.

If you answered mostly E's,
then you are a Polished Sophisticate.

Elegance drips from your pores just as certainly as other women drip saltwater after stepping out of the ocean. You've been tempted to smoke merely so you could hold a cigarette lighter and flick it about, a refined extension to your already graceful fingers. Your wedding will be the ultimate in polished elegance; from the sophisticated gown you wear to the oh-so-refined menu at your reception. Everyone will feel as if they've just been entertained by royalty.

If you answered mostly F's,
then you are a Glamour Queen.

You can make a terry cloth robe look like high fashion and are one of the few women you know to wear false eyelashes on a regular basis.

The spotlight was invented just for you, and your wedding is the perfect opportunity to showcase your flair and love of drama. You are at your most comfortable when all eyes are on you. Nothing is too grand for your day, not that haute couture wedding gown, nor the 3-carat engagement ring your fiancé had designed just for you. You will pull out all the stops for your wedding and it will be THE event of the decade, which is just exactly how you planned it.

CURRENT TRENDS

From splashy, grand affairs to smaller celebrations sporting unexpected atmospheres or lavish details, simple and elegant are the watchwords in today's weddings. No matter how practical, logical or matter-of-fact we may be in real life, every bride-to-be is enchanted with the idea of a romantic wedding. The beauty of it is that romance can be achieved in a variety of unique and individual ways.

Out Is In – From simple to spectacular, brides are taking their weddings outside to enjoy the splendors of nature; whether an elegant garden party at an estate garden, the sweeping Pacific, or a breathtaking mountaintop.

Grand Ballrooms Are Back – Embracing all the elegance and formality of yesterday, brides are opting for big, lavish celebrations, often including large live bands or orchestras.

The Wedding Cake as an Art Form – Wedding cakes and the artisans who create them have moved to the forefront of the wedding scene. The creators of wedding cakes are giving their imagination and artistic abilities free reign, creating masterpieces embellished with all manner of cascading sugar spun artwork, or breathtaking florals.

Food – Gone are the basic traditional chicken breast and prime rib, making way for sophisticated menu selections, with three-course sit-down dinners being the trend to watch for. Stylishly prepared fish and chicken, grilled meats, and elegant presentations are the choice du jour.

New Bars – The coffee bar and the martini bar have been popular for a while, and now the new kids in town are the champagne bar, hot chocolate bar, and dessert bar. Also, some couples are coming up with a signature drink, the Cosmopolitan, Kir Royale, flavored martinis, or having one designed especially for them to serve at their reception.

IF THE THEME FITS — WEAR IT

Themes are a great way to find an element or two and weave it throughout your festivities, making it a unified celebration.

SEASONS

Winter – Washes of silver or gold played out against the elegant and seasonal backdrop of white make for a festive, wintery wedding. Incorporate the trappings of your winter holiday celebration into the theme, giving ornaments as favors, or using evergreens as part of the decorations. And don't forget the twinkle lights or candles, the perfect way to perpetuate the iridescence of the season.

Spring – This season of new beginnings makes a charming theme for a wedding. Take advantage of the bounties that spring has to offer — plentiful flowers and foods just coming into season. Continue the theme throughout the reception with lots and lots of fresh flowers (sprinkle petals in the punch or place a petal or two in the champagne glasses) and perhaps prettily wrapped flower bulbs or seed packets for favors.

Summer – The long lazy days of summer just beg for a wedding in the splendor of the out of doors, with the beach or seashore enjoying a surge of popularity. These types of celebrations lend themselves to an easy, relaxed elegance, gently billowing tents, lots of shade-producing umbrellas, paper lanterns, and menus featuring fresh seafood and tropical fruit. More fresh fruit, exotic flowers, and seashells can be used for decorations.

Autumn – Autumn signifies the bounty of Mother Nature, resplendent in rich colors and varied textures. Use flowers in deep rich colors, adding foliage, autumn leaves, sheaths of wheat, and decorative grasses to take full advantage of the season. The added glow of candlelight keeps the look warm and welcoming.

*Some good movies
to inspire you
if you are
considering a historical
theme would be:*

>*Elizabeth*
>
>*Shakespeare in Love*
>
>*Emma*
>
>*Sense and Sensibility*
>
>*Jane Eyre*
>
>*Wuthering Heights*
>
>*The First Knight*
>
>*Bugsy*

HOLIDAY themes

Valentine's Day

Easter

May Day

Fourth of July

Halloween

Thanksgiving

Christmas

New Year's Eve

Mardi Gras

Carnival

SPORTS and hobbies

Nautical

Golf

Western

Derby Day

Ascot

Mystery

Aprés Ski

CULTURAL or ethnic

Scottish

Asian Tea Ceremony

Irish Gaelic

Native American

New Age

Viennese

French Provençal

Luau

Southern

Country

HISTORICAL themes

Victorian

Regency

Renaissance

Medieval

Roaring 20's

Midnight

Green-Eco

DECIDING ON FORMALITY

Traditionally, it was the degree of formality that determined the elements of your wedding, such as location, number of guests invited, time of the ceremony, and the bride's attire. While there is greater flexibility today, the degree of formality you select for your wedding will be helpful to you as you go forward in determining your wedding style. Here are some general guidelines as to what is standard with each degree of formality.

VERY FORMAL

Ceremony – House of worship or hotel.

Attendants – Eight to ten bridesmaids and eight to ten ushers, a maid or matron of honor, the best man, one or two flower girls and a ring bearer.

Attire – Bridal gown with long train and veil, long sleeves or gloves, and a full bouquet. Bridesmaids wear long gowns, which can be very dressy. Groom and ushers often wear cutaways or tailcoats. For a very formal wedding taking place after 6:00 PM, women guests dress in long or short evening dresses and the men in tuxedos. Before 6:00 PM, the women would wear elegant suits or short dresses, and the men suits.

Size – Usually 200 plus guests.

Reception – Large and elaborate sit-down dinner or buffet. Generally includes an orchestra for dancing and floral displays for the tables.

Details - Engraved invitations, formal photography.

FORMAL

Ceremony – House of worship, hotel, large home, or garden.

Attendants – Four to eight bridesmaids and four to eight ushers, a maid or matron of honor, the best man, a flower girl, and a ring bearer.

Attire – Bridal gown and veil in a complementary length, and a full bouquet. Bridesmaids' gowns can be floor, tea, or ballerina length. Groom and ushers – formal suits or tuxedos. Women guests would wear elegant suits, long or short dresses, and the men black tie or suits, depending on the time of the wedding.

Size – Usually 200 guests.

Reception – Sit-down dinner or buffet, usually includes an orchestra or live band for dancing and floral displays for the tables.

Details – Formal invitations, formal photography.

SEMI-FORMAL

Ceremony – Often takes place at the same location as the reception. Wide variety of locales, house of worship, church, chapel, hotel, club, banquet hall, home, or garden.

Attendants – Two to six bridesmaids and ushers, a maid or matron of honor, the best man, a flower girl, and a ring bearer.

Attire – Bridal gown may be long, ballet length or shorter. Bridesmaids' gowns should complement the style selected by the bride and can be of any length. Groom and ushers generally wear suits, as do male guests. Female guests can wear any length dress or suit.

Size – Usually 75 - 200 guests.

Reception – Buffet or cocktail party, small band, DJ, or orchestra.

DETAILS – Less traditional and individualized.

INFORMAL

Ceremony – Can take place in a wide variety of locations including parks, beaches, unusual locations.

Attendants – One to three bridesmaids and ushers, a maid or matron of honor, the best man.

Attire – Appropriate wedding attire might be a street or ankle length dress, or a suit in white or pastel. Does not even have to be a "wedding gown" per se. Let the overall style of the wedding dictate the attire requirements.

Size – 100 or fewer guests.

Reception – Restaurant, home, garden. Again, a wide variety of locales are options for the informal celebration. Refreshments may consist of champagne, punch and cake, or cocktails and hors d'oeuvres.

Details – Flowers and decorations optional, the invitations may be as informal as a handwritten note, background music from musician or tapes or CDs.

WHAT *is* your DEGREE *of* formality?

If you're still undecided, here's a quick quiz to help you sort through your choices.

1. *How much money do you have to spend on your wedding?*
   A. $8,000 or less
   B. $9,000 - $14,000
   C. $15,000 - $23,000
   D. $24,000 plus

2. *Your wedding will be paid for by:*
   A. You and your fiancé
   B. Your parents
   C. His parents
   D. All of the above

3. *Your first choice for a ceremony and reception location would be:*

A. Beach, park, garden, or an exotic locale like ski slopes or tropical destination

B. A private home, garden, restaurant, banquet hall, historical building

C. Hotel, banquet hall, private club, museum

D. House of worship, ballroom

4. *You plan to invite:*

A. Family and a few close intimate friends.

B. Your large extended families and lots and lots of friends.

C. In addition to the above, there are many additional acquaintances you wish to invite, perhaps a few business associates.

D. Everyone you, your fiancé, and your respective families ever met – you have quite large social obligations.

5. *You are:*

A. Shy and retiring

B. Neither shy nor outgoing

C. While not quite a party animal – you do love a good time

D. Very comfortable in large crowds

6. *In general, you feel that a wedding:*

A. Should be a small, intimate affair with lots of personal meaning.

B. Should be an incredibly romantic and personalized affair.

C. Should be a lavish celebration to celebrate your love for each other.

D. Is your shining moment to fulfill every fantasy you've ever dreamed.

If you answered mostly A's, you will most likely be comfortable with an informal wedding. Mostly B's suggest that a semi-formal celebration will be most in keeping with your personal tastes. If C was the answer you came up with the most often, then you should at least consider a formal wedding, and if you answered mostly D's, then you very likely will need a very formal wedding in order to be satisfied.

PRIORITIZING OR THE MINIMUM WEDDING REQUIREMENTS (MWRs)

Before you begin soliciting too many other opinions, especially from those with a vested interest such as your mother or your future mother-in-law, you and your fiancé should have your MWRs (Minimum Wedding Requirements) firmly established in your own mind. Other than those few issues, allow yourself to listen to the opinions of others who are involved. Decide if something is a show stopper and will keep you from enjoying your celebration. If the answer is no, then think about letting go.

Both of you will have some elements of the wedding that are vitally important to your idea of the perfect wedding. Each of you should firmly establish these in your own minds and then discuss them. Maybe you've always envisioned your wedding as a legitimate excuse to throw that debutante ball you secretly wanted. Or it will be your one chance to play Sleeping Beauty, Cinderella, or some other fairy princess. Fine. But suppose your fiancé becomes claustrophobic at the mere thought of a church or cathedral. Maybe he wants to get married in a hot air balloon, which is not exactly how you'd envisioned exchanging your vows.

Keep in mind, when determining your MWRs, this is where compromising comes in and you might as well get used to it because you will be doing a lot of it over the lifetime of your marriage.

WEDDING OPTIONS

What if one afternoon or evening just isn't enough time for the celebration you have in mind? What's an affianced couple to do?

Well you're in good company! More and more couples are choosing to host a Weekend Wedding, Destination Wedding, or Progressive Wedding. These alternate ways to wed are hugely popular today and work especially well for those wanting a small, truly unique experience, who are marrying for the second time, or whose guest list for a traditional wedding is towering near the 300 mark.

THE WEEKEND WEDDING

The perfect solution when your parents live in Portland, your sister, who is to be your maid of honor, in Los Angeles, his parents are based in Houston, and his four siblings are scattered across the country like a handful of wildflower seeds. In fact, now that you have your guest list in front of you, you realize that only you, your fiancé, and nine of your closest friends live in the town where you're planning your wedding.

This entry to the wedding scene is part mini-vacation, part wedding, part family reunion, part weekend-long party, and loads of fun for all your nearest and dearest who will be flying in from all points north and south. Devoting an entire weekend to the wedding and its related parties and events gives everyone a chance to spend more time together. You won't feel quite so much like everything went by in a four-hour blur, and you will all have an unforgettable time.

While it does involve a little extra planning on your part, many of your friends and family will most likely be willing to pitch in and help.

The "Wedding Weekend Plan" is just to give you an example; the options are endless. The following are some ideas for parties and activities:

→ Barbecue and pool party.
→ Picnic at the beach or a park.
→ Organize a golf or tennis tournament.
→ Play a softball game.
→ Hire a cartoonist, astrologer, tarot card reader, or magician to entertain guests at an evening event.
→ Host a Hawaiian luau.

Since guests will NOT want to miss this event of the decade, they'll need plenty of time to plan for this fun-filled weekend. It is a good idea to send a preliminary itinerary or announcement well in advance of the actual wedding invitation. As the date approaches, send a schedule of the activities and parties that are planned. Mention any additional cost guests might incur for an activity, and tip them off to the appropriate attire; shorts, jeans, bathing suits, or formal attire. Include information on travel or lodging arrangements. Even though guests are responsible for their own travel and hotel costs, you might reserve a group of rooms at a reduced rate. Any savings would be much appreciated. Additionally, if you have family that live in town, talk with them about the possibility of putting up some out-of-town relatives or friends.

A weekend *wedding*

FRIDAY
You might start the weekend by having a friend or relative host a welcoming party Friday evening. This could also be an outdoor barbecue, a catered picnic at a park, or take place at someone's home or a restaurant. Another option is to expand the rehearsal dinner to include your out-of-town guests.

SATURDAY
A luncheon, picnic, or barbecue, hosted by another relative or friend, can lead an afternoon of activities. Plan a golf tournament, touch football, bowling, tennis match, or game of croquet. Everyone is invited. Make sure to have a list of local attractions for guests to pursue on their own, if they're so inclined.

SATURDAY EVENING
A formal evening wedding and reception, starting at 6:00 or 6:30 PM, would make the perfect ending to a great day.

SUNDAY
The bride and groom stay in town to greet their guests at a late morning garden brunch, followed by an afternoon softball game.

SUNDAY EVENING
The bride and groom may choose to say their good-byes and leave for their honeymoon as guests leave at their leisure. Or they may all decide to stay for a Pizza Party that evening and say their good-byes over coffee and muffins the next morning.

DESTINATION WEDDINGS

Destination weddings are exactly what they sound like. Getting married at some far-away destination — usually a romantic vacation spot — is sort of like eloping, but with a few close friends and family along. You and your guests can enjoy a few memorable days at a beautiful beach in Mexico, Hawaii, or the Caribbean, or on a ski slope in Aspen or the French Alps. Consider a grand castle in England or Scotland, or a charming villa in Italy or the south of France. The options are limited only by your imagination, and the experience is one you and your guests will remember.

Destination weddings are one of the hottest trends going — and with good reason! They can be much simpler and (surprisingly!) less costly to plan than a traditional wedding. One drawback, however, is that their very nature dictates a somewhat smaller, more intimate circle of friends and family in attendance. Although for some, that may be an advantage.

Destination weddings work particularly well for people who feel obliged to invite 300 guests if they have their wedding anywhere near their hometown. This type of wedding allows them to keep the celebration small and intimate. However, a destination wedding can be as intimate and informal, or as large and elaborate, as you'd like it to be. Many are second marriages where the couple wants to include their children. It allows everyone to feel included and provides lots of opportunities for the two families to spend time together.

Wedding Ideas

The following are a few destination wedding ideas; the options are only limited by your imagination and your budget. Contact your travel agent to get ideas, surf the Net, consult our Weddinglocation.com website, or choose a location that already has a special meaning for you.

* A tropical location – Hawaii, Bermuda, the Caribbean, Mexico, Puerto Rico.

* A cruise ship or river boat.

* A train trip, perhaps the Orient Express.

* A bicycle tour in the Napa Valley wine country, if your hobby is bicycling.

* What about a dude ranch, camping at a favorite lake, or renting houseboats for those who prefer a rustic getaway?

* If your budget's unlimited, charter a plane and fly your guests to your favorite castle in Scotland, or cruise the Mediterranean on a private yacht.

* Plan a ski wedding — there are a large number of great resorts, both in the United States and abroad.

* Make it a cultural experience with a trip to Egypt, Israel, Greece, or Japan.
* Check local resort towns near your wedding site, to which guests could drive.
* For more ideas, pick up travel magazines, bridal magazines, or travel books about an area you're considering.

LOGISTICS

Before you set your heart on any one particular spot, you need to do a little investigating and research the rules and requirements for marrying there. Every state has different laws and regulations. Some countries make it almost impossible to be married there. France requires a thirty-day residency prior to the wedding, and other countries require even longer stays. Bermuda makes it easy by requiring only a "Notice of Intended Marriage" be published in the newspaper three weeks before the marriage, which can be arranged in advance, long distance. Make sure to thoroughly check out the legalities before you make your arrangements! The destination's embassy or tourist board would be a great place to begin.

PROGRESSIVE WEDDING

This type of wedding is a great alternative when not everyone you'd like to celebrate with can travel to the same location; the bride and groom simply travel to them. It's the perfect choice for couples whose families and friends live in different parts of the country, or for a bride or groom with divorced parents who don't want to attend the same event.

Let's say the bride's family lives in New York, the groom's family is in Los Angeles, and the couple now lives in Texas where many of their friends also reside. The wedding ceremony and reception hosted by the bride's parents would be in New York. Then the couple would travel to Los Angeles to a reception given by the groom's parents for his family and friends. Upon returning home to Texas, the newlyweds, or a close friend, host a reception for those friends who were unable to attend the other two.

Those receptions following the original ceremony may be as formal as the first wedding reception, informal, or anything in between. Some brides choose to repeat the original ceremony and wear their wedding gown again at a formal reception. Many others choose to wear an ankle length gown or a dressy cocktail dress instead.

The progressive wedding can relieve the financial burden of guests who wouldn't want to miss your celebration, but can't really afford travel and accommodation costs. This is becoming a practical alternative for today's brides. It can also be the perfect solution in a situation where the groom's family wants to invite more guests than the bride's family is able to accommodate.

DETAILS, *Details*

Be prepared to gather endless documents and certificates. Some that probably will be required would include: proof of citizenship; notarized birth certificate; affidavit stating neither person is currently married; blood test; proof of divorce or death certificate, if one of you was previously married. If you find the documentation and time requirements too much trouble to deal with, consider having a legal marriage at home immediately before traveling to the foreign country, where a ceremony and reception can then be held.

Couples who have their hearts set on marrying abroad, but have found requirements by foreign countries to be more than they care to handle, should consider Hawaii, the United States Virgin Islands, Jamaica, or Puerto Rico as alternatives. You'll find them much easier to deal with.

To marry at sea you would need to hold the ceremony while the ship is in port, or within three miles of land. You would need a marriage license from the state or country in whose waters you are to be married. Arrangements must be made with the ship's captain ahead of time. Check with your state to see if it recognizes out-of-country marriages.

Surprise Wedding

The surprise wedding is a perfect celebration for those who don't want family and friends to make a fuss, or feel obligated to send a gift. The spontaneity of this wedding ceremony turns the event into an emotional and festive occasion for all.

The couple may host the party themselves under the pretense of a birthday, housewarming, or no-special-occasion party. Or you may enlist the help of a friend who appears to be just having a party. A surprise wedding can be as informal and intimate, or large and elaborate, as you'd like it to be.

Surprise Your Guests

The following are some tips and imaginative ideas to surprise your guests and make a memorable day for both of you — and probably an occasion your guests won't forget either!

The party may be hosted at a home, restaurant, hotel, garden, on a yacht, or just about anywhere.

Host a Halloween costume party where you and your fiancé come dressed as bride and groom; invite the officiant to dress appropriately.

Invite your guests to a black tie New Year's Eve party. Say your vows just before the stroke of midnight; then everyone can join in the celebration by kissing the bride and groom.

Have guests arrive at your home for what they think is a party, offer them a glass of champagne, then load them into waiting limousines, vans, trolleys, or horse-drawn carriages that will take them to the church for a surprise ceremony. Afterward, they will be transported to an elaborately decorated reception site to continue celebrating with more champagne and food.

Invite guests to a barbecue, birthday, housewarming, or no-special-occasion party. Then surprise them with the wedding ceremony. To ensure that guests dress appropriately, state the dress on the invitation — casual, formal, or black tie.

Plan a family reunion with aunts, uncles, cousins, and grandparents. You may want to invite a few close friends to drop by just in time for the surprise ceremony.

Don't forget, even though it's a surprise, you will still need to make prior arrangements with an officiant and obtain your marriage license. ✳

WEDDING *information* worksheet

Wedding Date: _____   Time: _____

Style of Wedding: ❏ Very Formal   ❏ Formal   ❏ Semi-formal   ❏ Informal

Approximate Number of Guests: _____   Number of Bridal Attendants: _____   Number of Groom Attendants: _____

Additional Attendants: ❏ Flower Girl   ❏ Ring Bearer   ❏ Guestbook Attendant   ❏ Gift Attendant

Color Scheme: _____

Officiant: _____   Phone: _____

Special Classes, Requirements, or Pre-wedding Counseling: _____

_____

Dates _____   *Time:* _____   *Location:* _____

Dates _____   *Time:* _____   *Location:* _____

Dates _____   *Time:* _____   *Location:* _____

Ceremony Site: _____   Phone: _____

Address: _____

Restrictions: _____

Special Requirements: _____

Equipment Needed: _____

Decorating Ideas: _____

Rehearsal Date: _____   Time: _____

Reception Site: _____   Phone: _____

Address: _____

Reception Site Reserved: _____   From _____   Until _____

Restrictions: _____

Special Requirements: _____

Equipment Needed: _____

Decorating Ideas: _____

NOTES

Planning 101

TURNING *your* DREAM into *Reality*

As you begin planning your wedding, you'll need to start with the basics: who, what (style), where, when, and how (much). While these issues are somewhat related to style, they also factor heavily into the planning process.

Who – You'll need to come up with a preliminary guest list. You can pretty well count on it being far too long and needing lots of pruning.

What (Style) – Your wedding style will largely influence the planning process and degree of formality. A Zen wedding will most likely be less costly than a full-out Glamour Queen celebration, just as informal weddings tend to be less expensive (this is not set in stone, mind you) and have simpler location requirements than formal weddings.

Where – How many people you'll be inviting, how you envision your ceremony and reception will directly affect your location, which in turn affects every other aspect of the planning process, from setting the date to planning the budget.

When – Your date will somewhat be determined by where you want to get married, as some locations are booked eighteen to twenty-four months in advance. Also, some highly in demand wedding vendors can be booked up solid for months. Make sure to do a little preliminary research so you'll have some idea on the lead times involved.

How (Much) – That's very sweet of your parents to offer to take out a second mortgage on their house, but really, do you want them to have to work until they're seventy-five? Chances are you can plan the wedding you want at a fairly reasonable cost if you are just willing to do some research and compromise a little.

REALITY *check*

GETTING in *with* the *in-laws*

Okay. It is your wedding. But you also have to realize that parents take an extreme interest in their offspring's nuptials — it's an occupational hazard. Let them be involved. Gracefully. In fact, in many cases it's their money paying for the celebration. Find out what their MWRs are and try to work those in as best you can. Now, of course, that isn't always going to work, but make an honest effort. Even if they aren't your favorite people, remember, they did do one thing right. They raised the person you are going to marry.

The *date* YOU select

for you wedding can have a significant impact on your costs. If you book your wedding during the premium months, everything will just be that much more in demand. See if the off-season or less popular months work just as well for you. The time of day is also a critical factor in the ultimate cost of your wedding, with earlier in the day tending to be less expensive than late afternoon or evening.

HERE COMES THE PLAN

Some people can't wait to get started on the planning process. They set their wedding date at least eighteen months ahead of time, roll up their sleeves and set about planning every minute detail of their perfect day. Others have always wanted to be involved to some degree, but feel slightly overwhelmed when they realize how many details are actually involved in planning the perfect wedding. Then of course, there are those that grow faint at heart at the mere thought of all those phone calls, all those choices, all that organizational work that will be required of them when they can barely manage to balance their checkbook on a monthly basis. Well, have no fear. There are many tools and options available.

For those of you who are truly organizationally impaired, too busy, or just feel like you could use a little help, you may want to consider a bridal consultant. These are wonderful people who come in and organize everything for you. They can also be hired to handle only certain aspects of the wedding process. They usually have favorite vendors that they work with and respect, and they can be very valuable in helping to narrow down your choices. They are often walking encyclopedias of wedding etiquette and information and can offer you guidance, support, and a shoulder to cry on as you work your way toward The Big Day. They can serve as diplomatic consul to the whole affair, pay attention to all the pesky little details, be the traffic coordinator on the day of the wedding itself, and since they're professionals, often have access to information and contacts that you won't. These professionals have saved many a harried bride from elopement.

Brides have found hiring an experienced consultant especially helpful when planning a wedding out of town.

Bridal consultants/coordinators can be broken down into three main groups: professionals, semi-professional/volunteers, and site specific type coordinators.

Professionals – Just what the name claims, this is their full-time business and how they make a living.

Semi Professionals/Volunteers – This might include the wedding coordinator at the church you've selected or your Great Aunt Mary who has ended up doing this for a number of couples over the years. While it's not her main profession, she does have oodles of hands-on experience that you may lack.

Site-Specific Coordinators – This would be the site coordinator at the banquet hall, hotel ballroom, or Elk's Lodge where you will be holding your reception. Quite often they will help you as you plan, but only in those areas that pertain to the site.

Still not sure if a bridal consultant is for you? Take this quiz to help you decide.

Do you *need* A Bridal *Consultant*?

1. Is your spare time already at a premium?
2. Does your fiancé have little or no interest in helping with the planning?
3. Is your wedding going to be in a town other than where you live?
4. Do you balance your checkbook only twice a year whether it needs it or not?
5. Do you scratch your daily to-do lists on the back of old envelopes that you can never find again?
6. Is time rather than budget going to hold you back from having the wedding of your dreams?
7. Are you comfortable delegating?
8. Are you just interested in the results and don't give a fig for the process?

If you answered yes to five or more of these questions,
then you are a perfect candidate for hiring a wedding consultant to see you through the planning process. They can mastermind the whole thing, checking with you for approval on the details, or they can carry out your own pre-stated wishes and desires, whichever you choose.

If you answered yes to three or four of these questions,
then you are like most of us, capable of doing the job, but slightly intimidated by the enormity of it all. Rest assured. It can be done, and just be grateful that you bought this book.

If you answered yes to two or fewer questions,
then what are you waiting for? Plan away. You were born for just this sort of thing! The tools and techniques in this book will be second nature to you, but it will be helpful to have all the information handy in one place and at your fingertips.

WORKING WITH A BRIDAL CONSULTANT

There is only room for one star of the show in any wedding, and that's you! Your consultant is a hired professional and should leave any tendencies for histrionics at the door. She (or he) is there to see that YOU have the wedding of YOUR dreams. She's already gotten to plan lots and lots of weddings — this one is YOURS.

Make sure you feel comfortable with the consulting style of the consultant you've selected. Don't choose someone you feel might bowl you over at every turn (unless that's exactly what you are looking for, someone who will

KITCHEN *table* advice

TO LOVE, HONOR, AND COMPROMISE

With perfect poetic irony, planning a wedding together can be seen as a microcosm of your married life. Start good communication and negotiating habits now. And remember the Three L's: Love, Listen, and Let go.

The love part can seem obvious, but with all the planning, arranging, discussing, and maneuvering that will be required, it's easy to become so wrapped up in the planning process and getting your own way that you lose sight of that fact. Be prepared to really listen to others involved, your fiancé especially. Hear their concerns, suggestions, and ideas. Don't close your mind off to something just because it wasn't in your original wedding vision. And most importantly, when the pressures become too great — and they will — and you feel yourself digging in your heels a little too deeply — and you will — pause, take a deep breath, and let go. Remember, this whole celebration is to honor that wonderful, special love between the two of you. No planning detail should take precedence over that.

autocratically run the whole shebang).

Look for a good listener and one who you feel is strong enough to handle your family should they begin to interfere. Also search for someone with whom you can establish a good rapport.

The cost of hiring a bridal consultant will vary according to region and services rendered. Keep in mind that the fee may very well be offset by what the consultant will save you, in terms of time and money. Some charge a flat fee for their services. Others charge a percentage of the total wedding bill, usually between 10 and 20 percent. Or your consultant may charge an hourly rate, especially if hired for only limited services. Many use a combination of these methods, depending on the bride's needs. Some may also receive payment from vendors, rather than from the bride.

HOW TO FIND A BRIDAL CONSULTANT

As always, recommendations from people you know personally are always the best (and easiest!). If you are looking for a professional, there are a couple of highly respected professional organizations that will be happy to put you in touch with a professional consultant in your area.

For a list of bridal consultants, you can write to the Association of Bridal Consultants, 200 Chestnutland Road, New Milford, Connecticut 06776-2521. Send a legal size, self-addressed stamped envelope, and include your wedding date and phone number. They can also be reached at (860) 355-0464. Their email address is BridalAssn@aol.com.

Weddings Beautiful, a division of National Bridal Service will also provide you with information or names of Certified Wedding Specialists in your area. Contact Weddings Beautiful, 3122 West Cary Street, Richmond, Virginia 23221. Their telephone number is (804) 355-6945; FAX (804) 359-8001.

To make sure you find the consultant that is just perfect for you:

→ Interview more than one consultant.

→ Find a consultant you feel comfortable working closely with, and one who understands your desires.

→ Ask about the number of weddings the consultant has worked on.

→ Request client references if you feel you need further reassurance about the consultant's abilities. You must feel confident she can do the job.

→ Learn which specific services the consultant offers. Some may handle every detail; others may not.

→ Establish the fee structure up front. Is it a flat fee, an hourly rate, or a percentage of the wedding costs?

HAPPILY EVER AFTER

Remember to allow yourself enough time so you can enjoy the planning process. It is, with luck, a once-in-a-lifetime chance to plan a day that will uniquely reflect the emotions you are experiencing.

Of course, things will probably not come off exactly as planned, but the chances are it will still be an incredibly lovely day. Relax. Let yourself enjoy it. And remember that even Cinderella lost a glass slipper, and she still managed to have a great time!

INVITE THEM – INVITE THEM NOT

At first, you'll want to invite everybody. Toward the end of the planning process, you may end up wishing you'd invited nobody. Your actual guest list will end up somewhere in the middle. In order to go forward and select a location and plan other major details of your wedding, you will need to have at least a rough idea of how many people you intend to invite.

THE THREE ELEMENTS OF GUEST LIST COMPOSITION

Personal Style – This is somewhat covered by the wedding style you decide on but speaks more to the actual quantity and quality of time you wish to spend with your guests. Obviously, you will be able to spend more time with each of your nearest and dearest if it is a smaller, intimate gathering.

Budget – Unless you're one of the lucky few for whom money is no object, this is where nasty old reality intrudes on the lovely fantasy wedding you've been planning in your head. While it is true that the more the merrier, it is equally true, the more the costlier. It may be that you can afford a sit-down dinner for 150 guests, or a buffet luncheon for 250.

Families – This encompasses both size and closeness. There is a chance that either one or both of your parents will have their hearts set on inviting a large number of their friends. If they're helping out with the cost, you at least need to hear them out (remember the three L's!). If you and your fiancé have huge extended families that you just have to invite, there goes a big chunk of your list right there.

The first step in the guest list process is for you and your fiancé to make up your dream lists individually. Invite your parents to do the same. When you merge the four lists together, you'll have a good idea of just how overgrown it's become and will see how much trimming has to be done. Of course, it may be possible to invite everyone on the original dream lists, just by slightly altering

---

PLANNING *strategies*

Much of what is done while planning a wedding would be called work if it was done with a different end result in mind. It makes sense to look to the corporate world for the strategies that allow us to squeeze sixty hours of work into a mere forty-hour week. I'm talking delegating, time management, budgeting, and follow up. I'm talking about bringing those very skills that you use to get ahead in the real world and applying them to your ultimate wedding fantasy.

Delegate – Why do we all have so much trouble asking for help? But we do. We tend to feel it's an imposition or that everyone else is as busy as we are. While it's true that everyone is busy, that's what involved family members and bridesmaids are for. (They did realize they were going to have to earn that frilly dress that they'll never wear again, didn't they?) By delegating you allow everyone to feel a part of the fun and excitement leading up to the big day. Do choose your delegates wisely and take their inherent strengths and weaknesses into account or you'll spend more time following up on them than planning your wedding.

Give Deadlines – When you delegate tasks, make sure you clearly communicate what time those tasks need to be completed by, otherwise you'll have only yourself to blame if things aren't done on time.

Follow Up – Do not forget this critical aspect of planning your wedding. Confirm (or have someone else confirm – see Delegate) all the details with your vendor and wedding party.

Budgeting – You know that painful budget you hammered out? Stick to it. Seriously. Sticking to that budget is the one thing that stands between you and Wedding Day Mania.

Networking – In the business world, some of the best tips come from networking.

Time Management – Set goals for yourself, a timeline in which to complete specified tasks. Use the calendar to plan out the larger, overall picture of when things will get done, then follow up with monthly, weekly, and daily to-do lists.

Ceremony

Allow 8 square feet per person. (200 people = 1,600 sq. ft.)

Cocktails

8 square feet per person.

Cocktails with hors d'oeuvre stations set up — 10 square feet per person.

Cocktails with hors d'oeuvre stations set up and dancing — 12–13 square feet.

Dancing

Allow 2.5 square feet per person. NOTE: This allows for only half of your guests to be dancing at any one time. If you have a dance-the-night-away crowd, allow more space.

Reception with fully seated meal, buffet — 16–20 square feet per person. (This figure includes room for dancing.)

Reception with fully seated meal, served — 13–15 square feet per person. (This figure includes room for dancing.)

elements of your celebration. Select a luncheon buffet instead of dinner and dancing, or perhaps serve only wine, beer, and punch instead of having full bar service.

PRUNING TIPS

Invitations extended to single friends do not need to include a date. Engaged couples, those living together, or those who have dated steadily for several years should be invited as a couple.

Consider eliminating children from your guest list. If you do this, however, you need to make no exceptions or they may result in hurt feelings. If you absolutely HAVE to have your twelve-year-old nephew there or your ten-year-old sister, then make them part of the wedding party, either a junior usher or junior bridesmaid, or if even younger, a ring bearer or flower girl.

Don't invite coworkers.

Divide the list into four parts, either equal or determined by financial contribution. One part goes to each the bride, the groom, and their respective sets of parents. Let the individuals do their own pruning. Divorced or separated parents will need to divide their portion.

WHAT A SITE!

Before you can begin researching your site, you'll want to have some idea of how big your guest list will be and what type of celebration you'll be having. A sit-down dinner with dancing will have much different site requirements than a breakfast buffet or a cocktail hour reception.

LOCATION OPTIONS

One of the first choices you'll need to make is what town to have your ceremony and reception in — yours, his, your parents, his parents, an old hometown, or somewhere completely neutral. Then you can determine if you'll want to have your reception and ceremony at the same location, or if they will be at two separate locations. How about indoors or outdoors?

PICK A DATE, ANY DATE

Well, okay. NOT just any date. This will need to be a well-thought-out, scientifically analyzed, consult the stars, tea leaves, numbers, and every person who's important to you kind of date. You'll need to determine if any close friends or relatives have conflicts, or if you and your fiancé can actually get time off from work at that time of year. Have your heart set on a particular honeymoon location? Make sure your wedding (and therefore your honeymoon) does not happen to coincide with their hurricane season.

Another prime consideration is to allow enough lead time to plan your wedding the way you want it. Are the reception and ceremony sites you want actually available on the dates you want them? How about the florist, caterer, baker, limousines, musical band, and photographer? Many of the popular sites need to be reserved anywhere from twelve to twenty-four months ahead of time, especially for popular months or days. The same applies to in-demand wedding vendors and professionals.

The most popular months for weddings are June, August, and September, with May, July, October, and December following closely on their heels. If you are looking to get married in those months, you will be smart to allow a little extra planning time or make your reservations NOW. This minute! Saturdays are the preferred days for weddings, with Sunday and Friday nights in second place. Time of day can play an important role in setting the tone of your wedding and establishing a budget. Generally, weddings that take place earlier in the day are somewhat lower in cost than evening, dinner, or drink-and-dance-until-dawn weddings.

TRY TO AVOID:

→ Tourist season and rush hour traffic, if you can help it.

→ Days with sad or poignant memories.

→ Religious restrictions as determined by your faith. For example, the Catholic Church discourages weddings on Sundays and holy days. Jewish weddings may not take place on the Sabbath, major festivals, other holy days, or during the forty-nine days between Passover and Shavuot, with the exception of the 33rd day. *

Keep *in* MIND that smaller weddings can usually be planned in less time than it takes to orchestrate a large one.

BRIDAL *consultant* worksheet

ESTIMATE #1

Name _____ Phone _____

Address _____ Zip _____

Recommended By _____

Appointment Date _____

Services Provided _____

Fee is based on: ❏ Hourly Rate   ❏ Flat Fee   ❏ Percentage   ❏ Per Guest

Consultant Choice: ❏ Yes ❏ No   Number of hours of service: _____

Contract Signed: ❏ Yes ❏ No   Date: _____   Total Cost $ _____

                                                  Deposit $ _____

                                                  Balance Due $ _____

ESTIMATE #2

Name _____ Phone _____

Address _____ Zip _____

Recommended By _____

Appointment Date _____

Services Provided _____

Fee is based on: ❏ Hourly Rate   ❏ Flat Fee   ❏ Percentage   ❏ Per Guest

Consultant Choice: ❏ Yes ❏ No   Number of hours of service: _____

Contract Signed: ❏ Yes ❏ No   Date: _____   Total Cost $ _____

                                                  Deposit $ _____

                                                  Balance Due $ _____

                                                  Contract Signed _____

Wedding Date		Time
Number of Guests		
Rehearsal Date		Time

Name	*Home Phone*	*Work Phone*
Bride:		
Groom:		
Bride's Parents:		
Bride's Parents:		
Groom's Parents:		
Groom's Parents:		

Bride's Attendants	*Arrival Time*	*Phone*
Maid/Matron of Honor:		
Bridesmaid:		
Bridesmaid:		
Bridesmaid:		
Bridesmaid:		
Bridesmaid:		
Bridesmaid:		
Bridesmaid:		
Junior Bridesmaid:		
Junior Bridesmaid:		
Flower Girl:		
Other:		

Groom's Attendants	*Home Phone*	*Work Phone*
Best Man:		
Usher:		
Usher:		
Usher:		
Usher:		
Usher:		
Usher:		
Usher		
Ring Bearer:		
Other:		

bridal CONSULTANT'S *information* worksheet

Ceremony Site: _____ Phone: _____

Address: _____

Area to Dress: Bride and Attendants ❏ Yes ❏ No   Groom and Attendants ❏ Yes ❏ No

Reception Site: _____ Phone: _____

Address: _____

Area to Dress: Bride and Attendants ❏ Yes ❏ No   Groom and Attendants ❏ Yes ❏ No

Ceremony Services	*Arrival Time*	*Phone*
Officiant:		
Officiant:		
Site Coordinator:		
Organist:		
Soloist:		
Other Musicians:		
Photographer:		
Videographer:		
Florist:		
Wedding Transportation:		
Other:		

Reception Services	*Arrival Time*	*Phone*
Site Coordinator:		
Guest Book Attendant:		
Gift Attendant:		
Florist:		
Caterer:		
Bakery:		
Bartender:		
Rent Equipment:		
Special Transportation:		
Musicians:		
Other:		
Other:		

Virtual Planning

USING *the* World Wide Web *and* OTHER Computer *Tools*

Never before has the concept of letting your fingers do the walking been more far reaching or all encompassing. Between the information and resources provided by the World Wide Web and the tools available on home computers, the planning process has never been more streamlined.

Most computers come with basic software packages that include Internet access, spreadsheets, and calendar programs. If not, they can usually be purchased relatively inexpensively and used later, when you need to coordinate your busy married life schedules or work out a family budget. Use the calendar program to keep your to-do list current and mark appointments on your monthly schedules. Worksheets can be used to streamline everything from wedding budgets to guest lists to keeping track of deposits made to which vendors and what balance is owed when. Use the worksheets in this book as templates for the information you will want to include on the spreadsheets.

WORLD WIDE WEDDING

A whole world's worth of information, resources, planning tools, and research is now a mere mouse click away. Virtually every step of the planning process can benefit from what the Web has to offer. Just pick your favorite search engine and voila! Now, in the comfort of your own home at ten o'clock at night, you can:

➜ Search for the perfect location site.

➜ Check its availability.

➜ Take a virtual tour of the premises.

➜ Find the perfect words to use to write your own vows.

➜ Check out caterers' menus, musicians' repertoires, photographers' portfolios, invitations designs, and the latest designer bridal fashions.

➜ Find out which stores in your area carry the above so you can go in and try them on.

3 THINGS *you* must NEVER *use your* COMPUTER *to* Do

→ Don't create mailing labels for your invitations or any other wedding correspondence.

→ Don't write your thank you notes on a word processing program. They must be hand written.

→ Don't e-mail your thank you notes or wedding invitations. They must go out regular (snail) mail.

→ Research accurate historical information for your medieval themed wedding, and even locate a gown company that specializes in medieval gowns.

→ See the difference between a peony and a tulip.

→ Log into chat rooms and get advice and support from others going through the wedding planning process.

→ Get the happy news to your friends via e-mail.

→ Keep friends and family informed with your own personal website.

Some people find this wealth of information too overwhelming, while others feel like a kid in a candy store with so much knowledge at their fingertips. Even if the research possibilities are more than you think you can handle, there are other Web tools that can be invaluable. The Web boasts hard logistical data such as national telephone directories and map information and directions that can get anyone from point A to point B.

Many gift registries are available online, allowing you to register from the comfort of your own home, and your wedding guests to buy you a gift from the comfort of theirs.

The Web is also a great place to research travel options. You can do tons of research on various destinations and different ways to get there. You can even look at photos of potential hotels and resorts. By comparing price and package information, you can find great travel deals on the Web.

Internet access is a virtual necessity for anyone planning an out-of-town or location wedding. E-mail leaps time zones in a single bound, is as efficient as a quick telephone call, without the long distance charges, and provides you with a written record of the correspondence sent. It's a great way to follow up on details with vendors, confirm arrangements, and keep everyone informed of any change in plans. You can even demo music for your wedding online and e-mail digital images back and forth, confirm colors, textures, styles, and other visual details of your wedding.

A WEBSITE BUILT FOR TWO

One of the most fun tools available on the Web for wedding couples is the ability to build their own website, one for friends and family to visit to keep updated on the latest and greatest in the wedding process. The depth of the information and the degree of maintenance for the sight are up to you. You can put one together in fifteen minutes or spend the better part of three days. Your choice. There are many websites and services that will host your site for free and give you the tools and templates needed to do it.

WHAT TO INCLUDE

A picture of the two of you would be nice, as well as bios so those who know only one of you can get up to speed on the other. Details about your engagement, how he proposed, funny stories about your first blind date, or how you met when he ran a red light — straight into your car, all make for great website content.

Logistical details are good, too: the name of the church or hotel where you're planning to get married. How about posting links to local information such as weather, community attractions, driving instructions and maps, hotel accommodations, or where you're registered? Whatever you can think of that your friends and family will want to know, or will make their life easier, is perfect for your website. ✳

KITCHEN *table* advice

We are *not* recommending or even suggesting that you would hire a wedding professional or vendor sight unseen over the Internet. It is merely a tool for you to screen your choices and narrow the field down to two or three options you wish to pursue. You absolutely MUST contact them in person and have a conversation, or two, before agreeing to hire them. Nor do we recommend buying over the Internet unless it is from a reputable vendor that has a good recommendation from friends or family. Even then, it is difficult to purchase something from a picture on a computer screen. Make sure and check their return policy before risking it.

WE *Don't* mean *to be* A Tease . . .

The Internet is a volatile, ever evolving resource and due to its very nature, subject to rapid change. From website companies going out of business to changing servers, there are any number of reasons why a website address here today may be gone tomorrow. In an effort to avoid frustrating our readers with information we couldn't guarantee would be accurate for more than a week, we have avoided listing e-mail addresses. Run a search using your favorite search engine on any number of topics: weddings, bridal fashion, bridal shoes, engagement rings, honeymoon, wedding accessories, musicians, florists, caterers, etc., and you'll get pages and pages of e-mail addresses to pore over. Most major manufacturers and retailers have a website as well, so try searching under those names also.

REALITY *check*

Using the Web is a great way to get the groom more involved. While his knees may wobble at the idea of interviewing a florist face to face, using a search engine to scan a website for information is probably something he is familiar with.

NOTES

chapter
SIX

Asset Management

COMING up *with* A budget *you* CAN *live* with

*I*f only money grew on trees! But it doesn't. And the only way to keep from spending way too much of it, or worse — money you don't even have — is to create a budget. Put this budget in writing and keep to it. It will be your reality check as you go forward, shopping for the ultimate wedding experience. Sure, the florist will show you samples of incredible flowers that can be yours for a mere $3,000. Check your budget and you may see that you only have $1,200 to spend on flowers. This is when you will either need to cut back on your floral vision or decide to cut back in some other category in order to afford the flowers of your dreams. Consult your MWRs and remind yourself what you're absolutely committed to. Budget the must-have items first.

This would be a good time to discuss your joint financial plan for yourselves as a couple. If you intend to buy a house in the next few years, or go back to graduate school, or start a family, this may affect just how much you're willing to spend or go into debt.

Your only hope of staying on budget is to write everything down, both in the estimation process and in the actual spending process. Use the estimation worksheets for trying to grasp the amount of funds you'll need, and the actual budget record for monies spent.

Create a payment schedule showing the amount contracted for each service, the date the deposit is due, the date you pay the deposit, when subsequent payments are due, and note when you make them.

If you put items on your credit card, log them onto this sheet. A great tip for keeping on top of your credit card balance is that each time you charge something, enter it in your checkbook register as if it were a check. When that bill comes, you will already have recorded the money as spent and can pay off the debt immediately to avoid costly interest charges.

Okay, let's say you've made up a budget. After much paring and pruning, negotiating, wheedling, and mourning over what you can't have, you both agree you need $18,000 for the perfect wedding. You have $2,000 in savings, and your sweetie has $175. Now what?

Traditionally it has been the bride's family who has paid for the wedding, but no more. A much larger portion of weddings are being paid for by the couple themselves or a combination of everyone pooling their resources, including the groom's parents. This is a much more modern and equitable solution.

Just remember, when people are paying toward something, they tend to feel they have a "say" in the decision making process. If either of your parents offer to help with the finances, or better yet — insist — accept the help gracefully, but try to establish some ground rules. It's always a nice gesture to ask your families for input and opinions, keeping in mind that it is your wedding and you get to have the final say. Try to identify any strings that may be attached right up front. It may help if you specify which area of the wedding your parents' money is going toward and let them have some input in that section.

If your parents don't immediately offer financial help, you may want to at least have a conversation with them about contributing. This will most likely feel more comfortable if each of you talk to your families separately. Financial issues are emotional hotbeds, often centering around issues of personal power and control. Being aware of this is half the battle. The other half is keeping the conversation neutral and calm.

JUST THE FACTS

Your conversation with your parents will go much more smoothly if you have some idea on how much you'll need. Have those facts and figures in hand when you sit down to talk. "Our wedding is going to cost around $18,000. We have $2,500 saved and think we can save an additional $4,000 before the wedding. We were wondering if there was any way you could help with some of the remaining costs."

TREAD LIGHTLY

Be sensitive to your parents' financial situation. Sometimes this is difficult because parents guard this sort of information from their children as effectively as Fort Knox. You should still use your eyes and ears and fabulous powers of perception to try and assess their ability to help. If your parents are still paying for your Ivy League education, or are putting siblings through college, you can be fairly confident that money is tight. That doesn't mean they won't want to help, just be aware they might not be able to help as much as they would like. If your future father-in-law just got cut in the most recent corporate reshuffling, be sensitive to the fact that whatever savings they have may need to be used just to get by in the next few months as he looks for a new job. There are many other ways he can contribute over the next few months, and with cash tight, they will most likely be more realistic for him to manage.

Perhaps he has a green thumb that has been put to good use tending a spectacular garden that would make an ideal setting for your wedding. Or maybe he belongs to an auto club with owners of exotic cars who would be willing to offer the use of their vehicles for your wedding transportation. If he's a great negotiator, put him to work on negotiating with some of your prospective vendors. There's so much to do when planning a wedding that there will be plenty of non-monetary ways for Dad and others to help.

WHO (TRADITIONALLY) PAYS FOR WHAT?

Being the tradition-steeped celebrations that they are, weddings do have some general, traditional guidelines as to who pays for what.

BRIDE

→ Wedding ring for the groom

→ A wedding gift for the groom

→ Gifts for the bridal attendants

→ Personal stationery

→ Medical examination and blood test

→ Accommodations for out-of-town attendants

→ Bachelorette party

GROOM

→ The bride's engagement and wedding rings

→ A wedding gift for the bride

→ Gifts for the best man and ushers

→ Groom's wedding attire

→ Bride's bouquet and going away corsage

→ Mothers' corsages

→ Boutonnieres for attendants and fathers

→ Medical examination and blood test

→ Marriage license

→ Clergyman's fee

→ The honeymoon expenses

→ Bachelor dinner (if not given by the best man, optional)

BRIDE'S FAMILY

→ Engagement party (optional)

→ Ceremony cost: location, music, rentals, and all related expenses

→ Entire cost of reception: food, beverage, entertainment, rental items, decorations, and wedding cake

→ Bride's wedding attire and accessories

→ A wedding gift for the couple

→ Wedding invitations, announcements, and mailing costs

→ Bridesmaids' bouquets

→ Transportation for bridal party from bride's home to the site of ceremony

→ Bridesmaids' luncheon

→ Photography (groom's parents may pay for the pictures they would like)

→ Personal wedding attire

→ Floral decorations

→ Special item they may wish to purchase: toasting goblets, ring pillow, etc.

GROOM'S FAMILY

→ Rehearsal dinner party

→ Personal wedding attire

→ Travel and accommodations for groom's family

→ Wedding gift for the bride and groom

→ Special item they may wish to purchase: toasting goblets, ring pillow, etc.

→ Any general expenses they may wish to contribute

ATTENDANTS

→ Wedding attire for themselves

→ Any travel expenses

→ Wedding gift for bride and groom

→ Showers given by maid of honor or bridesmaids

→ Bachelor party given by best man or ushers

BRIDE AND GROOM

→ Gifts of appreciation for parents or others who helped with your wedding

→ Expenses of items desired, which have exceeded original budget allocations

OPTIONAL EXPENSES

→ Attendants' dresses are traditionally bought by each bridesmaid, but may be purchased by the bride or her family.

→ Bridesmaids' luncheon is generally given by the bride's family; may be given by the bride.

→ Bride's bouquet has traditionally been a gift from the groom, but may be purchased by the bride's family, along with the other flowers.

→ Corsages for mothers and grandmothers have been the responsibility of the groom; the bride may opt to pay for her own mother's and grandmothers' corsages, or the bride's family may pay for all of them.

→ The groom's family usually hosts rehearsal dinner, but the bride's family or a close friend may host it.

JUST HOW MUCH DO YOU NEED, ANYWAY?

The average amount spent on a wedding today is in the $18,000 to $20,000 range. Of course, this varies widely depending on where you live and your personal taste and expectations. The higher the cost of living in your area, the more you can expect to pay for wedding related services.

FOUR WEDDINGS AND A BUDGET

On the following pages, to give you an idea of how many different ways the same number of dollars can be spent, we've put together four completely different weddings with divergent themes, degrees of formality, and budgeting priorities, yet all in the $10,000 range.

WEDDING EXPENSES	Percentage of Budget Allocated	Sample Budget $10,000	Sample Budget $20,000	Sample Budget $30,000
Food	40%	$ 4,000	$ 8,000	$ 12,000
Reception and Other Rentals	10%	$ 1,000	$ 2,000	$ 3,000
Attire	12%	$ 1,200	$ 2,400	$ 3,600
Flowers	8%	$ 800	$ 1,600	$ 2,400
Photography	5%	$ 500	$ 1,000	$ 1,500
Videography	2%	$ 200	$ 400	$ 600
Music	7%	$ 700	$ 1,400	$ 2,100
Invitations	3%	$ 300	$ 600	$ 900
Gifts & Favors	4%	$ 400	$ 800	$ 1,200
Wedding Rings	2%	$ 200	$ 400	$ 600
Ceremony	2%	$ 200	$ 400	$ 600
Transportation	1%	$ 100	$ 200	$ 300
Miscellaneous	4%	$ 400	$ 800	$ 1,200

Planning a Wedding to Remember

Four Weddings and a Budget

Ah, the Romance of Spring

Perfect for Hopelessly Romantic Brides, or with a few modifications, the Zen Minimalist.

150 Guests

11:00 Ceremony —

12:00 Luncheon Reception

This is an informal wedding that will be taking full advantage of the season, therefore saving money in a variety of ways. By having this wedding outdoors, you immediately reduce your cost for florals and greenery because nature provides the backdrop. By choosing an earlier time of day for the celebration, the food and entertainment costs are reduced dramatically. Almost all flowers are available during the spring months, so you most likely won't incur any additional costs there.

$ 350 — **Ceremony Site and Officiant Fee**
This allows for getting married in a small country chapel and driving to the ceremony site or performing the ceremony at the reception site itself.

$ 200 — **Reception Site**
A large public garden or park is the perfect backdrop for this type of wedding. If more privacy is needed or desired, consider someone's (large) backyard.

$ 1,500 — **Rentals**
This fee includes chairs, tables, linens, as well as a ceremony arch (if you get married at the reception site). This also covers china and utensils. Tents or umbrellas are optional, depending on the site you've chosen and the weather, but are also factored in.

$ 500 — **Wedding Cake**

$ 1,100 — **Floral Arrangements**
This includes a stunning bouquet for the bride, three bridesmaids' bouquets, boutonnieres for the groom and ushers, as well as centerpieces for each of the twenty tables.

$ 400 — **Music**
Can be a harpist, string quartet, violinist, or a sound system.

$ 400 — **Invitations**

$ 650 — **Photographer**

$ 1,150 — **Wedding dress and accessories**

$ 200 — **Horse-drawn carriage**
For ride from chapel to the reception site.

$ 400 — **Favors and Attendant Gifts**

$ 3,750 — **Food and Beverages,**
including tax and gratuities

This includes cold lemon chicken with rice pilaf, Greek green salad, and fresh fruit. Other affordable options would be a quiche bar, pasta dishes, salad buffet. This only allows for wine, beer, champagne, and non-alcoholic drinks.

$ 10,600 — **Total Cost**

Four Weddings and a Budget

The Classic Wedding

Classic Traditionalists, Need We Say More?

200 guests

6:00 Ceremony —

7:00 Dinner and Dancing Reception

This is a formal wedding incorporating all the classic hallmarks of this most hallowed of celebrations. The ceremony is held in a church, as tradition dictates, followed by a sit-down or buffet-style dinner, after which the bride and groom and their guests can dance the night away. Since the bride and groom invite 200 guests, and they are adamant about wanting to serve a meal, complete with dancing, those became their budget priorities and they had to cut back in other areas. They opted for a less expensive dress for the bride, a no-host bar for those guests who wanted more than the beer and wine provided, a less fancy wedding cake, and a DJ instead of live music.

$ 350 — Ceremony Site and Officiant Fee
This allows for getting married in a small country chapel and driving to the ceremony site or performing the ceremony at the reception site itself.

$ 250 — Reception Site
A hotel banquet room that is, most often, provided with the cost of the food.

$ 0 — Rentals
One advantage to a hotel banquet room is that all the chairs, tables, linens, china, and utensils are included.

$ 500 — Wedding Cake

$ 1,000 — Floral Arrangements
This includes bouquets for the bride, three bridesmaids' bouquets, boutonnieres for the groom, and ushers, as well as centerpieces for each of the tables.

$ 750 — Music

$ 400 — Invitations
Since they invited so many people, invitations were kept to a simple, classic style that were still elegant, but had no cost-adding extras.

$ 650 — Photographer
Never scrimp on a photographer! It's too risky.

$ 800 — Wedding Dress and Accessories

$ 0 — Transportation
The couple used his father's Lincoln instead of renting an expensive limousine.

$ 560 — Favors and Attendant Gifts

$ 5,000 — Food and Beverages, including tax and gratuities
This includes a dinner — probably chicken, with two or three side dishes or salads, and only allows for wine, beer, champagne, and non-alcoholic drinks.

$ 10,260 — Total Cost

Four Weddings and a Budget

An Elegant Wine Tasting

Either a Polished Sophisticate or a Zen Minimalist would appreciate the sophisticated simplicity of this celebration.

100 guests

3:00 CEREMONY —

 4:00 WINE AND HORS D' OEUVRES

This is a semi-formal wedding that is made all the more elegant for its intimate look and feel. A wine tasting, or wine country theme, can be used anytime of the year and lends itself particularly well to a casual elegance without being over the top expensive. If you happen to live near a winery, research their availability and pricing, otherwise use a home setting — your house or someone else's (the bigger the better!). Funds have been allocated in case a home needs to be rented for the afternoon. No fuss and no muss, this wedding is a quiet statement of personal style that will captivate your guests.

$ 150 — CEREMONY SITE AND OFFICIANT FEE

$ 1,000 — RECEPTION SITE

A private home, hopefully yours, your parents, or another acquaintance whose home lends itself to this type of entertaining. You can also consider consulting a location service to find a home for you to rent for the afternoon.

$ 1,800 — RENTALS

Includes chairs, tables, linens, china, and utensils.

$ 500 — WEDDING CAKE

$ 1,000 — FLORAL ARRANGEMENTS

This includes bouquets for the bride, three bridesmaids' bouquets, boutonnieres for the groom, and ushers, as well as centerpieces for each of the tables.

$ 375 — MUSIC

A harpist or violinist works especially well for this theme.

$ 300 — INVITATIONS

$ 600 — PHOTOGRAPHER

$ 900 — WEDDING DRESS AND ACCESSORIES

$ 0 — TRANSPORTATION

$ 400 — FAVORS AND ATTENDANT GIFTS

$ 3,000 — FOOD AND BEVERAGES, INCLUDING TAX AND GRATUITIES

This includes a variety of wine and hors d'oeuvre stations placed around the room.

$ 10,025 — TOTAL COST

Four Weddings and a Budget

Winter Wonderland

Weddings for Glamour Queens are hard to do on a budget, but they can be done! Also works well for the Polished Sophisticate or a Hopelessly Romantic bride wanting to get married in the winter months.

150 guests

8:00 Ceremony —

    9:00 Champagne and Hors d' oeuvres

Lots of winter white, silver, and twinkling lights give this formal wedding its wonderful brand of sophisticated magic. It works well for any winter months, but is especially suited to the days surrounding the holidays. What better way to toast in the New Year than at your wedding reception!

$ 150 — Ceremony Site and Officiant Fee

$ 1,250 — Reception Site

Rent a lodge for the day, or a gathering room at a quaint local inn. If there is nothing like that available in your area, consider a more traditional ballroom, banquet hall, or large home. If using a lodge or inn, or restaurant, the rental items will most likely be included in the cost. If using a different locale, then you will need to use some of the reception site fee to pay for the rental fees.

$ 750 — Wedding Cake

$ 1,400 — Floral Arrangements
                and Decorations

$ 1,000 — Music

You'll want a live band or small orchestra for a night of dancing

$ 450 — Invitations

$ 700 — Photographer

$ 700 — Wedding Dress and Accessories

$ 200 — Transportation

$ 400 — Favors and Attendant Gifts

$ 3,000 — Food and Beverages,
including tax and gratuities

This includes champagne and hors d'oeuvre stations placed around the room.

$ 10,000 — Total Cost

TEN WAYS TO SAVE

one As soon as you're engaged, or earlier if you can, set up a savings plan and try to put away 10-20 percent of every paycheck. Think that's impossible? Think again. Here are nine ways to save up money for your wedding. While we don't expect you to use all of them all of the time, they are a good illustration of just how quickly expenses add up.

two Give up designer coffee. Or at least modify it. A three-dollar-a-day habit adds up to $1,095 per year! Buy a pound of grocery store coffee and save big time. Or consider buying a pound of your favorite designer coffee beans and brew it yourself. You'll still save close to $800-900 over the course of the year. If two of you do this, double your savings.

three Brown-bag it. It's much, much cheaper to make your lunch, and often less calories as well. In fact, this might help you with two common wedding goals: saving money and losing weight. If you spend $7 a day on lunch, that equals $1,750 per year!

four Cut down on dinners out. Really, do you need to go out to dinner every Friday and Saturday night? (Annual Cost - $5,200) How about just one of those? (Save $2,600) How about once every two weeks? (Save $3,900) Once a month? (Save $4,600) Dinner with drinks easily runs $50 for the two of you.

five Consider car-pooling or taking public transportation to work. You know you should be doing it anyway, to help out with the environment. Now you can accomplish two things at once. Transportation costs can add up, there is the cost of gas plus wear and tear on the car. If you commute thirty miles to work each day, that's 300 miles for the week! That's a savings of $30 per week on gas, not to mention that wear and tear on your car, which equals $1,500 per year.

six Remember the library. You don't have to go out and purchase every new bestseller that hits the stands. Same for magazines.

seven Choose a credit card with the lowest possible interest rate.

eight Utilize the automatic withdrawal service at your bank to put money in your savings account each pay period.

nine Shop the bargains at the grocery store. That doesn't mean feasting on ramen noodles and Hamburger Helper for the entire week. Rather, pick the orange juice that's on sale this week or try the bargain yogurt instead of your normal brand that sells for $1 a carton. If chicken breasts are on sale, eat those this week and stock up for the future. (You're going to need the extra chicken to pack your brown bag lunches anyway.) Doing this can shave 15-25 percent off your weekly grocery bill, adding up to nearly $1,000 per year in savings.

ten Adjust your utilities. Do you really need to set your thermostat at 68 degrees in the summer months? Wouldn't you be just as comfortable at 72 degrees? How about in the winter? Try for 65 degrees and put on that darling sweater you got at last year's department store sale. Depending on which part of the country you live in, the savings can be significant.

There are some big decisions you can make at the very beginning that will dramatically cut your wedding costs. Additional cost-whittling ideas will be featured in the chapters focusing on that category.

Think small, intimate and meaningful, not large, lavish, and loud.

Go over that guest list with a fine-tooth comb. Cull it down from 175 to 125 guests. Choose three bridesmaids instead of six. A three-course meal instead of five. You get the picture.

De-formalize it.

Very formal affairs are almost always more costly than those that are more relaxed. Think buffet instead of sit-down dinner, think outdoors instead of ballroom, think early in the day rather than late at night. Earlier is better. Breakfast is traditionally less expensive than luncheon, which is also less expensive than dinner and dancing.

Formulate your Minimum Wedding Requirements.

Know what is absolutely essential to your wedding happiness and focus your splurges in those areas. Compromise in all others. *

WEDDING *expense* record

Wedding Items & Services	TOTAL COST *(cost to be paid by)*				Deposit Paid	Balance Due
	Bride's Family	Groom's Family	Bride	Groom		
CEREMONY						
Site Fee						
Marriage License						
Officiant's Fee						
Ceremony Music						
Guest Book and Pen						
Ring Bearer Pillow						
Flower Girl Basket						
Other						
BRIDAL CONSULTANT						
STATIONERY						
Invitations						
Reception Cards						
Response Cards						
Pew or Rain Cards						
Announcements						
Thank You Notes						
Stamps						
Programs						
Calligraphy						
WEDDING ATTIRE						
Bridal Dress						
Headpiece/Accessories						
Gloves/Shoes						
Jewelry						
Hairdresser						
Hosiery/Garter						
Other						
Groom's Formal Wear						
RINGS						
Engagement Ring						
Bride's Wedding Ring						
Groom's Wedding Ring						
GIFTS						
Bride's gift						
Groom's gift						
Bridal Attendants						

WEDDING *expense* record

Wedding Items & Services	Bride's Family	Groom's Family	Bride	Groom	Deposit Paid	Balance Due
TOTAL COST *(cost to be paid by)*						
FLOWERS						
Ceremony Site						
Reception Site						
Bride's Flowers						
Bridesmaids' Bouquets						
Men's Boutonnieres						
Mothers/Grandmothers						
RECEPTION						
Site Fee						
Caterer						
Liquor/Beverage						
Equipment						
Rentals Items *(Tent, Arches, Chairs, Linens, Tableware)*						
Bartending/Corkage Fee						
Cake						
Cake Cutting Fee						
Cake Top						
Cake Knife and Server						
Toasting Glasses						
Favors						
Music						
Parking/Valet Service						
PHOTOGRAPHY						
Formal Portrait						
Parents' Albums						
Extra Pictures						
VIDEOGRAPHY						
TRANSPORTATION						
Limousines, etc.						
Parking Attendants						
PARTIES						
Engagement						
Bridesmaids' Luncheon						
Bachelor's Party						
Rehearsal Dinner						
HONEYMOON						
PRENUPTIAL AGREEMENT						

Planning a Wedding to Remember

The Ceremony

THE *Heart* and SOUL of YOUR *Wedding*

*I*f couples were to pick a defining moment on their wedding day, it would no doubt be the one when they stare into each other's eyes and, as the rest of the world falls away, say, "I do." Make no mistake, the ceremony is the heart and soul of your wedding. Without it, the reception would be just another great party. And as you can guess, any issue dealing with heart and soul requires some deep thought and, well, soul searching.

Because receptions require so many decisions and arrangements affecting a large number of guests, it's easy to let the planning of that event overshadow the planning of the ceremony. Don't let that happen. The ceremony will affect both of you, (profoundly, we hope) and you should devote as much time as possible to making the ceremony as meaningful to the two of you as you can. From the music and candles to the words you speak, let the details bring your emotional commitment to life.

RELIGIOUS VS. CIVIL

The first decision you need to make is what type of ceremony you'd like to have — civil or religious.

CIVIL CEREMONIES

A civil ceremony is a secular ceremony that occurs within the legal proceedings determined by the state instead of being determined and governed by the laws of a church or temple. Civil ceremonies can be performed by judges, mayors, or other authorized officials of the state. They may take place in a judge's chamber, courtroom, home, garden, club, or hotel. While there are very few rules and regulations regarding the civil ceremony, it's a good idea to check with the marriage bureau to confirm the procedures for a civil ceremony in your particular state.

Civil ceremonies work particularly well for those with no strong religious ties or preferences, or for those whom religious differences are so extreme that this is the most neutral solution. They are also a good choice for second marriages, or if the ceremony of your dreams is just a little too unconventional, either content-wise or location-wise, for a member of the clergy.

RELIGIOUS CEREMONIES

Religious ceremonies are governed by the covenants and laws of a particular religious faith or denomination. They may or may not take place in a house of worship, as many clergy members are willing to perform ceremonies at other locations. If you want your religion, or your deeply religious family, to recognize your union, then you'll need to opt for a religious ceremony.

Religious ceremonies usually follow a prescribed format, incorporating the traditions, rites, and customs of that particular faith. It's vitally important that you find an officiant who understands your religious viewpoint and respects your beliefs. This, of course, means the two of you have thoroughly discussed your religious views and have come to some agreement as to what those beliefs are. (If not, see Civil Ceremonies.) This is much easier if both of you come from similar religious backgrounds, or compatible ones. If not, this will be the first of many discussions you'll have over the course of your lifetime together as to how to blend your religious rituals. Look for two officiants who are willing to conduct an interfaith marriage ceremony.

Roman Catholic Ceremonies

According to the Catholic Church, marriage is one of the seven sacraments and considered a serious and lasting commitment. Most parishes require pre-marital counseling so the couple can prepare for this lifelong commitment.

The church requires that traditional vows be said, although slight changes may be possible as long as the meaning remains the same. The most traditional and religious ceremony is one that takes place at high noon — a Nuptial Mass. You may also want to include one or both of the following symbolic rituals: the bride places the bouquet at the shrine or statue of Mary while a prayer is said, or you both light one larger unity candle from two smaller ones to signify your new life as one.

The Catholic Church discourages weddings from taking place on Sunday or holy days and after 6:00 PM on Saturdays.

In the case of an interfaith marriage, a priest will usually agree to co-officiate with a Protestant minister. The two ceremonies are similar. However, in the traditional Catholic procession, the father escorts the bride down the aisle but doesn't "give her away." Most interfaith marriages do not have a Nuptial Mass; in those that do, non-Catholics do not take Holy Communion. With an interfaith ceremony, a combination of both religious traditions is best.

If both are Catholic, marriage banns, a public announcement of the proposed marriage, are announced three times — during Mass on Sundays or holy days, or in the church calendar of both the bride and groom's parishes. With an interfaith marriage, banns are not published. The Catholic must obtain dispensation from the bishop of the diocese. In the case of divorced Catholics, a church-sanctioned annulment is required before they may remarry.

Eastern Orthodox

The churches of the Eastern rite, including Russian and Greek Orthodox, are similar in many ways to the Catholic tradition. While not encouraged, interfaith marriages are allowed, providing that the non-Orthodox party is a baptized Christian. Remarriages are also acceptable if religious decrees of annulment have been received, followed by a civil divorce. The banns of marriage may be published or not, as desired.

The Orthodox ceremony is long and full of symbolism. It usually takes place in the afternoon or early evening, but not during seasons of fasting or certain holy days. The ceremony begins with a betrothal ritual in which the rings are blessed, exchanged three times to signify the Holy Trinity, and then placed on the bride's and groom's right hands.

At the close of the betrothal ritual, two crowns

are placed on the heads of the bride and groom and exchanged three times. A Gospel is read. The couple then drinks from the same glass of wine three times. This signifies their everlasting love and commitment to share both the happy and sad times in marriage. The ceremony closes with the bride and groom, hands bound together, being led around a ceremonial table three times while the congregation sings *God Grant Them Many Years*.

Jewish Ceremonies

Orthodox, Conservative, Reform, and Reconstructionist are the four main groups within the Jewish religion, with Orthodox being the strictest in following Jewish law. Conservative falls in the middle, while Reform and Reconstructionist adherents are the most liberal of the four.

Some of the differences between the traditions are as follows: In the Orthodox interpretation the rabbi will not marry divorced persons unless they have a religious as well as civil decree. The men and women are seated in separate areas of the synagogue. Even though the Conservative ceremony is less rigid in adhering to the Jewish law, many of the traditions are the same as the Orthodox. With both, the service is in Hebrew and English. Neither a Conservative nor Orthodox rabbi will officiate at a marriage of mixed faiths. The wedding attire is very conventional. The men wear caps or yarmulkes in these ceremonies. Another similarity is that the ring is placed on the index finger of the bride's right hand during the ceremony (it may be switched to the left hand after the ceremony). The ceremonies are performed under a chuppah by a rabbi. The chuppah is a canopy, which symbolizes cohabitation and consummation.

The Reform service is usually in English though some Hebrew may be used. The ceremony is generally performed under a chuppah, but this is not mandatory. Men may wear yarmulkes, if they desire.

The ceremony begins and ends with the blessing of the wine, and the bride and groom taking a sip from a joint cup. The exchange of rings in the Jewish ceremony has slightly different significance in that it represents the exchange of material goods, which must take place in order to validate a Jewish wedding.

The Ketubah is a marriage contract, usually finely decorated, that lists the bride's rights in the marriage. It is given to the bride after the ring exchange, and then she usually hands it off to her honor attendant for the rest of the ceremony.

The ceremony ends with the reciting of the seven blessings. The bride and groom drink the blessed wine from a glass; the glass is wrapped in a napkin and then smashed beneath the groom's foot. Many times, *mazel tov* is said at the end of the ceremony. This means good star or good position of your stars, which, over the years, has come to mean good fortune.

The bride and groom then withdraw for a few minutes of seclusion, known as the Yichud. It is a few private moments in which the bride and groom have an opportunity to savor their new union. In the past, the bride and groom withdrew to consummate their marriage, but luckily that's no longer the case!

The Jewish wedding may take place at any time, other than on the Sabbath, major festivals, or other holy days. It may not take place during the forty-nine days between Passover and Shavuot, with the exception of the thirty-third day.

Protestant Ceremonies

While most Protestant churches have similar marriage ceremonies, each denomination has its own practices and traditions. It is best to go over the regulations of the church with the clergy member that you select. Some are reluctant to perform a marriage on Sundays or holy days, although it is allowed. Then, too, churches may have restrictions against certain music, the use of candles, or photography. And many churches will require both of you to attend pre-marital counseling sessions with a clergyman.

MILITARY
Ceremonies

Military ceremonies can take place at military chapels in addition to the other traditional locations. The groom and military attendants dress in full ceremonial dress uniforms (white in summer, blue in winter), complete with sword or saber. Boutonnieres are not worn. However, brides choosing to wear their military uniform may carry a bouquet.

The basic ceremony is the same except for the dramatic arch of steel during the recession. The honor guard forms the arch of steel by raising their sabers or swords, which the new couple passes through, symbolizing a safe passage into married life.

Non-military attendants, fathers, and the bride should dress in traditional formal attire. If the bride is a military officer, she may opt to wear her dress uniform or she may prefer to wear a long formal bridal gown, with train and veil, to complement the formality of the military dress uniform.

Make sure to verify your wedding plans with the appropriate military authorities and get permission for all facets of your wedding — flowers, music, photographers, and so forth — because military chapels and bases have their own rules and guidelines.

Interfaith marriages are accepted in most denominations, as long as one partner is a baptized member of that denomination. In the case of divorced persons, a "church judgment" as well as civil divorce papers may be required.

In Protestant ceremonies the bride is escorted down the aisle and given away by her father. If he's not available, a brother, relative, or close friend may escort her, or she may choose to walk down the aisle alone.

Most fathers look forward to the moment when they are asked, "Who giveth this woman to be married to this man?" Traditionally, he answers "Her mother and I do," places her hand in the groom's, and then takes his seat in the front left row. The marriage vows end with "'til death do us part." And many go on to finish the ceremony with the Lord's Prayer.

Note:
Creating interfaith ceremonies that work for both religions involved requires more research, counseling, and tact, but can make for an absolutely moving and meaningful ceremony.

YOUR OFFICIANT

Once you've decided on the nature of your ceremony, you'll need to locate an officiant to perform it. If one or both of you, or your families, are members of a church that is in keeping with how you want to conduct your ceremony, then that's the most logical place to start your search. If there is no church that immediately comes to mind, then you'll need to begin researching churches of your faith in the town in which you're planning to marry.

Some clergy members will only conduct ceremonies for members of their church, so you may need to consider joining if you plan on marrying there. Other considerations would be any restrictions the house of worship may place on attire, music, decorations, or readings. You should also find out whether or not pre-marital counseling is required and just how much personalization can be done to the ceremony or even the vows themselves.

Once you decide on an officiant, you'll need to meet with them in order to go over these and other issues.

QUESTIONS TO ASK YOUR OFFICIANT

→ What are the house of worship's marriage requirements?

→ Are there any special rules or regulations regarding required membership, music, attire, photography, videotaping, vows, or decorations?

→ Can the officiant perform off-site marriages?

- → Is the date and time you want available?
- → Can vows and ceremonies be personalized? To what degree?
- → How many guests can the facility accommodate?
- → Is pre-marital counseling required? How much?
- → What is the site fee? Officiant fee?
- → Does the house of worship provide any aisle runners, chuppahs, or other standard equipment?
- → Is the officiant available for the rehearsal?
- → Is there a dressing room available?
- → How much church parking is there?
- → How many weddings will be scheduled on the same day as yours?
- → Can birdseed, rose petals, or bubbles be used?

WHERE to FIND *an* Officiant

Church you or your future spouse attends

Family's church or faith

Recommendations from friends

Wedding consultants or site coordinators

Churches either of you attended as a child

Marriage license bureau referrals

Directories, under specific faith listings or weddings and churches

PRE-WEDDING COUNSELING

Since churches view marriage as a lifelong commitment, they are eager to see them succeed. They offer couples pre-marital counseling in order to make sure the couple has discussed issues that can be critical to the success of a marriage. You can expect one to four sessions in which you will discuss how you met, what marriage means to you, whether or not your families are supportive, why you want to get married, what kind of religious life you want to build for yourselves, your views on money, children, sex, and other make-or-break issues.

CEREMONY BASICS

The basic components of a ceremony are:
- → The processional
- → Opening remarks by the officiant
- → Exchange of vows by the bride and groom
- → Ring ceremony
- → Pronouncement complete with permission to kiss
- → The recessional

THE PROCESSIONAL

This is the part where you all enter the church and find your way to the altar. The wedding party proceeds (thus processional) down the aisle toward the altar, where the groom and best man may or may not be waiting. In the traditional Jewish ceremony, both the bride and groom are escorted down the aisle by both of their parents.

It's a good idea to have any ring bearers or flower girls take their seat at the end of the processional. They are usually too young to be able to stand throughout the entire ceremony without fidgeting or growing tired.

Processional Order – Christian Ceremony

→ Officiant, groom, and best man wait on the right side of the altar, facing the aisle, although in some ceremonies they do precede the bridal party down the aisle before taking up their positions

→ Ushers (Usually in order of height, walking in pairs or single file)

→ Bridesmaids (Usually in order of height, walking in pairs or single file)

→ Maid or matron of honor

→ Ring bearer

→ Flower girl

→ Bride, with her escort on her right

Processional Order – Jewish Ceremony

→ Cantor or rabbi

→ Groom's grandparents

→ Bride's grandparents

→ Ushers walking singly or in pairs

→ Best man

→ Groom and his parents, with his mother on his right and his father on his left

→ Bridesmaids, walking singly or in pairs

→ Maid or matron of honor

→ Ring bearer or flower girl

→ Bride escorted by both her parents, mother on right, father on left

WHO STANDS WHERE?

The traditional placement of people at the altar in a Christian ceremony is as follows, although this can be arranged to suit your individual ceremony needs.

The traditional placement in a Jewish ceremony is as follows:

OPENING REMARKS

This is where the officiant welcomes your guests and invites them to share in this momentous event in your lives.

EXCHANGE OF VOWS

The bride and groom exchange vows, either traditional ones or those they have written themselves.

RING CEREMONY

The officiant blesses the rings, explains their significance, then the bride and groom exchange them.

THE PRONOUNCEMENT

The officiant pronounces you man and wife, usually introducing you to the crowd by the names you've chosen for your married names. You are then instructed to kiss (as if you needed any prompting!).

THE RECESSIONAL

The bridal party prances out of the church to the sound of the joyful music the two of you have selected.

Christian Recessional

Bride and groom

Best man and maid/matron of honor

Bridesmaids and ushers, in pairs

Parents are the first to leave the pews, following the bridal party out of the church

Jewish Recessional

Bride and groom

Bride's parents

Groom's parents

Best man and maid/matron of honor

Bridesmaids and ushers, in pairs

Cantor and rabbi

PERSONALIZING YOUR CEREMONY

Some couples love to say vows that are steeped in tradition and significant historical custom. Others can't imagine saying words that someone else put in their mouth for such a personal, meaningful part of their lives. Luckily, you can personalize your wedding – or not – to any degree you'd like. You can choose to use the traditional ceremony, vows, and readings, taking deep satisfaction in those traditions, or you can personalize some readings, hymns, or musical selections. It's your choice. Just make sure you've discussed any desired personalization with your officiant well beforehand so there is no misunderstanding as to what you can change and what you cannot.

CREATIVE IDEAS

THE PROCESSIONAL

* Rather than have your back to the guests, change places with the officiant and face your guests.

* At a small, intimate ceremony, have the guests join you at the altar or have them join hands encircling you.

* Consider including both sets of parents in the processional.

* Have the groom meet you halfway down the aisle.

* The bride can part from her father by kissing him on the cheek when they reach his seat, then walk alone to meet the groom.

THE CEREMONY ITSELF

❉ Have the officiant ask, "Who blesses this union?" or "Who blesses this marriage?" Have both sets of parents or all the guests join in saying, "We do."

❉ Involve children from previous marriages by acknowledging them in the ceremony through special readings, prayers, or the presentation of the "Family Medallion."(More on this in the chapter on second marriages.)

❉ Have a favorite piece of music played or sung during the ceremony, or as you leave. But check with your church or synagogue as to any music restrictions they might have.

❉ Write your own poem or prayer and read it, or have quotations from a favorite poem or prayer read by the officiant or a family member.

ACCEPTANCE CEREMONY

If you're looking for an alternative to being "given away," you may want to consider the acceptance ceremony. Many older brides, those marrying for a second time, or those who don't have a father in attendance, feel being given away doesn't work for their situations. This makes a nice alternative.

In the acceptance ceremony, the officiant asks if there are members from both the bride and groom's families who wish to stand and express a few words, accepting the new spouse into their family. The officiant may start with either the bride or groom's family first. Ahead of time, select one or two relatives from each side to speak, that way they'll have something prepared. Others may choose to join in after the originally chosen members have spoken. If either the bride or groom has children from a previous marriage, those children should be included in the ceremony and should be accepted into the new family along with the parent. Be sure they are mentioned by name in the speech.

CANDLELIGHT CEREMONIES

The romantic glow of candlelight can be absolutely breathtaking in evening or late afternoon ceremonies. If this idea appeals to you, you will need to check with proper church authorities to see if this type of ceremony is allowed and what fire regulations will apply, possibly affecting the location and number of candles you may use.

Have two candle stands decorated with ribbons and flowers on either side of the altar. You may want to complement that with a similar single candle stand at the end of several rows. You can have the candles lit by a pair of ushers before the ceremony, or have each attendant carry a candle down the aisle to make a dramatic entrance.

If you want additional symbolism in your ceremony, consider having a lit candle on both the bride's and groom's side, with a single unlit candle in the center. Once pronounced husband and wife, you each take your respective candles and, with their flames blending together, light the Unity Candle, joining your lives as one. Whichever type of candlelight you choose to enhance your ceremony, double-check to make sure all candles are securely placed in their holders before the ceremony begins.

SHARING OF THE CUP

A cup of wine (or other beverage) is symbolic of the cup of life. During the sharing of the cup, both the bride and groom drink from the same cup, symbolizing their commitment to share all that the future may bring. All the sweetness life's cup may hold for you should be sweeter because you drink it together; whatever bitterness it may contain should be less bitter because you share it together.

PRESENTATION OF ROSES

The presentation of roses (or other gifts) by the bride and groom to their parents symbolizes their affection and appreciation for the love that has brought them to this day. Together the couple presents roses to the groom's parents and then to the bride's parents, uniting the families in this joyous celebration. Surprise them by keeping this part of the ceremony a secret until the moment the roses are presented.

INVOLVING YOUR GUESTS

✳ Depending on your budget and the number of people, a single rose could be handed to every guest, or a candle for each guest to light during an evening ceremony.

✳ If you're not too nervous, you can stop at the end of the aisle, take a single rose from your bouquet, and hand it to your mother. Then take another and hand it to his mother. Keep this move as a little surprise for them.

OTHER SPECIAL TOUCHES

✳ Incorporate symbolism in some way by carrying a family Bible, handkerchief, or fan that was carried by your or the groom's mother.

✳ In a church wedding, you can find out about having the church bells rung after you say your vows.

✳ There are creative alternatives to throwing rice. Since rice is harmful to birds, consider throwing birdseed instead. Dried flower petals and colorful confetti or streamers (in bio-degradable material) are affordable alternatives. Or add some fun by having the guests blow bubbles as the newlyweds leave the church. Sparklers (when carefully used and discarded) can be spectacular for an evening wedding.

✳ After being pronounced man and wife, add a romantic touch with the centuries-old European tradition of releasing white doves, the symbol of love, unity, and devotion. With a church ceremony, stage the dove release outside. Re-exit the church, and have the doves released as your guests look on. A flock of white doves makes a great alternative to throwing rice, and a spectacular send-off. For information on white dove releases, check the wedding section of your phone book's yellow pages or call local florists and pet stores. This special touch may not be available in your area.

✳ Today's ecology-minded brides, who are looking for new ways to do something special for their weddings and the environment, might consider the newest concept in weddings, and release dozens of Monarch butterflies. These butterflies are specifically raised for this purpose, then carefully shipped overnight and released into the environment at the proper time during the ceremony. This not only helps increase our diminishing butterfly population but also adds a dazzling touch to a garden wedding.

WRITING YOUR OWN VOWS

Most couples feel that their love is truly unique, a special bond between the two of them that no one else will ever experience in quite the same way. They're right. Writing your own vows can be an intensely moving and intimate way to create a ceremony that truly reflects the way you feel about each other.

Before you can effectively express your feelings, you'll need to identify them. It's important to talk to each other about your marriage, discussing your beliefs, dreams, and expectations. Take notes on

The vows themselves should only take two or three minutes to say to one another. This is a public declaration of your commitment, not a private conversation between the two of you.

Don't embarrass your friends and family with details that are too intimate or lengthy.

Sincerity is the key; the words should come from your heart.

Decide whether or not the two of you will recite the same vows or different ones.

Incorporate your wedding guests into your vows by having them respond with their blessings and support.

Discuss your personal vows with your officiant beforehand.

Read your vows out loud, which is a surprisingly effective way to catch errors, glitches, or awkward phrasing.

Additional thoughts on your commitment to marriage may be expressed in the main body of the ceremony or through the use of special poems and prayers.

this conversation and use it as the foundation for building your own custom made vows. Once you identify the things that are the most important to you, then you can decide how best to express them.

HERE ARE SOME QUESTIONS TO GET YOU STARTED

→ *When and where did you first meet?*

→ *What was the state of your life before the two of you met?*

→ *At what point did you realize you were in love? Describe the feeling.*

→ *What inspires you about your loved one?*

→ *What life goals and dreams do you share?*

→ *What have you learned from each other?*

→ *What qualities make your love unique? What qualities will keep it strong?*

→ *How has your view of the world changed since you fell in love?*

→ *What do you most look forward to about life with this person?*

→ *What are some special moments in your relationship, either happy or sad, humorous or profound?*

ALL YOU NEED IS WORDS

When searching for the right words to use, don't forget poetry, books, or song lyrics that touch your heart. These are a great place to begin.

Also consider taking some of the typical words used in ceremonies — cherish, love, honor, support, obey — and brainstorm around them, finding your own unique words with just the right nuance of meaning. Just in case you're stuck, we've provided a Wedding Vow Thesaurus, a list of phrases and words that will get you started.

PHRASES

In sickness and in health
In sunshine and in shadow
For all eternity
From the deepest recesses of my heart
The full measure of my love
Built on mutual love and honesty
A symbol of my love
All the days of our lives
Dearer than life itself
I give myself to you
Light of my life
May our love flourish and grow

VERBS

Accept	Endeavor	Promise
Adore	Endure	Protect
Challenge	Experience	Respect
Cherish	Give	Share
Comfort	Honor	Stand
Commit	Join	Strive
Cry	Laugh	Support
Declare	Learn	Swear
Desire	Love	Uplift
Develop	Nurture	Wonder
Embrace	Offer	
Encourage	Pledge	

NOUNS

Accomplice	Fears	Permanent
Adversity	Frailty	Problems
Ally	Freedom	Reverence
Angel	Friend	Sickness
Beauty	Good fortune	Sorrow
Beloved	Growth	Soul mate
Best friend	Hero	Spirit
Companion	Humor	Sweetheart
Darling	Joy	Symbol
Dearest	Lover	Teacher
Despair	Neglect	Treasure
Eternity	Partner	True counterpart
Faith	Peace	Understanding

QUALITIES

Beauty	Generosity	New
Candor	Gentility	Partnership
Charisma	Grace	Playfulness
Charm	Happy	Priceless
Cheerfulness	Holy	Pride
Chivalry	Honesty	Purity
Courage	Hopeful	Simplicity
Dearest	Humility	Sincerity
Dependability	Humor	Sweetness
Determination	Independence	Tenderness
Elegance	Innocence	True
Enduring	Integrity	Trust
Eternal	Joyful	Unknown
Everlasting	Long	Virtue
Fidelity	Loveliest	Worth
Forever	Loyalty	

DESCRIPTIONS

Alive	Emotional	Predestined
Ardent	Enduring	Pure
Attractive	Fair	Reliable
Beautiful	Faithful	Romantic
Beholden	Forgiving	Safe
Binding	Genuine	Significant
Caring	Glowing	Sincere
Charming	Glorious	Soft
Complete	Growing	Solemn
Considerate	Happy	Staunch
Constant	Hopeful	Sweet
Courageous	Innocent	Triumphant
Cozy	Jubilant	Unconditional
Dauntless	Lasting	Virtuous
Deserving	Lovely	Wonderful
Desirable	Mutual	Worthy
Devoted	Noble	
Ecstatic	Precious	*

CEREMONY *wording* and IDEAS *worksheet*

Prelude:

_____

Processional (participants order)*:*

_____

_____

Welcome or Call to Worship:

_____

_____

Readings or Prayer:

_____

_____

Music (optional)*:*

_____

Wedding Meditation (additional comments on marriage, optional)*:*

_____

_____

_____

Declaration of Consent (directed to bride's father, or both sets of parents)*:*

_____

_____

Readings or Prayer (optional)*:*

_____

_____

_____

_____

Introduction to the Vows:

_____

_____

CEREMONY *wording* and IDEAS *worksheet*

Bride's Vows:

_____

_____

Groom's Vows:

_____

_____

Affirmation by Guests:

_____

Exchange of Rings:

_____

Blessing of the Rings (optional):

_____

Pronouncement of the Union:

_____

Music (optional):

_____

Recognition of the Children (see chapter on Second Marriages for ideas, optional):

_____

_____

Prayer of Hope or Lord's Prayer (optional):

_____

_____

Special Acts of Celebration (lighting of the Unity Candle, Sharing of the Cup, Presentation of Roses, or other symbolic celebration; optional):

_____

_____

CEREMONY *wording* and IDEAS *worksheet*

Benediction and Blessing:

_____

_____

Presentation of the New Couple:

_____

_____

Recessional:

_____

_____

_____

_____

NOTES:

_____

_____

_____

_____

_____

_____

_____

_____

_____

_____

_____

_____

_____

_____

Is There a Contract in the House?

Avoiding consumer fraud

Your florist promised you white tulips and peonies for your wedding bouquet and you received calla lilies and roses. Your baker promised you a wedding cake of chocolate with raspberry flavored filling and you received a cake with brown frosting and raspberries on it for decoration that reminds you far too much of that volcano you made for the sixth grade science fair. Now what?

Never underestimate the power of a good contract.

It's been proven that quite often, no two people hear the same thing the same way. (Remember the game Telephone where you all sat around in a circle and watched as a whispered phrase became mutilated beyond recognition?) You may think you've been quite clear in communicating your wants and needs to your wedding vendors, and they may be equally certain they understood you. Unfortunately, while you said chocolate cake, they heard chocolate frosting. They were completely taken aback when it turns out it was NOT what you had specified.

Also, you would hope that weddings — being such optimistic, cheerful, romantic affairs — would only attract equally optimistic, cheerful, and romantic people. Unfortunately, that's not the case. Weddings are a multibillion-dollar-a-year industry and as such attracts its share of unscrupulous vendors. How can you protect yourself? How can you be sure that you get exactly what you're planning on come the big day?

In a word, contracts. Always put everything in writing.

There is no real way to make this subject interesting, but like root canals and income taxes, contracts are a necessary part of life. Especially if you want to avoid being taken to the cleaners, or at the very least, ensure you get exactly what you bargained for on your wedding day. In fact, a clear, well-drawn-up contract is one of the few tools you have available to guarantee that the wedding vendor delivers exactly what you asked for.

Once you've decided which wedding professionals you plan to use, it's time to firm up the details in the form of a contract or letter of agreement. Having things in writing with each of your providers will give both of you peace of mind as the wedding day approaches and will help ensure there are no misunderstandings. Or, if something should go wrong, you have the written contract to help renegotiate the price or provide evidence in case of litigation.

CONTRACTS

Most wedding professionals will have standard contracts. If they don't, they can write the details out in a letter of agreement. The contract or agreement should describe the details of merchandise or service they are to provide, the costs agreed upon, and should be signed by both parties.

You should have contracts or letters of agreement with the following professionals, or anyone else providing services for your wedding.

- Baker
- Bridal consultant
- Bridal salon
- Caterer
- Ceremony location
- Florist
- Musicians
- Photographer
- Reception hall
- Rental equipment company
- Stationery provider
- Transportation service
- Tuxedo rental store

CONTRACT TIPS

Specify all the details, from the size and type of flowers in your bouquet to the appropriate dress and number of breaks the musicians will take. The following list contains some of the general items that should be included in your contract.

- Day, date, and time
- Delivery dates, times, and locations
- Detailed list of merchandise ordered
- List of services to be provided, number of hours, breaks, etc.
- Appropriate dress
- Name of person in charge of your wedding
- Alternative merchandise or service, if needed
- Deposits or payment schedules
- Last date to make changes or provide final guest count
- Cancellation and refund policy

Read the contract carefully, especially the fine print. Make sure you understand and agree to everything; if not, ask questions or make changes—now's the time! Don't overlook the refund or cancellation policy.

Make sure both parties sign and date the contract. You won't have a valid contract if the party promising to provide the merchandise or service doesn't sign it. This may only become an issue if something goes wrong, but then of course, it's too late.

Consider putting your deposit on a credit card. Putting all deposits and purchases on a credit card is one of the best ways to protect yourself as a consumer. Special federal consumer protection laws protect all payments made with credit cards. You, as a consumer, have recourse with your credit card companies if you receive merchandise or services that do not live up to those you contracted for. You must first make an effort to correct the problem with the provider, or renegotiate the terms or price (do this in writing and keep copies). If this does not prove satisfactory, send a copy of your contract, correspondence, and a letter explaining the problem, and pictures or any proof that will strengthen your case to your credit card company. If, after their investigation, they find the merchant did not live up to the terms of your contract, they will not release funds to his or her account (or will deduct them from the account) and will credit your account. If the retailer wishes to dispute this, he or she will have to file a claim against you for payment.

Avoid large cancellation fees by reading the fine print of the contract, or ask exactly what the cancellation policy is. Will the deposit be refunded if you cancel six months in advance, or if the provider is able to rebook the date with another wedding? Does the contract state that, if the wedding is canceled, you are liable for 50 percent of the cost or for the total cost of the wedding, even if the original deposit was for much less than that cost?

Last-minute cancellation fees are understandable and fair; just beware of what you are agreeing to before signing the contract. In the event you do have to cancel, notify all services as soon as possible.

WEDDING INSURANCE

Now you can protect what you have invested in your wedding day with Weddingsurance, offered by Fireman's Fund. You may find this insurance to be a small price to pay for peace of mind. The company has a variety of plans available that offer coverage and protection against wedding cancellations (they don't cover change of heart). They may include wedding photographs, wedding attire, personal liability, and more. Contact Weddingsurance for information on reimbursement policy and restrictions. For more information call 1-800-ENGAGED (1-800-364-2433). ✳

NOTES

Setting your *Sites*

FINDING the perfect CEREMONY *and* RECEPTION *Location*

W hen trying to decide on a location for your wedding, the sky's the limit. Literally. Couples have been known to get married while skydiving or up in a hot air balloon, floating in a sea of blue sky and clouds. While you and your honey might not want to go to such extremes, it's nice to keep in mind that just about anything is possible. In fact, that's part of what makes this decision so tough — all the choices.

The setting you choose is the stage on which the drama of your nuptials will play itself out. Do you envision an elegant formal wedding in a grand old cathedral with dinner and dancing afterwards at a stately ballroom? How about marrying in a charming garden, surrounded by lush flowers, greenery, and all your family and friends invited to an al fresco reception immediately following? Maybe your style leans more toward a quaint country chapel with the reception at a charming country inn. Or perhaps you're one of the lucky ones and already have a perfect location in mind: the place where he proposed, where you first met, in front of the massive oak tree in your parents backyard where you used to climb and dream of your wedding, or at the small chapel you went every Sunday while growing up.

If you're having a tough time coming up with the perfect place or are unable to settle on a style, visiting a variety of sites can be both inspiring and motivating. You'll need to move quickly, however, because the most popular spots are reserved anywhere from twelve to twenty-four months in advance. So hop to it!

Hopefully, you did a little homework back in Chapter Four, Planning 101, and you have some idea of how many people you'll need to accommodate and what type of reception you want: sit-down dinner with dancing, buffet, or cake and champagne only. This will give you some idea as to how big a space you'll need.

The next critical factor in determining location is whether or not you want to have your ceremony and reception at different places, or whether you'd like the convenience of having them both at the same venue. That, in turn, will be decided by whether or not you want to have your ceremony in a house of worship, or are open to having it someplace else.

HOUSE OF WORSHIP

When planning a religious wedding in a house of worship, the location selection will depend on either your, your fiancé's, or your family's personal affiliation with a particular church or synagogue. Keep in mind the location's distance from the reception, and its size and style in relation to your overall wedding plans. When considering locations, make sure the space will accommodate all your guests. However, don't select a large church or temple if there are very few guests. A small place of worship would be more intimate.

Some houses of worship also have banquet or meeting halls that work well for a catered reception right there on the church premises, which will somewhat simplify things. Make sure to ask about that when researching the church or synagogue.

It's also possible to have a religious ceremony in a secular location, as many officiants are willing to perform ceremonies at other locations such as homes, gardens, or hotels.

QUESTIONS TO ASK

Before making a commitment to a particular place of worship, set up an appointment to discuss the following:

➼ Is proof of divorce or special permission from the church needed when remarrying?

➼ Must we be members of the church, or may a friend sponsor us?

➼ What are the fees for the church or synagogue? And how much time does that allow us?

➼ Is a small chapel available for smaller ceremonies?

➼ Are there any restrictions regarding ceremony attire, such as bare shoulders or yarmulkes?

➼ How many people will the church or synagogue hold?

➼ Is there a hall or social room available for a reception? If so, is there an additional fee? If you plan to serve alcoholic beverages or wine, be sure to inquire about the policies.

➼ Will they supply tables, chairs, linens, china, and silver?

➼ May rice, birdseed, or rose petals be thrown?

➼ Are there accommodations for wheelchairs?

➼ Is an aisle runner, chuppah, candelabra, or kneeling cushion available, if needed?

➼ May the wording of the religious ceremony be changed at all?

➼ Are there facilities for the bridal party to get dressed in?

➼ Are there any restrictions regarding flowers or candles?

➼ What are the rules regarding photography inside the place of worship?

➼ Are there music restrictions that interfere with music or songs you may want?

➼ Do you need approval for special vows you may want to incorporate?

➼ Are there restrictions regarding the day of the week, or the time the ceremony can take place? What about religious holidays?

➼ What are the policies on interfaith marriages? Can you combine two religious ceremonies, or have both clergymen officiate jointly?

➼ Can you have the caterer of your choice?

OTHER CEREMONY AND RECEPTION LOCATIONS

In addition to your personal taste and desires, the location you select will be determined by the availability on your date, the number of people to be accommodated, and the price. Because all these factors don't always line up exactly right, it helps to have a few sites in mind. As you research your location choices, remember to find out precisely what is, or is not, included in the price. Unexpected extras can add up quickly. Don't delay in reserving the location once you've made your decision; popular places are reserved early. The following are some things to keep in mind when selecting a location.

Space – Either wide open or cozy and intimate, whichever works best with the wedding you envision for yourself.

Parking options – This is more of a factor if you're inviting two hundred guests rather than fifty, but either way, remember they'll need to park their cars somewhere.

Privacy – Do you want anyone out walking his or her dog to be able to look over and see your wedding? Usually, even hotels and banquet facilities have more than one function going on at a time, so there's a possibility of Lookey Loos there as well.

Lighting – This can be a terrific mood enhancer or mood breaker. Try to view the location around the same time of day you are planning your ceremony or reception. If you're having a daytime wedding, the facility should be bright and cheerful, not dim and gloomy. If you're planning an evening wedding, try to envision your different lighting options, whether special effects or merely soft and romantic.

Color and décor – If the room has lots of personality in this regard, that's great! Just make sure it jives with your desired colors and decorating themes. If the room is a Plain Jane of a room, how much work (and money) will be required to bring it up to par.

Surroundings – What type of neighborhood is it in? Does it have a spectacular view of the ocean or mountains? Or docs it look out over a chain link fence and narrow alley?

Usage of space – Does the room lend itself well to all the facets of the wedding you're planning? Does it have a nice focal point for your ceremony? Is there adequate room for setting up dining tables, mingling with cocktails, and dancing?

Technical support – Can the location support all of the various electronics that you'll be plugging in? Amplifiers, speakers, special lighting, etc?

Acoustics – If music is going to be an important part of your reception, do the room acoustics help or hinder this goal?

TWO SITES – TWO TIMINGS

It's always best to have your reception immediately following the ceremony. If you decide on two separate sites, you'll need to be certain the timings coordinate. If the ceremony is held at a house of worship and is over at 4:30, but your reception site isn't available until 5:30, you will have a timing problem. Or perhaps your ceremony site is only available at 3:00 PM, but you have your heart set on a sit-down dinner with dancing reception. That will be a huge time gap to bridge, so you'll need to move to your second choice, or come up with an especially creative (and time consuming) activity for your guests.

TURNING A ROOM

If you have your ceremony and reception in the same room, an expression you'll need to become familiar with is, turning a room. Turning a room is when you have to rearrange it after one activity in order to prepare it for another. For example, breaking down the chairs and arch used for the ceremony to make room for buffet tables and table rounds for dining. While the room is being turned, you can have your receiving line outside on the patio or in another room or foyer that is close by. Or you might want to consider serving cocktails in a separate room instead.

On-Site Catering vs. Off-Site Catering

Most hotels, restaurants, banquet halls, and private clubs will have on-site chefs, menus, and wait staff that they will insist on using for your event. Normally, there isn't too much flexibility here. Very few hotels, restaurants, etc. will allow you to bring in an off-site caterer. Usually, however, a facility's on-site catering service has played a major role in why you've selected that location in the first place.

Private homes, estates, gardens, museums, and other locations will most likely not have any catering facilities of their own. In this case, you'll need to find your own caterer, which is known as an off-site caterer.

Don't forget to factor in the cost of rentals when deciding between all-inclusive packages that are offered by hotels and banquet halls versus those coordinated at a home, garden, or other location. Often, such things as tables, chairs, linens, china, tableware, and glasses are included when having a reception at a hotel or banquet hall. While at first it may seem more expensive, make sure to add up all the rental costs before planning an off-site reception. You may find out it is no deal.

Home or Garden Weddings

There's a special warmth and uniqueness that can be derived from a home wedding. A home or garden wedding can range from a more formal ceremony and catered affair to an informal ceremony and a do-it-yourself reception (with a little help from your friends). If your home isn't large enough, maybe some friends or relatives would offer the use of theirs. If none of theirs are suitable or available, sometimes you can find private homes to rent through real-estate companies, wedding consultants, or local newspapers. It may be possible to go through a film location company, one that scouts locations for advertisements or television commercials. So check to see if there is this type of a location company in your area.

If the ceremony is in the home, coming down a stairway and then having the ceremony take place in front of a fireplace can make a nice arrival. If in the garden, what about having the ceremony under a stately old tree, decorated arch, or gazebo? Whatever the focal point is, try to position it so the sun will not shine in the guests' eyes. Depending on space, guests may be seated or they may stand. If the latter is the case, don't make the ceremony too long. Even if you keep the ceremony short, do remember to provide seating for any elderly guests that will be attending.

Private homes and gardens can offer more flexibility with regard to personal desires and time schedules. However, the burden of coordinating is on you and may require the assistance of a wedding coordinator.

Things to think about when considering a home wedding:

- Can the home or garden comfortably accommodate all the guests you want to invite?
- Is there adequate parking?
- Is the kitchen large enough to accommodate the caterer's needs?
- What about the toilet and septic facilities? Are they adequate for the needs of two hundred guests?
- Are there enough electrical outlets for the lights, heating, band equipment, etc.?
- Can the area be tented or moved inside in the event of bad weather?
- Have you thoroughly considered the rental costs associated with bringing in tables, chairs, sufficient linens, and dinnerware?

→ Do consider sending a note letting your neighbors know that a wedding reception will be taking place, especially for an evening reception with a band. This may prevent any problems that might otherwise occur. Even better — invite them!

→ Unless the house has extremely large rooms, or an enormous cultivated lawn space, you'll need to consider renting a tent in order to set up rows and rows of chairs for the ceremony or to provide a Plan B in case of rain.

GOOD IN-TENT-IONS

Tenting is a critical consideration when planning an outdoor wedding, whether in a private garden or in a public outside space. Tents can be expensive, running anywhere from $500 all the way up to $2,000 plus, not including set up and delivery! You may or may not need a floor, depending on how level and stable the ground is, and what you want to do on said ground (i.e., dance). Flooring adds considerably to the expense. But, if your only other option is drenched guests and water logged hors d'oeuvres, they are the best deal going.

If at all possible, it's a good idea to have a separate tent for the caterer and their staff. If it rains, you need to work out how the caterers will get from their tent to the main tent without getting soaked or ending up with a soggy supper.

Decorating the tent can be expensive, and most brides do prefer something other than blank canvas and tent poles for their wedding decorations.

The weather also plays a part. You'll want a tent sturdy enough to stand up to rain, but not so heavy that all your guests feel as if they're wearing a tarp. In warm weather, you need to decide if it will be hot enough to warrant air conditioning. If there's a chance the weather will turn nippy, how about supplying heaters?

Make sure you've thoroughly discussed sound system hook-ups, flooring or ground cover, set up and delivery charges, generators, and back up generators. You'll also need to check if there is a local permit required to erect a tent in your area.

MOUNTAINS, PARKS, BEACHES

For some, there is nothing more romantic than saying your vows under a beautiful blue sky with towering redwoods, majestic mountain peaks, or the sparkling ocean as a backdrop. The parks and recreation department in your area can help you find that perfect spot, and it will work equally well for your reception. Again, you'll need to have a back up plan in case of inclement weather. Often, public outdoor locations will have a clubhouse, gazebo, or pavilion you can use. Just be sure to check first. You will also need to consider the following.

→ Do you need a permit to have your reception in a public outdoor place?

→ Do you need to reserve the space? How far in advance?

→ Can you have a band or DJ?

→ Can you have cooking fires?

→ What types of electrical hook-ups can they accommodate?

→ What equipment will you need to rent? Tables, chairs, portable toilets, tents, dinnerware, etc.

→ Is lighting an issue?

→ What about bugs, your uninvited guests?

WEDDINGS HELD AT PRIVATE CLUBS, HOTELS, RESTAURANTS, OR BANQUET FACILITIES

Most hotels, private clubs, and banquet facilities can accommodate both the ceremony and reception, which can significantly reduce the logistic juggling involved with planning a wedding. Many will even furnish altars, aisle, canvas, canopies, and chairs. Before committing yourself, check on whether or not these items are provided and if not, see what the availability and cost will be through a rental company. Hotel facilities tend to book up rapidly, especially in the traditionally busy wedding months of June, July, and August. Keep in mind that few private clubs open their facilities to non-members. If your family doesn't have a membership, you might have a relative or close friend who would be honored to sponsor (not pay for) your wedding.

These facilities are popular for a reason: they do a lot of weddings, often offering complete wedding packages, and they've acquired a hefty degree of experience. They've done things like set up and break down hundreds of times. They've got it all down to a science, which can make things wonderfully easy for the bride and groom. This ease of planning and stepping into their polished template can be fabulous or miserable, depending upon how well their standard approach suits your wedding vision. You may find yourself having to conform to their time schedule and pre-established menus, which allow little or no flexibility.

Your main point of contact will be the catering or banquet manager, and you'll need to know right from the beginning what they will and won't do and how much flexibility you'll be allowed.

PRIVATE CLUBS, HOTELS, OR RESTAURANTS

→ These locations are probably the easiest to consider. They offer complete service and facilities and they will coordinate all phases of your reception.

→ See the actual room or location where the reception would take place.

→ Discuss the menu selections and the costs per person of each. Does it include the cake?

→ Check liquor and beverage fees. What is the charge per drink for an open bar? Is there a corking fee if you provide your own champagne? Do they charge extra to pour coffee with the cake?

→ Find out what equipment is included, what will be extra, and what will be rented — dance floor, microphone, etc.

→ Check on music restrictions.

→ Know exactly how long you may have the facilities.

→ Make sure they have adequate serving people. Most commercial places add a service fee, so find out what that will be.

→ See if decorations and flowers are handled separately or if they are provided.

WINERIES

If you have wineries in your area, many of them will rent their grounds. The prices can vary so it may be wise to check a few before making a decision. Many are old, steeped in tradition, and make a beautiful setting for a unique wedding. Some wineries in California's Napa Valley are known for the hot-air balloons, which land at the winery in time for a champagne brunch. You can plan an early morning ceremony, then take a hot-air balloon ride to a winery where you'll meet your guests for this special occasion.

HISTORICAL OR PUBLIC SITES

There are many beautiful old mansions that, over the years, have been donated to cities or states, and are open to the public for tours. Many of these mansions can be rented. The cost varies so check their fees and availability. To imagine using such a location, just think of having a Gatsby style wedding at the Astors' mansion in Newport, Rhode Island, where the movie The Great Gatsby was filmed.

Planning a Wedding to Remember

There are also many museums, arboretums, and formal gardens that make beautiful settings for a wedding. To find locations available in your area check local newspapers and phone books, or call the chamber of commerce in your vicinity.

IMPORTANT CONTRACT NOTES

→ Booking receptions too close together is a common problem that can occur. When another wedding is booked for the same day in the same room as yours, make sure you specify your exact time, from which hour to which hour, allowing enough time for clean up. If you feel the catering manager or reception coordinator has not allowed enough time for clean up or overstaying by those attending the first reception, point this out. You don't want your guests to arrive and have to wait in the wings. Remember, the more weddings the managers book, the more money they make, and sometimes they try to squeeze too many in on the same day.

→ Cancellation policies. Read the fine print and fully understand the cancellation policy. Are you liable for 50 percent of the entire reception cost, or just the small deposit you made, if you cancel months before the wedding? What if you cancel at the last minute? Do you get your deposit back if they are able to rebook the room? Check these things out. Put your deposit on a credit card; you'll have a better chance of having it refunded in case there's a dispute.

→ Avoid hidden extras by reading the fine print of the contract. If the contract doesn't specify certain fees such as set up, clean up, overtime fees or gratuities, ask about them. Inquire about charges for cake cutting, coat check, and corkage fees. Itemize all the costs, and then state on the contract that no additional fees are to be added. If anything should change, initial and date the new charge.

WHERE TO FIND SITES

→ Yellow Pages → Web directories

→ Local newspapers → Tourism boards

→ Historical societies → Chambers of commerce

→ Personal references → Wedding professionals

→ Regional bridal magazines

MORE GREAT IDEAS FOR CEREMONY AND RECEPTION LOCATIONS

A romantic resort	Civic or private theaters	Hotel ballrooms	Private club facilities	Yachts, boats, or barges
Aquariums	Community centers	Lighthouses	Private homes and estates for rent	Your home or a friend's home
Art galleries	Concert halls	Luxury or historic hotels	Public beaches and parks	Zoos or amusement parks
Banks or larger lobbies of grand old buildings	Condominium or private estate clubhouse facilities	Military club facilities	Public or private gardens	Any place beautiful, interesting, or romantic in your area ✳
Bed and breakfast inns	Elks or women's club facilities	Mountain or beach resorts	Racetracks	
Castles and private estates	Fairgrounds	Movie studio lots	Romantic restaurants	
Church or synagogue halls	Historical buildings or mansions	Museums	University facilities	
		Observatories	Wineries	
		Orchards		

QUESTIONS to Ask the RECEPTION site coordinator

Photocopy and use one for each location interviewed.

RECEPTION SITE

_____

What type of hall or
social rooms are available? _____

What is the maximum number
their room can accommodate? _____

What is the fee? _____

For how many hours? _____

Are there overtime charges? _____

What is included? _____

Do they provide tables,
chairs, linens, china, and silver? _____

Is there any additional fee? _____

Are there certain days of the week,
or times of the day, when the price
is discounted? _____

Can the site be used for both the
ceremony and reception? _____

Can you use your own caterer
or is there an in-house caterer
that must be used? _____

Are there music restrictions
concerning the type of music or
length of time it may be played? _____

Is there a piano or are other
musical instruments at the site? _____

Is there a charge to use them? _____

Are there regulations on
photography or videotaping? _____

Are there rooms available for the
bride, groom, and attendants to
change into wedding attire or
going-away clothes? _____

Are there restrictions on alcohol? _____

Can hard liquor, beer, wine,
or champagne be served? _____

Can you provide your own liquor? _____

With wine or champagne,
is there a corkage fee? _____

If they provide the liquor,
what is the per drink or
per person charge? _____

Is there an adequate kitchen? _____

Is there a dance floor? _____

Do they provide a microphone? _____

If outside, are there
heaters and lights? _____

If not, is there sufficient electrical
power available to use them there? _____

Are there adequate
restroom facilities? _____

Is liability insurance,
including liquor liability,
included in the rental fee? _____

Do they provide a coat check? _____

What is the fee, if any? _____

Do they have adequate parking? _____

Is there an additional fee? _____

What is the deposit? _____

What is the cancellation policy? _____

If reception is to be in a garden,
can the area be tented? _____

Is there an alternative location
that can accommodate the guests
in the event of bad weather? _____

With a private reception site, do
neighbors, police, or security
companies need to be notified? _____

Is there a special area for guests
to wait for the arrival of the bride
and groom? _____

Is there a good location for the
receiving line, guest book,
and gift tables? _____

Is a security deposit required? _____

  If so, how much? _____

  When is it refunded? _____

Is the clean up included in
the rental fee? _____

RECEPTION site *worksheet*

	Estimate #1	Estimate #2
	Name _____	Name _____
	_____	_____
	Phone _____	Phone _____

	Description Cost	Description Cost
ROOM/HALL Date Available Time Occupancy Fee		
EQUIPMENT Tables Chairs Linens		
FOOD Hors d'oeuvres Buffet Sit-down Wedding Cake		
BEVERAGES Open Bar Champagne/Wine Non-alcoholic		
NUMBER OF SERVERS Waiters Bartenders Valet Attendants Tips		
MISCELLANEOUS		
TOTAL		
GRATUITIES INCLUDED	❑ Yes ❑ No	❑ Yes ❑ No
SALES TAX INCLUDED	❑ Yes ❑ No	❑ Yes ❑ No
NUMBER OF HOURS		
OVERTIME COST per hour		
CANCELLATION Policy Fee		
DEPOSIT REQUIRED Amount Date Required		

RECEPTION site *worksheet*

	Estimate #3		Estimate #4	
	Name _____		Name _____	
	Phone _____		Phone _____	
	Description	*Cost*	*Description*	*Cost*
ROOM/HALL Date Available Time Occupancy Fee				
EQUIPMENT Tables Chairs Linens				
FOOD Hors d'oeuvres Buffet Sit-down Wedding Cake				
BEVERAGES Open Bar Champagne/Wine Non-alcoholic				
NUMBER OF SERVERS Waiters Bartenders Valet Attendants Tips				
MISCELLANEOUS				
TOTAL				
GRATUITIES INCLUDED	❏ Yes ❏ No		❏ Yes ❏ No	
SALES TAX INCLUDED	❏ Yes ❏ No		❏ Yes ❏ No	
NUMBER OF HOURS				
OVERTIME COST per hour				
CANCELLATION Policy Fee				
DEPOSIT REQUIRED Amount Date Required				

Your Supporting *Cast*

SELECTING wedding *Attendants*

*L*uckily, no one expects the two of you to stand up there at the altar in front of God and everyone all alone. You're allowed to take reinforcements with you. These stalwart, supportive souls are known as your wedding attendants. They attend the wedding, they attend the parties, they (hopefully) attend to their duties, and they most definitely attend to you!

These people will be your support system, your network of helping hands, and sympathetic ears. Use them wisely and use them well, but most importantly, use this circle of friends to help keep your wedding planning a joyous and filled-with-laughter time of your life.

IT'S A CHICK THING – SELECTING YOUR BRIDESMAIDS

Girlfriends. How could you possibly get by without them? Whether she was the one who showed you how to wad up tissue paper and stuff it into your bra so it wouldn't show and explained to you what French kissing was, or introduced you to Vodka martinis and male strip clubs, life would be a dull gray without them. Who else would you call, squealing like an eleven-year-old at an 'N Sync concert after your first big promotion? Who else could tell you exactly what to do when your latest color rinse turned your hair a brassy green?

Your girlfriends are the anchors in your sea of life. Of course they'll play a major part in your wedding. They might even be partially responsible for you getting married in the first place, whether due to their advice, skills as a venting board, meddling, or fixing you up with a blind date.

When selecting your attendants, keep in mind their basic personalities and abilities. The friend who introduced you to male dance clubs and vodka martinis might not be your best choice for maid of honor, but you can bet she'd be awesome at throwing a great bachelorette party. No matter how close you and your youngest sister are, if she is known more for her whimsical flights of fancy than her dependable and assisting nature, think twice before choosing her to be your maid of honor. Review the lists of duties required by each member of the wedding party and make sure the people you have in mind have the ability and the willingness to perform those functions. The last thing you want to do is strain close relationships during this highly emotional time. If those who are near and dear to you aren't particularly well suited to the tasks you have in mind, remember that there are other wedding functions they can perform.

Another consideration in your selection process is the state of your friends' bank accounts. If bridesmaids or ushers will be coming from out of town, bear in mind that they'll incur travel expenses as well as the normal expense of attendant attire and party giving. Also, they may not be as available to help with the pre-wedding activities, such as addressing envelopes or assembling favors.

MAID OR MATRON OF HONOR

Remember when you were younger, how you had one — and only one, there couldn't be a tie — best friend. As long as you had her to turn to, the other cliques could come and go, because you had each other, and really, when you had a best friend, the world was a great place to be.

Well, wedding etiquette and tradition has allowed for this female bonding phenomena and created the position of maid or matron of honor. She can be your biological sister, or the sister of your heart, someone who has shared in both your good times and bad with equal love and support. If you're the director of this whole production, then your maid or matron of honor is your assistant director. Just make sure she's up to the task. Keep in mind that while physical availability is a consideration, emotional availability is equally or even more so.

As maid or matron of honor, she will:
→ Help with details of wedding planning, such as addressing envelopes, making favors, and going on shopping excursions.

→ Pay for her own wedding attire.

→ Host a shower for the bride, either alone or with bridesmaids.

→ Host a shower for the bride and groom, with the help of the best man.

→ Organize or appoint someone to organize the bachelorette party, if you're having one.

→ Help organize the bridesmaids with their fittings.

→ Keep bridesmaids informed of all parties, functions, and rehearsals.

→ Attend the rehearsal dinner.

→ Oversee the bridesmaids on the wedding day by coordinating gowns, makeup, jewelry, and flowers.

→ Assist the bride in dressing before the ceremony and at the reception before the bride leaves.

→ Keep the groom's ring until the appropriate time in the ceremony, when she will exchange it for the bride's bouquet.

→ Sign the wedding certificate as a legal witness.

→ Assist the bride with the train and veil at the altar.

→ Be a member of the receiving line and be seated in a place of honor at the reception.

→ Make a toast in honor of the bride and groom, if she so chooses.

→ Make sure that the bride takes care of herself, especially at the reception; getting her something to eat and drink occasionally.

→ Hold the bride's hand throughout the long months of planning and be her shoulder to lean on during times of crisis.

BRIDESMAIDS

Girlfriends are like gourmet potato chips — no one can have just one. That would be like having to wear the same color lipstick for the rest of your life, or the same pair of shoes, or, well you get the idea. Variety is the spice of life and most women have a circle of close friends that they will want to include in this bridesmaid thing. There are no definite rules on the number of bridesmaids you should have, although most weddings do not have more than eight. For a semi-formal or informal wedding, you will probably want fewer. It's perfectly acceptable to have an uneven number.

With three or less, the bridesmaids walk single file down the aisle and precede the maid of honor. With an even number of four or more, you may want them to walk in pairs. If the bridesmaids outnumber the ushers in the recessional, the extras can pair up or walk alone. Most brides try to keep the same number of bridesmaids and ushers because it makes for symmetry at the altar and in the pictures.

The bridesmaids will:

→ Help with pre-wedding errands and tasks, specifically addressing invitations and making favors.

→ Pay for their own wedding attire.

→ Have a shower for the bride. This can be arranged by one or more of the bridesmaids.

→ Host a bachelorette party. Also can be held by one or more of them.

→ Attend all pre-wedding parties.

→ Attend the rehearsal and rehearsal dinner party.

→ Precede the bride down the aisle.

→ Participate in the receiving line.

→ Be generally supportive and ooh! and ah! over all the bride's painstaking and careful choices.

IT'S A GUY THING – SELECTING THE GROOMSMEN

THE BEST MAN

This is the groom's counterpart to the maid or matron of honor, lending him support, an ear, or a place to escape to when wedding planning threatens to overtake his life. Usually a brother, relative, or best friend, the best man is the groom's right-hand man in organizing activities and handling important duties. You'll want to select somebody who is dependable and who's not mourning the groom's passing from the stage of being a bachelor into matrimony.

The best man will:

→ Coordinate a shower for the couple with the maid or matron of honor.

→ Organize the bachelor party.

→ Pay for his own wedding attire.

→ Supervise the ushers' fittings.

→ Attend the rehearsal dinner.

→ Transport the groom to the church and help him dress.

→ Coordinate the groomsmen or ushers on the wedding day.

→ Keep the bride's wedding ring until the appropriate time during the ceremony.

→ Stand next to the groom at the altar to offer moral support and catch him in case he faints at the sight of his stunningly beautiful bride.

→ Deliver the officiant's fee before or after the ceremony.

→ Sign the wedding certificate as a witness.

→ Stand in the receiving line.

→ Make the first toast to the bride and groom at the reception and read any telegrams.

→ Dance with the bride and maid or matron of honor.

→ See that the suitcases are loaded into the honeymoon car and that the groom has his plane ticket, itinerary, and traveler's checks.

→ Take the groom's wedding attire to the cleaners or return it to the rental shop.

→ Hold the groom's hand throughout the entire process (mentally, of course, because Real Men don't hold hands).

THE USHERS OR GROOMSMEN

Like the bridesmaids, there is no definite number of ushers. Generally, the size of the wedding determines the number. For example, you wouldn't want ten ushers with only seventy-five guests. A good guide to follow is one usher for every fifty guests.

It's not necessary to have the same number of ushers as bridesmaids, however, it is better balanced if they are close in number. If there are less than four ushers, they walk down the aisle in the processional single file. If there are four or more, they may be paired with the bridesmaids, or each other, if you like.

The ushers or groomsmen are usually brothers, relatives, or close buddies of the bride and/or groom. Their responsibilities are to:

→ Pay for their wedding attire.

→ Arrive at the church one hour before the ceremony to seat the early guests.

→ Seat people with pew cards in the reserved or special section.

→ Distribute wedding service programs, if any.

→ Seat the bride's guests, usually on the left and the groom's on the right. (In the Orthodox Jewish wedding, the sides are reversed.)

→ Direct the placement of wedding gifts.

→ Seat the groom's parents in the right front pew and then the bride's mother in the left front row. She is the last person seated before the processional begins.

→ Unroll the aisle carpet, then take their places.

→ Escort the bridesmaids out of the church after the recessional.

→ Decorate the getaway car.

→ Act as if their buddy's transition to the married state is the best thing that ever happened to him.

THE FLOWER GIRL

These are adorable little cherubs masquerading as little girls (or little girls masquerading as cherubs — depends on whether or not they've had their nap) who precede the bride down the aisle. Usually, they range in age is from four to eight and they will skip, waltz, or pirouette their way down the aisle scattering flower petals for the bride to walk on. If rose petals are prohibited in your church, a great alternative is to have the flower girl carry baby roses and pass them out as she walks down the aisle.

RING BEARER OR TRAIN BEARER

It's not necessary to have either a ring bearer or train bearer. However, if you do know one or two cute little boys about four or five, you may want to include them just for the sheer adorability factor. The ring bearer or train bearer may also be a little girl. If so, she should be dressed the same as the flower girl. The duties are minimal, but the children look adorable and add a special touch. Note: If you're worried about the child losing the rings, it's perfectly acceptable to have "dummy" rings on the pillow with the real ones safely tucked away in the best man's pocket.

Responsibilities of the ring bearer and train bearer:

→ Carry the ring or rings tied by a ribbon on a satin or lacy pillow.

→ Walk alone or with the flower girl, preceding the bride.

→ Carry the bridal gown train, following the bride down the aisle.

MOTHER OF THE BRIDE

She is probably just as excited as you are and will want to be involved whenever possible. Her participation will depend on where she is geographically located in relation to you or the wedding and how close your relationship is. If you are close, she can help you with just about everything. Even if there's a distance (emotional or physical), she can help with advice and decisions. The two of you can review what needs to be done and decide where her biggest contribution will be.

Traditionally, the mother of the bride will:

→ Assist with the selection of the gown, accessories, and attendants' attire.

→ Compile her portion of the guest list and help address invitations.

→ Assist in the ceremony and reception details.

→ Attend most of the showers and parties given in her daughter's honor.

→ Attend the rehearsal dinner.

→ Purchase her own dress. She has the first choice in color, but consults with the groom's mother.

→ Keep the father of the bride informed of wedding plans.

→ Be the official hostess at the wedding reception.

→ Be the last person seated at the ceremony and the first to greet the guests in the receiving line.

→ Be seated in a place of honor at the reception.

→ Dance with your father and the groom.

→ Cry a lot — after all, her darling, sweet baby is getting married.

FATHER OF THE BRIDE

Many fathers prefer to be involved in more ways than merely writing the checks and escorting their daughters down the aisle. Make sure to discuss your dad's wishes. If he wants to be more involved — wonderful! You can either come up with separate duties for him or he can assist your mother with her list.

Many proud fathers have waited anxiously for this big day and the chance to escort their cherished daughter down the aisle to the new life that awaits her. While some brides prefer to walk alone, you might want to give it some thought before denying your father this pleasure.

With this is mind, the father of the bride will:

→ Conform, more or less, to the groom's and other attendants' apparel.

→ Drive to the wedding ceremony with the bride.

→ Escort his daughter down the aisle, and either stay there or sit in the front left pew.

→ Stand in the receiving line or mingle with guests as the host of the reception.

→ Take care of final payments of caterers, musicians, etc., and, generally, be the last person to leave the reception.

→ Look wistful a lot. After all, his beloved little girl is getting married, and he can't understand where the time went.

Groom's Parents

Once upon a time, the groom's parents were minimally involved, but no longer. Whether their involvement is of the financial, emotional, or task-oriented variety, do make full use of whatever assistance they are willing to offer.

Commonly, the groom's parents will:

→ Send a note or phone the bride and her parents welcoming her into their family.

→ Host the rehearsal dinner party.

→ Stand in the receiving line; the father may or may not do this.

Other Participants

Chances are good that there will not be room for everyone who is important and meaningful to you to stand up at the altar with you. As mentioned earlier, there are a number of ways to include other friends or relatives in the celebration. Here are some ideas to get you started.

→ Help decorate the ceremony or reception locations.

→ Read a scripture or poem, or serve as candle lighters.

→ Be in charge of the guest book and the gifts.

→ Oversee the production of the wedding program.

→ If musically talented, play a selection during the ceremony or reception.

Thanking Your Attendants

After all your attendants do to help you in planning and executing your wedding, you'll want to thank them with a special gift. It can be a memento of your wedding day or an indulgent gift for them to enjoy. It's usually given at the rehearsal dinner, the bridesmaids' luncheon, or at the bachelor or bachelorette party.

Some Suggestions for Her

→ Jewelry, either for the wedding or after:

Small crystal bangle bracelets

Delicate necklace

Locket

Earrings

→ A purse that either matches or coordinates with her gown:

Satin bag decorated with silk flowers

Small decorated evening bags on delicate chains

Drawstring pouches

→ Compacts

→ Indulgent spa or beauty kits, containing loofahs, bath salts, creams, aromatherapy candles, body scrubs, etc.

→ A beautiful jeweled frame to hold a picture of them decked out in the wedding day finery (and you've selected such great gowns that they look truly stunning!)

→ Coffee or tea basket personalized with their favorite types of tea, coffee beans, syrups, biscotti, or shortbread

→ A striking journal to record their innermost thoughts

→ A commemorative book of poems, sayings, or wisdom that they will turn to again and again for comfort and inspiration

→ Scent, either in the form of elegant little sachets or cologne

→ Cosmetic or toiletry bag

→ Fine stationery

→ A gift pertaining to a particular hobby or interest of hers: ballet tickets, a gift certificate at a cycle shop, tickets to an art museum, a spa day

→ Payment for a portion of her bridesmaid dress

Some Unisex Suggestions

→ Day planner

→ Luggage tags

→ A truly stunning pen

→ Sake cups

→ Watch

→ Espresso cups

→ Business card holder

Some Suggestions for Him

→ Leather travel, toiletry, or shave kit

→ A really great bottle of wine

→ Cuff links

→ Pocket watch

→ Shaving brush and a fine shaving cream

→ Martini shaker

→ Bar accessories set, like a jigger, corkscrew, bottle opener, etc.

→ Golf balls and tees

→ Tickets to a hot sporting event or concert

→ A nice poker chip and card set

→ Aftershave

→ Pilsner glasses

→ Desk clock

→ Small portable tool kit

→ Pocket tool with many uses

→ Grooming kit

→ CDs ✳

BRIDE'S *Attendants* list

Maid of Honor

Address

City

Phone

Duties

Sizes

Bridesmaid

Address

City

Phone

Duties

Sizes

Bridesmaid

Address

City

Phone

Duties

Sizes

Bridesmaid

Address

City

Phone

Duties

Sizes

Bridesmaid

Address

City

Phone

Duties

Sizes

Flower Girl

Address

City

Phone

Duties

Sizes

Bridesmaid

Address

City

Phone

Duties

Sizes

Bridesmaid

Address

City

Phone

Duties

Sizes

Bridesmaid

Address

City

Phone

Duties

Sizes

Bridesmaid

Address

City

Phone

Duties

Sizes

Planning a Wedding to Remember

BRIDE'S *Attendants* information

Photocopy and give a copy to each attendant.

FIRST FITTING *date/time* _____   FINAL FITTING *date/time* _____

  Location _____

→   Make sure you have everything for the wedding day

    ❏ Dress   ❏ Shoes   ❏ Lingerie   ❏ Hosiery

    ❏ Gloves   ❏ Hat   ❏ Jewelry   ❏ Makeup

→   Break in your shoes, if they are new.

→   Have your hair washed and your nails done.

→   Get plenty of rest the night before.

BRIDAL LUNCHEON

    Date _____ Time _____ Phone _____

    Location _____

    Address _____

CEREMONY REHEARSAL

    Date _____ Time _____ Phone _____

    Location _____

    Address _____

REHEARSAL DINNER

    Date _____ Time _____ Phone _____

    Location _____

    Address _____

WEDDING DAY

    Arrival time _____ Phone _____

    Location _____

    Where to dress _____

    Photograph location _____ Time _____

TRANSPORTATION

    To the ceremony _____

    To the reception _____

OTHER

_____

_____

_____

Groom's *Attendants* list

Best Man

Address

City

Phone

Duties

Sizes

Ring Bearer

Address

City

Phone

Duties

Sizes

Usher

Address

City

Phone

Duties

Sizes

Usher

Address

City

Phone

Duties

Sizes

Usher

Address

City

Phone

Duties

Sizes

Usher

Address

City

Phone

Duties

Sizes

Usher

Address

City

Phone

Duties

Sizes

Usher

Address

City

Phone

Duties

Sizes

Ring Bearer

Address

City

Phone

Duties

Sizes

Train Bearer or Page

Address

City

Phone

Duties

Sizes

GROOM'S *Attendants* information

Photocopy and give a copy to each attendant.

FIRST FITTING   *date/time* _____   FINAL FITTING   *date/time* _____

Location _____

→   Make sure you have everything for the wedding day

❏ Coat   ❏ Shoes   ❏ Shirt   ❏ Vest or Cumberbund

❏ Suspenders   ❏ Trousers   ❏ Socks   ❏ Studs/Cuff Links

→   Have your hair trimmed and your hands groomed.

→   Get plenty of rest the night before.

BACHELOR PARTY

Date _____   Time _____   Phone _____

Location _____

Address _____

CEREMONY REHEARSAL

Date _____   Time _____   Phone _____

Location _____

Address _____

REHEARSAL DINNER

Date _____   Time _____   Phone _____

Location _____

Address _____

WEDDING DAY

Arrival time _____   Phone _____

Location _____

Where to dress _____

Photograph location _____   Time _____

TRANSPORTATION

To the ceremony _____

To the reception _____

OTHER

_____

_____

_____

NOTES

_____

_____

_____

_____

_____

_____

_____

_____

_____

_____

_____

_____

_____

_____

_____

_____

_____

_____

_____

_____

_____

_____

_____

_____

_____

_____

_____

_____

_____

_____

The Couture *Connection*

A *Guide* to WEDDING *Attire*

That spark of recognition from across the room, the lights dim, the music crescendos, and you just know, this is the one for you.

No, we're not talking about your fiancé, silly, we're talking about your wedding dress!

Finding the perfect wedding gown is a lot like falling in love. Like dating, it can be time consuming, seemingly worthless, and discouraging (remember that old adage about kissing a lot of frogs?), but, ultimately, when you find the one of your dreams — bliss.

Besides, after you've spent so much time planning for all that reality, isn't it time you treated yourself to a bit of fantasy. Cinderella? Queen for a day? A dewy-eyed ballerina? A seductive siren? The picture of elegance? You name it, there's a wedding gown out there that fits the bill.

The first requirement is that you curl up in a comfy spot and pore over the bridal fashion magazines, cheerfully ripping out the dress photos that you think you'll like. Notice that we said think. It's incredibly difficult to second-guess which wedding gowns will look good on you.

Next, familiarize yourself with wedding dress lingo and know-how so that you can understand exactly what you're looking for, not to mention what the sales consultants are talking about. You'll feel more informed, and remember, knowledge is power.

FABRICS

Consider the wedding style you've decided on, the season, and the setting, then let common sense prevail. Pass on velvet for a summer afternoon wedding (you'll die of heat prostration), and, most of the time, things that sparkle look best at night. Here's a list, and definitions, of some of the more common fabrics used in wedding gowns. Each fabric has its own drape and feel, which will create a distinctly different look and effect on your body.

Brocade – thick fabric with all-over raised design woven into it. Has a rich, heavy feel to it. Best for fall and winter.

Charmeuse – extra lightweight silk or polyester with a softer, more slippery feel to it than satin or silk. A little more luster as well.

Chiffon – sheer, delicate, and transparent, this light fabric is hugely popular in bridal designs. Works well for all seasons.

Moiré – usually polyester or silk, this fabric has a watermark pattern woven into it.

Organza – sheer like chiffon, but has a slightly stiffer feel.

Peau de soie – a heavy, satin-like fabric but with less shine. Also used on handbags, shoes, and accessories.

Satin – usually man-made, this smooth, popular fabric has a lustrous sheen.

Silk – a luxurious, natural fiber in high demand for weddings. Comes in many finishes ranging from a soft luster to nubby raw textures.

Shantung – a silk or polyester with a hand woven, nubby feel.

Taffeta – a crisp, textured fabric with mid to low degree of sheen.

Tulle – a fine, open weave netting used for everything from wedding favors to veils to bridal gown skirts.

Velvet – made of nylon, rayon, or silk, velvet has a soft thick nap to it.

Usually a heavier fabric is selected for fall or winter weddings: satins, rich taffetas, brocade, a moiré, velvet, or a heavy lace. For spring or summer weddings, a lighter fabric such as chiffon, lightweight satin, organza, silk charmeuse, eyelet linen, dotted Swiss, or a lightweight lace may be used.

SILHOUETTES

Silhouettes are the general shape of the gown and the overall way they do just that — silhouette your body.

A-Line/Princess – slim fitting from shoulder to hem, but less fitted, therefore, more forgiving than a sheath. This shape is universally flattering.

Ball gown – the quintessential fairy tale wedding gown. It has a fitted bodice and a full skirt flaring out from the natural waist. Works well on tall or slender figures, or else it is apt to make you look too curvy.

Basque waist – the Basque waist is similar to the ball gown but the waist dips down below your natural waist in a U or V shape. Downplays the hips and slims and elongates the waist.

Empire –this style has a tiny bodice that ends just below the bust line. (Think Jane Austen.) Slightly A-shaped skirt falls to the floor. Works well for thick waists, but large-busted women tend to avoid it since it accentuates that area.

Sheath – a sleek, form-fitting silhouette that follows the lines of the body. Works for slim and petite figures.

Mermaid – a very form-fitting gown that hugs (as opposed to follows) the body before flaring out around the knees.

LENGTH

Generally, there are three standard lengths that bridal dresses come in: floor or full length, tea, ankle, or ballerina length, and knee length.

Planning a Wedding to Remember

SLEEVE OPTIONS

The sleeves of your gown are another design element that has significant impact on the overall style and appearance of your dress. Some of the more common are:

Balloon – wide, elbow length sleeves.

Cap – short, fitted sleeves that cover the shoulders.

Dolman – wide sleeves at the armhole, then tapering in at the wrist. Think batwings.

Fitted point – long and fitted, these sleeves end at a V point at the hand.

Juliet – puffed near the shoulder, but fitted the rest of the way down the arm.

Three-quarter length – straight sleeves that stop just below the elbow.

Leg-o-mutton – rounded pouf from the shoulder to the elbow, then tightly fitted from the elbow to the wrist.

Off-the-shoulder – the name says it all.

Puff – short sleeves gathered into a puff.

Spaghetti straps – thin little straps.

Strapless – you guessed it – no straps, leaving the shoulders beautifully bare.

NECKLINES

Consider the neckline of your dress as a beautiful frame that will accentuate your neck and face. Your choices will depend on how daring you want to be and what looks good on you.

Bateau – a neckline that runs straight across the line of the collarbone.

Décolletage – a plunging, cleavage-exposing, neckline.

Halter – two straps of fabric originating at the bodice and wrapping around the neck.

Jewel – simple, slightly rounded neckline.

Off-the-shoulder – neckline sits just below the shoulders, leaving them bare.

Sabrina – similar to the bateau, but running from shoulder to shoulder in a nearly straight line.

Sweetheart – somewhat revealing, it dips downward in a heart shape.

Scoop – a low, scooped neckline with round lines.

V-neck – a neckline that ends in a V.

Wedding band collar – a collar that sits high on the neck.

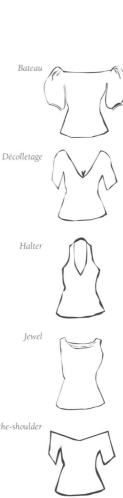

Bateau

Décolletage

Halter

Jewel

Off-the-shoulder

Sabrina

Sweetheart

Scoop

V-neck

Wedding band collar

A Whiter Shade of Pale

White has many different shades, hues, and tones, so be sure to find the one that is the most flattering to your skin tone.

Stark or blue white is the whitest of all whites, usually with a touch of blue in it. It works well with darker skin tones as it will completely wash out those with fairer skin.

Soft, diamond, or natural white is the most wearable of all the whites and is the whitest white that most natural fibers come in. It flatters most skin tones.

Cream, eggshell, and candelight are the whites that aren't quite white but not yet dark enough to be called ivory. They usually have slightly yellowish undertones. Keep in mind that the pinker your natural skin tone, the less yellow you'll want in your white.

Ivory – a soft creamier choice than pure white, it comes in a variety of shades with varying degrees of yellow undertones.

Where to Shop

Now that you know all the elements of bridal gown-ese, where on earth can you find this most perfect of dresses?

Bridal Salons – For the ultimate in shopping experiences, be sure to visit a full-service bridal salon. Most have gowns to fit all budgets and, as a general rule, you'll find excellent customer service as well as helpful, knowledgeable salespeople. Consider making an appointment during the middle of the week in order to avoid the inevitable weekend crowd and to receive the most personalized attention. Let the salesperson know your budget, but ask to see gowns both slightly below and slightly above your budget, just to get a good feel for what's out there. Most bridal salons handle the fittings and alterations in order to get the most custom fit of your gown. Some will charge for this service. At other places, it will be included in the cost of the gown. Be sure to ask.

Pros: Great expertise and customer service.

Cons: Can be more expensive.

Bridal Warehouses and Outlets – These are huge stores that stock enormous inventories of gowns with the majority of them being in the low to mid price range. They may include last year's designs of the top designers, lower priced designer lines, or lesser known gowns by non "name" designers or manufacturers. Part of it will boil down to how intrepid a shopper you are and whether or not you have the fortitude to plow through racks and racks of gowns (this is that kissing a lot of frogs part). Great finds can be had, but only if you're willing to devote the time and energy to looking. Sometimes the sales staff can be helpful; sometimes they're not particularly knowledgeable. Dress styles might not be available in all sizes, which can be frustrating, and there's usually no alteration service. Carefully examine any dress you choose to make sure it hasn't been manhandled too badly during its life on the rack. Check for tears, rips, dirt smudges, heel marks, lipstick, or other makeup stains. Examine it closely because most of these types of stores don't allow returns.

Pros: Great prices.

Cons: Lack of knowledgeable staff and customer service and the need to paw through many unsuitable choices.

Department Stores – Some department stores have bridal salons or departments that are certainly worth a visit. Oftentimes, they combine the best of the salon and warehouse experiences. Even if the department store doesn't have a bridal section, consider checking out the evening and formal wear section. One of its gowns in white or ivory may be just perfect for you and will most likely be a fraction of the cost of a true bridal gown. This is also a great place to look for bridesmaid dresses.

Pros: Prices and a familiar shopping environment.

Cons: Generally, they have a smaller selection than warehouses or bridal salons.

Custom Made – Perhaps you have a specific vision of the gown you want, but aren't able to find it anywhere. Or the only gowns you seem to be attracted to are $3,000 plus. Consider finding a qualified and experienced (*qualified* and *experienced* being the operative words here) seamstress and showing her the pictures of what you have in mind. She might be able to create your perfect bridal vision at a fraction of the cost required to purchase it. Simple designs will be less expensive to make than highly ornate ones, and fabric costs can be up there, anywhere from $30 per yard to $150 plus. It's highly recommended that you have the seamstress make a test gown out of muslin first so you can work out all the design and fitting bugs before cutting into that costly fabric.

NOTE: If you, your mother, aunt, sister, or dear friend is an EXCELLENT seamstress, then you might consider taking on the project of making your own gown, but only if you're very, very handy with a needle and thread.

Pros: Unique, one-of-a-kind designer gown at a fraction of the cost.

Cons: Can't see the final result until it's done and, if you don't like it, you're either stuck with it or have to shell out for a new gown.

IF YOUR SOMETHING OLD IS YOUR GOWN

Some brides-to-be are drawn to lovely, antique things. Perhaps you're set on wearing your mother's or grandmother's wedding dress, which will make for an especially emotional ceremony. Often, there will need to be some restoration or refitting involved. There are all sorts of creative ways to use a dress that is in less than perfect shape, either by strengthening its structure from underneath (where it won't show) or by using elements of the gown in a custom creation. Make sure to consult with a knowledgeable seamstress.

THE SHOPPING TRIP

Now you're ready to shop for a gown that will make you look not just beautiful, but beautifully YOU, harmonizing not only with your skin tone, but with your Inner Self.

How Early to Start: Nine to ten months before the wedding.

When to Go: Weekdays are best to avoid crowds.

Who to Take: One highly trusted person: your mother, maid of honor, best friend, someone who has taste similar to yours.

What to Bring: Have your pictures from magazines in hand. Also, bring shoes similar to those you plan on wearing, and a strapless or backless bra, if you have one. The salon may or may not have bras, but will usually have a full slip to try on with the gown. If you're wearing a special necklace, earrings, or heirloom gloves, bring those too.

WHAT Size is Your Fantasy? Wedding gown sizes run notoriously small, so don't be dismayed if you're normally a size six and you end up in a ten. Don't insist on ordering your "normal" size because of vanity.

The *alteration* cost for letting out a too-small gown will be much higher than those of taking in a too-large gown. Remind yourself it's all a numbers game anyway.

IMPORTANT SHOPPING TIPS

→ Confirm the store's refund, cancellation, and return policies before you walk out with a gown or plunk down your non-refundable 50 percent deposit.

→ Find out if there are any hidden shipping costs.

→ Don't buy the first time out. At least sleep on it.

→ Be certain you are comfortable in the dress, both emotionally and physically. Move around, mimic poses you will be striking on your wedding day, dancing with your arms up, bending over, sitting down, etc. Be certain the gown affords you the necessary range of motion. Equally important, make sure you feel like YOU in the dress (an especially dressed up and romantic you to be sure). If you don't feel you belong in the dress, then you don't. Listen to your intuition.

→ Also, listen to experienced and knowledgeable salespeople. Remember, this is probably your first time shopping for a wedding dress, and they have most likely helped hundreds of brides choose their perfect dress. Let them put their years of experience to work for you.

→ Have the style number, dress size, and color ordered written on the receipt, along with the deposit amount and promised delivery date.

→ A couple of weeks after the gown is ordered, call to verify that the order has been placed with the manufacturer, and confirm a delivery date.

→ Stay in touch with the salon periodically. Some salons have been known to close their doors after taking deposits from brides. They may not have ordered the dress or made any arrangements for the bride to take delivery of her gown. Who needs a last minute surprise like that!?

→ When ordering a gown, be sure you are measured properly with a cloth tape, then ask to see the manufacturer's size charts and order the size according to your largest measurement. This will help minimize costly, unnecessary alterations. Remember, it's better to order the dress a little larger than too small. And don't order a dress one or two sizes smaller than you normally wear based on the idea that you'll lose twenty pounds. If you don't lose it, you're in real trouble.

→ Pay the smallest deposit you can, and put your deposit on a credit card. If you have a problem, you can dispute the charges, and subsequently, often have the disputed charges taken off your bill.

→ Your contract or receipt should include a cancellation clause, stating that the deposit will be refunded if the gown ordered doesn't arrive in good condition by the desired date.

MONEY SAVINGS TIPS

- Consider wearing a bridesmaid's dress in white for an informal wedding.

- Order bridesmaid dresses from ready-to-wear designers. There may be little or no savings, but your bridesmaids will have a dress they are more inclined to wear again.

- Rent a gown. Many stores rent both dressy formal wear and bridal gowns; others just specialize in bridal attire. Check the yellow pages in your area or in a large city nearby.

- Check out consignment shops and newspapers. Sometimes weddings are canceled, or newly married brides are looking to recoup some of the money they just spent. The gown may need alterations and cleaning, so figure that into the cost and take the time to inspect the dress carefully. Start looking months in advance; you need to allow yourself plenty of time to order a gown if you don't find one using these sources.

- Check with bridal salons in your area to see if they have gowns that have never been picked up. Sometimes a bride will put a deposit on a gown, the wedding is canceled, and she never returns to pick it up. The salon may be willing to sell the gown for the 50 percent balance that's owed, since they've already collected a 50 percent deposit from the first bride.

- Wear the gown that your mother, sister, or friend wore at their wedding. This is not only cost saving, but it also adds a touch of sentiment to the ceremony.

- Ask about package discounts. Some salons may offer a discount on your gown if you purchase all the bridesmaids' dresses from them. Although this is often negotiable, it never hurts to ask!

- Add your own touch. Buy a simple, inexpensive gown from a salon, bead your own lace appliques, and add them to the gown in order to give it a more elaborate look. Check local fabric stores for prices and availability of lace before taking this route.

- Save on shoes. Buy shoes that can be dyed another color and worn again, or borrow shoes from a friend.

- Order the gown in a less expensive fabric. If the dress style you like is out of your price range, see if the dress can be made in a less expensive fabric.

- Avoid expensive design changes. Find a gown that has the design elements you want, and avoid expensive changes, such as changing the train length or style of sleeve.

- Minimize alterations. Keep alterations to a minimum; order the closest size, to your largest measurement, from the manufacturer's size chart (each manufacturer's size chart varies).

REALITY *check*

Many times the gowns we envision ourselves in aren't the ones that look the most flattering on us. Be flexible in what you're willing to try on, especially if you're having no luck with your own choices. Often things that look so-so on a hanger end up looking WOW! on the bride.

Warning! Be *cautious* when ordering your dress at a discount over the Internet or by mail. Some of the problems that can arise are: not getting the style, color, or size dress you ordered; getting a knock-off, or cheaper version of the dress you saw in the picture; running a greater chance of not getting your dress on time. Since you'll be dealing with these problems long distance, and you've already paid them all the money in advance, it's not as easy to get problems resolved. You will also have to make your own arrangements for alterations and pressing. Weigh the cost savings and the advantages and disadvantages of ordering from a discount place with whom you have no relationship versus a full-service salon that will handle any problems at their expense. Don't forget about shipping charges and long distance calls. The charges can add up, especially if there should be a problem.

CARE and Feeding of YOUR Gown

Before the Wedding

It most likely won't fit in your closet without some major restructuring and consolidating first, so you'll need to spend a little time thinking about where you're going to put it when you bring it home from the bridal salon. Be sure you have an adequate protective covering and that you've cleared out a space wide enough in your closet so that it won't be crushed by other clothes hanging too closely to it.

PRESERVING the gown

After the wedding, have your mother or maid of honor take the dress to a reliable cleaner. They will clean it. If you wish, have it wrapped and sealed in a special box. This will preserve your gown for possible future use by a friend or family member, or perhaps for you to wear again in a reaffirmation ceremony.

If you choose to preserve the gown yourself, here are some helpful hints. Never leave it on a hanger, and don't store it in a plastic bag. Fold the dress with layers of acid-free tissue (ask your cleaner where to purchase it). Then wrap it with unbleached muslin, which allows it to breathe. Store the gown in a cedar chest or a lined wooden drawer. Air it out yearly and fold it in different places before restoring. Make sure it's stored in a dark, dry place.

THE CROWNING TOUCH – CHOOSING YOUR HEADPIECE

Today's headpieces run the gamut from the traditional veil to the simple headband or barrette — all the way to sparkly tiaras. Selecting the one that's not too hot and not too cold, but just right, depends on the style of your gown, your personal wedding style and formality, and your overall flair for the dramatic.

The salon where you ordered your gown may have a nice selection of headpieces, making it easy for you to try on your options while wearing your gown. Some will even offer custom headpieces. If not, see if you can obtain a fabric swatch of your gown and use it when shopping at other locations for your accessories in order to match those tricky shades of white or ivory.

VEILS

Veils vary mainly in length, with the longer of the veils being the more formal. While many brides opt not to wear a veil, at least remind yourself that this is possibly the only time in your life when it will be appropriate.

OTHER HEADPIECES

✳ **Tiaras** – delicate and airy, with crystals, colored rhinestones, pearls, and other sparkles, they make every bride look like a dream come true. These princess-for-a-day headpieces are back in a big way. Several clever designers are also making tiaras that can be converted into stunning chokers or other jewelry after the wedding.

✳ **Hair gems** – sparkling little bits of glamour at the end of a pin or barrette that can be secured in your hair. Often made of rhinestones, crystals, or semi-precious stones, these are extremely versatile and are perfect for achieving a scattered, whimsical effect.

✳ **Headbands** – thick or thin, satin, pearled, or jeweled, these are a great, understated look.

✳ **Wreaths** – circlets of delicate blossoms or strikingly elegant flowers in a very romantic headpiece option, especially for an informal or outdoor wedding.

flyaway

blusher

fingertip

ballerina

sweep

cathedral

* *Combs* – usually worn to one side of the head, they can be decorated with fresh flowers, pearls, crystals, ribbons, or sequins. They can also be worn at the back of the head near the nape.

* *Barrettes* – fancy ones that coordinate with your gown make easy hair accents without being overwhelming.

HEADPIECE TIPS

→ If you wear a veil, either alone or in combination with a comb, barrette, or headband, consider making it detachable so that you can put it aside after the ceremony. Veils have been known to get in the way of dancing, drinking, eating, and hugging your guests.

→ Do a run-through or two before the wedding, using your headpiece so you can work out any kinks beforehand.

→ Make sure your headpiece flatters your face and doesn't overwhelm. Very petite brides can get lost in a floor-length veil.

→ Make sure your gown and headpiece coordinate with each other.

SHOES

Since you'll probably not be sitting down much on your wedding day, chant this mantra to yourself as you shop for wedding shoes: comfort first, beauty second. (There's a reason many brides opt for ballet slippers or decorated sneakers.) With all the shoe styles available, there should be no problem finding something both stunning and comfy for your feet.

Wedding shoes range from pumps to stilettos, from open back slings to strappy sandals, and everything in between. Generally, an ornate dress calls for a subtler shoe and an unadorned skirt allows for more style elements in your footwear. You can try for an exact match in terms of white tones or consider mixing textures and tones. Complementing is good.

GLOVES — THE LONG AND SHORT OF IT

You may or may not be interested in wearing gloves with your gown, but, for many women, this is the perfect finishing touch. The degree of wedding formality and the type of gown you are wearing will influence your glove selection. Kid, silk, matte satin, spandex, velvet, and organza all make elegant gloves. Just make sure they truly complement your dress style.

Long gloves are most often worn in formal weddings with short sleeved or sleeveless dresses. Short gloves would be worn at a less formal wedding with three-quarter length sleeves.

CONSIDER *this*

You might wear one pair of shoes for the ceremony, pictures, and receiving line, then change into a super-comfy pair before cutting up the dance floor.

KITCHEN *table* advice

The second most important thing to remember about your wedding day shoes is to break them in prior to the big day. And make sure to scuff up the bottoms so you won't slip-slide your way down the aisle!

CONSIDER *this*

Gently remove the seam stitching along the ring finger of your left hand glove to allow for the exchange of rings during the ceremony. That way you can slip your finger out during this part of the ceremony, then discreetly tuck it in later. Some glove manufacturers have begun making bridal gloves with the finger seam left open. It is also perfectly acceptable to remove the gloves and hand them to the maid of honor along with the bridal bouquet.

Hosiery

The most important hosiery tip? Buy at least two pairs, just in case. Or, if you know you're personally hard on stockings, opt for three or four pair.

Sheer beige, ivory, white, and champagne all work well for wedding day hosiery, as do the special bridal hosiery with embroidered or sequined embellishments. This special type of hosiery is usually available at bridal salons.

The second most important tip? Wear pantyhose that will stay up. Control top (even if you're tres svelte) is wonderful to prevent stockings from slip-sliding away during the day.

Jewelry

If jewelry is to be worn, it's best to keep it simple. You may want to wear a single pendant or a strand of pearls if the neckline is open. You may wear pearl or diamond earrings. They add a nice touch if your ears show. If you don't have this type of jewelry, it can be your something borrowed, rather than something you purchased. Don't wear watches or heavy bracelets.

Garters

What about a pretty lace garter? This could be your something blue. There are some beautiful, hand-detailed garters available, so pretty you'll hate to toss them. Buy one to keep and one to toss.

Hankies or Bibles

It might be a nice touch of sentiment to carry an antique lace hanky or a family prayer book. This could be your something old.

Hair – Your Crowning Glory

Don't forget to try out any new hairstyle well ahead of time to see how you like it. Also, try it with any headpiece or veil you'll be wearing so you know it all works together. There's nothing worse than having to face your wedding day with stiff, uncomfortable hair that just doesn't feel like you. Perhaps the single most important advice on hair is to wear something that feels comfortable and that you won't feel the need to fiddle with. Your day will be busy enough without having to check on your hairdo every few minutes. It's also hard to look your best when you're worried that your hair is tipping over or falling down.

If you're planning any treatments (coloring, highlighting, weaving, perms), have them done well before your wedding day to allow plenty of time to relax and look their best.

The Beautiful Bride

Every bride is so beautiful and radiant that she makes the moon and stars weep with envy. But just in case you want some reassurances, here are some surefire tips to guarantee your wedding day radiance.

The best way to beauty and good health is with preventative measures. And yes, we've all heard them before but they bear repeating, especially because in the busy months ahead you'll no doubt be tempted to let some good habits slide.

Health Habits to Remember:

➜ Eat well and stick to complex carbohydrates and protein to give you lasting energy.

➜ Eat smaller meals, more often.

➜ Don't overdo the caffeine.

➜ Don't rely on sugar boosts to give you energy.

➜ Drink plenty of water.

➜ Exercise daily. Remember that any exercise is a great way to rid your body of stress. Better yet, consider signing up, perhaps as a couple, for a good yoga class to help you deal with the ongoing happy stress of planning your wedding.

➜ Try to get regular sleep.

➜ Don't overdo the alcohol at your pre-wedding parties.

MAKEUP

Now's not the time to experiment with wild, avant-garde looks or to take the opportunity to wear considerably more makeup than you normally do. You want to avoid looking so different that no one at the wedding will recognize you! You need to find the balance between looking natural but not overdone or washed out. Natural looking tones that bring out your own individual coloring are what's in order for your wedding day. Steer clear of anything harsh. Check the lighting where your ceremony and reception will be held, and keep it in mind as you plan your makeup. The difference between daylight, soft indoor lighting used in a reception hall, and fluorescent lighting can be extreme, and will affect how your makeup looks.

Experiment – Try different foundations, tones, and blushes. Get free makeovers at cosmetic counters. You might even consider having your makeup professionally done, but schedule the consultation with the makeup artist well ahead of time so that you'll have time to work together. Look at and take full advantage of the wide range of makeup now offered in long-lasting, stay-all-day formulas. These are ideal for minimal touch-ups to your wedding makeup.

MAKEUP TIPS AND SUGGESTIONS

→ Do a complete dry run of your full wedding day makeup and hair routine at least once.

→ Don't try new facial treatments, products, or facials just before your wedding. You don't know how your skin will react.

→ Discover the wonders of blotting papers, now widely available, to remove the shine without adding yet another caked-on layer of powder.

→ Build on a good foundation.

→ Let moisturizer "set" for at least twenty minutes before applying foundation.

→ Use long-lasting foundation closely matched to your skin type. Set with loose powder.

→ Try out (well beforehand) some of the fun, romantic shimmer lotions and powders. They give an all-over glow and come in a wide array of tones and colors: pearl, pink, bronze, lilac, peach, champagne, gold, and silver. Use them to accent your cheekbones or collarbones, perhaps even your shoulders.

→ Use a long-lasting cream blush, a powder blush, or a gel cheek tint to add that rosy glow. It doesn't have to be rose-colored, however, whatever best accents your own skin coloring: rose, plum, café mocha, shell pink, or peach, to name a few.

THE EYES HAVE IT

→ Try using an eye shadow primer base before applying eye shadow. Colors will go on truer and not slip or crease as much.

→ Usually, powder or won't-budge cream shadows in neutral colors are best. Taupe, brown, smoky lavender, and gray all emphasize your eyes without detracting.

→ Use eyeliner of your choice, either a pencil or liquid liner, whichever you normally use. Next, dust some eye shadow powder in a similar color over pencil eyeliner to "set."

→ In a nutshell — waterproof mascara. It may take a while to locate one that you really like, so try out a few different ones before your wedding day. Take a shower, swim, and watch an old tear-jerker movie while wearing it. Try to give the stuff a real workout and see how it stands up.

BLACK
and
white
PHOTO
beauty tip

Use lipstick in a shade or two darker than you normally wear, or else it will barely show.

HOT LIPS

☞ Consider avoiding high-maintenance shades like fire engine red or deep berry. Stick to neutral shades like rose, pink, or dark peach.

☞ Try lip stain. It needs to be reapplied less often.

☞ Try a long-lasting lip pencil instead of lipstick. It won't budge.

☞ Slick a bit of long-lasting lip gloss on top of your long-wearing lip color for a dewy finish.

☞ For very dry lips, use a moisturizing lipstick.

☞ Put your lipstick on last, after you've slipped into your dress, in order to avoid any accidental stains.

BRIDAL BEAUTY EMERGENCY PRIMER

No matter how hard you work to avoid it, there's a good chance that at some point you'll stress out over your wedding. Chances are, it'll be the night before. And as we all know, stress does really bad things to your looks and health.

PREVENTIVE MEASURES - GENERAL

☞ Use sun block religiously before your wedding. You don't want a sunburned nose in your wedding photos, or, worse yet, peeling skin.

☞ If you even suspect a pimple or blemish might be forming, use one of the on-the-spot type overnight acne medications immediately to keep it from truly blossoming.

☞ Don't try any new procedures just before your wedding. If you've never tried a facial peel, mustache wax or bleach, or permanent wave in your hair, DON'T try them two days before your wedding.

PREVENTATIVE MEASURES – THE NIGHT BEFORE

☞ Don't drink any caffeine after noontime, and try not to consume any alcohol either, because both of those (or either one alone) can disrupt sleep patterns, and you really, really want a good night's sleep.

☞ Allow yourself enough time in your schedule to wind down before bed. A quiet hour with a cup of herbal tea and a relaxing aromatherapy candle can help you to calm down.

☞ Consider writing in a journal to help empty your mind of its nervous jitters the night before. Besides, being able to go back and read your thoughts just before your wedding day will make for a fabulous keepsake years later.

☞ Don't exercise heavily or eat a big meal too close to bedtime.

☞ If it's getting later and later and you're still wide awake, consider one of the over-the-counter sleep aids, just this once.

QUICK FIXES

Emergency Crying Tip – Brighten red eyes with white eyeliner on the inside of your bottom lid.

Puffy eyes from either a sentimental evening or too little sleep — Cold tea bags, cucumber, or potato slices are very good for reducing puffiness. Drink lots of water and use just a touch of concealer.

Broken nail – Clip the broken nail to as even a length as you can (without removing polish), then file smooth. Reapply a quick coat of polish.

You over tweezed your eyebrows – Fill them in with eyebrow powder and an eyebrow brush that closely matches your own brow's coloring. Use small, light-handed strokes for the most natural effect.

While curling your lashes, you accidentally yank out a few too many of them – Ask a dear friend to dash to the store and pick up a set of the lightest weight false eyelashes she can find. Using tiny scissors, trim off a piece approximately the same size as your missing lashes. Glue into place with eyelash glue. If you need to balance the look, add a couple to the other eye as well.

ATTENDANT ATTIRE

They've stood by you through thick and thin, offering support, humor, and friendship in times of need. They are your nearest and dearest, the friends who mean the most to you in the whole world. The least you owe them is a decent bridesmaid's dress! Luckily for you, there are now more fabulous styles available than ever. (You may even want to consider one of these types of gowns in ivory or white for your own dress.)

The attendants' dresses should complement the bride's gown and the overall look of the wedding, but they should make the bridesmaids feel comfortable and attractive, too. Traditionally, this has translated into identical gowns in identical colors. This works best if all your attendants are of similar height, build, and coloring — and we all know how unlikely that is. Fortunately, times and trends have changed and there are many fun, creative, and more individual ways to outfit your bridesmaids so that all of you are happy, comfortable, and beautiful.

Have all the attendants wear gowns that are of the same type and color

FIX *yourself*

Create A *beauty* EMERGENCY kit which contains these can't-live-without items:

Antacid
Band Aids
Blotting papers
Bobby pins
Breath spray or mints
Brush
Cell phone
Clear fingernail polish for runs
Concealing makeup
Cotton swabs
Dental floss
Deodorant
Emery board
Extra stockings
Eye drops
Hairspray
Lipstick
Nail clippers
Pain reliever of choice
Powder
Safety pins
Small sewing kit
Spot remover
Tissues
Tweezers

of fabric, yet each one in a different style, whichever is the most flattering to the individual bridesmaid.

Have each of them wear completely individual gowns, but all in the same fabric and color family. For example, pale sherbet tones in organza or chiffon, or deep jewel tones in silk or satin.

If all your maids own a little black dress, consider that for their wedding attire. While the neckline, sleeves, and hemlines will vary, they will also achieve a surprising degree of harmony. You can use their bouquets to dress them up and pull in the wedding colors and themes.

ORDERING BRIDESMAIDS' DRESSES

Bridesmaids' dresses should be ordered at least six months before the wedding to allow for alterations and fittings. The gowns are usually ordered through a bridal salon or bridal warehouse. Another great place to look for a gown is in the evening wear or formal dress section of a better department store in your area. You may find something your attendants love and that they'll have a ghost of a chance of wearing in the future.

Have all the bridesmaids order their gowns at the same time from the same shop in order to ensure that the fabric is of the same dye lot and that it will match. The same goes for shoes. There can be a surprising degree of variation from dye lot to dye lot of the (supposedly) same color.

For long distance bridesmaids, send them magazine tear outs so they can see what style of dress you're considering. Have them go to a bridal salon, tailor, or seamstress to be measured (the measurements will be more accurate that way). When the gowns come in, have it sent to the long distance bridesmaid so she can have it fitted in her own town.

HOT TRENDS IN BRIDESMAIDS' GOWNS

Hot, fruit punch colors

Rich jewel tones

Pale pastels

Iridescent two-tone fabrics

Two-piece ensembles

Plaids and florals for spring and summer

JUNIOR BRIDESMAID

A junior bridesmaid's dress would be exactly the same as her older counterparts. If going for one of the more individuated looks, then she would select something that would be complementary. If low necklines or plunging backs are a part of your bridesmaids' gowns, you might want to alter the junior bridesmaids' gowns slightly so they will be more age appropriate.

THE FLOWER GIRL

The flower girl's dress may match the bridesmaids' dresses in color and may be short or floor length. Some wedding dresses have flower girl dresses that match. Or a short lace party dress may be worn. Ballet slippers are often worn in either white or pastel. A nice touch is to add lace and baby pearls around the opening of the slipper. Flower girls always look darling, especially carrying a basket of rose petals that has been decorated with ribbons. Add a flowered wreath woven with colored ribbons to her hair and she'll look just like a little angel.

THE MOTHERS

No one wants to look like the mother of the bride. Luckily, they don't have to with the current crop of mother-of-the-bride dresses achieving a high degree of style and panache that was unheard of years ago. Today's moms are active, fit, and rarely match the old concept of matronly. Designers have been only too eager to meet these new demands.

The only requirements should be that the dresses of the bride's and the groom's mother harmonize and complement the overall look of the wedding in regard to style and color. This is also important for a consistent look to the wedding pictures. Let them know whether or not they'll need to wear gloves or a hat, and what length gown will be most appropriate.

MEN'S FORMAL WEAR

In most weddings, the groom, best man, ushers, and even fathers rent their formal wear. A wide selection is available so it's best to look in a few shops before making a final decision. If possible, rent everything from the same shop and, if not, at least get the same type of suit. There are many choices available: single and double-breasted jackets with notch, peak, or shawl lapels; double inverted pleated or merely pleated trousers with or without a fabric strip running down the side. Select something to fit your formality and the season, and one that will blend nicely with the other colors. Most of the originality and color will come from the myriad choices of cummerbunds, ties, vests, and shirts that are available. They should coordinate with or complement the bridesmaids' colors.

Consider having the groom's father in the same outfit as the others. This looks better for pictures and in the receiving line. The bride's father should always be dressed in accordance with the groom and the attendants.

MEN'S SEMI-FORMAL WEAR

For a great look at a less formal wedding, put the groom and attendants in suits and ties. For evening or winter, generally navy, black, or dark gray is worn. A light white or ivory suit is worn for summer afternoons. If the groom's suit is white or ivory, it should match the bride's dress. If she wears ivory, then he should not wear stark white.

With many wonderful things to select from, remember to keep the overall look in mind. This goes without saying: dark shoes and socks with dark suits, and light shoes and socks with light ones.

MEN'S WEAR TIPS

Shop for and reserve your formal wear from six to eight months in advance, in order to ensure availability, especially if you're getting married in the more popular months.

Pick up the tuxes the day before the wedding so that if there's a fit problem, there will be time to fix it.

Have all the men try on their whole outfit when they pick it up so they can check for potential fit problems and have them fixed in time.

Most men will want to wear their own dress shoes (newly polished) for the highest degree of comfort.

RING BEARER OR TRAIN BEARER

Usually, the ring bearer and train bearer are little boys. If this is the case, dress them the same as, or similar to, the groom or his attendants. If not identical, then keep in the same color scheme. Depending on the formality, and the size of the boy, he can wear a tuxedo, light or dark suit, or perhaps knickers with knee socks for a less formal garden wedding.

If you're having a ring bearer, you'll want to find just the right pillow for him or her to carry. That shouldn't be a problem; they can be found at many bridal salons or specialty shops that make pillows. There are many styles, colors, and shapes to choose from — round, square, rectangular, and heart-shaped — all equally beautiful. Many of the nicer ones will coordinate with your wedding colors or a design element of your bridal gown.

If you're talented, you may want to make your own, and then personalize it with your names or the date of the wedding. *

Wedding Style	Bride	Bridesmaids	Groom & Attendants	Mothers
Very Formal Daytime 200 guests or more, daytime	Same as very formal evening, but a short train is also appropriate.	Four to twelve. Same overall style as very formal evening, but dresses are often less elaborate.	Traditional: Cutaway coat, gray striped trousers, gray waistcoat, wing-collared shirt, ascot or striped tie. (Optional: Top hat, spats, gray gloves.) Contemporary: Contoured long or short jacket, wing collared shirt.	Floor-length dresses not as formal as those for evening. Same accessories as those worn for evening.
Formal Daytime 100 guests	Same as formal evening, but an elaborate, short dress worn with a bridal headpiece and short veil is also acceptable.	Two to six. Dresses either long or street length, but not too elaborate. Matching or harmonizing accessories, including bouquet.	Traditional: Gray stroller, waistcoat, striped trousers, shirt, striped tie. (Optional: Homburg, gloves.) Contemporary: Formal suit in white or light colors for summer, darker shades for fall, dress shirt, bow tie, vest or cummerbund. Groomsmen coordinate with similar ensembles.	Elegant dress or suit, usually street length. Flowers to wear, other accessories to match or harmonize.
Semi-formal Daytime 100 guests or fewer, often at home	Street-length dress, white or pastel color, short veil. Small bouquet or flower-trimmed prayer book.	Seldom more than one. Same as semi-formal evening, but dresses are simpler.	Traditional: Favorite suit, white, colored or striped shirt, four-in-hand tie. Contemporary: Dinner jacket or formal suit, dress shirt, bow tie, vest, or cummerbund.	Same as semi-formal evening dress, but less elaborate.
Informal Daytime	Suit or street dress. Hat, gloves, shoes, and bag. Nosegay or flowers to wear.	Maid of honor only. Dress or suit similar to bride's. Flowers to wear.	Same as semi-formal.	Dresses or suits, similar to honor attendant's.

GUIDE TO evening *Wedding* ATTIRE

Wedding Style	Bride	Bridesmaids	Groom & Attendants	Mothers
Very Formal Evening 200 guests or more After 6 PM	Dress with a long train. Veil to complement dress, often long or full. Long sleeves or gloves to cover arms. Shoes to match dress. Full bouquet or flower-trimmed prayer book.	Four to twelve. Long dresses, short veils, or other headpieces, gloves to complement sleeve length. Any style bouquet, shoes to match or harmonize.	Traditional: Full dress tailcoat with matching trousers, white waistcoat, white bow tie, wing-collared shirt. (Optional: Black top hat, white gloves.) Contemporary: Black contoured long or short jacket, wing collared shirt.	Floor length evening dinner dresses. Small hats. Shoes, gloves, and flowers harmonize.
Formal Evening 100 guests or more, After 6 PM	Long dress with a chapel or sweep train. Veil of a length to complement dress. Accessories the same as those for very formal wedding.	Two to six. Similar to very formal, but dresses are sometimes short. Gloves are optional.	Traditional: Dark dinner jacket with matching trousers, dress shirt, bow tie, vest, or cummerbund. (Optional: White or ivory jackets in summery climate.) Contemporary: Same as formal daytime. Groomsmen coordinate with similar ensembles.	Dinner dresses, usually long. Small hats, shoes, gloves, and flowers harmonizing with dresses.
Semi-formal Evening 100 guests or fewer, home chapel	Trainless, floor length or shorter dress white or pastel. Veil, elbow length or shorter. Same accessories as for a formal wedding, but simpler bouquet is used.	Seldom more than one, plus an honor attendant. Elaborate, street length dresses. Small bouquets.	Traditional: Favorite suit, white, colored, or striped shirt, four-in-hand tie. Contemporary: Dinner jacket of formal suit, dress shirt, bow tie, vest, or cummerbund.	Elaborate street length dresses with appropriate accessories.
Informal Evening	Suit or street dress. Hat, gloves, shoes, and bag. Nosegay or flowers to wear.	Maid of honor only. Dress or suit similar to brides. Flowers to wear.	Same as semi-formal.	Dresses or suits similar to honor attendant's.

Bridal *attire* shopping WORKSHEET

Option #1

Item _____ Store _____

Description _____

Manufacturer _____

Style # _____ Color _____ Size _____ Cost _____

Sales Contact _____ Phone _____

Option #2

Item _____ Store _____

Description _____

Manufacturer _____

Style # _____ Color _____ Size _____ Cost _____

Sales Contact _____ Phone _____

Option #3

Item _____ Store _____

Description _____

Manufacturer _____

Style # _____ Color _____ Size _____ Cost _____

Sales Contact _____ Phone _____

Option #4

Item _____ Store _____

Description _____

Manufacturer _____

Style # _____ Color _____ Size _____ Cost _____

Sales Contact _____ Phone _____

Option #5

Item _____ Store _____

Description _____

Manufacturer _____

Style # _____ Color _____ Size _____ Cost _____

Sales Contact _____ Phone _____

Option #6

Item _____ Store _____

Description _____

Manufacturer _____

Style # _____ Color _____ Size _____ Cost _____

Sales Contact _____ Phone _____

BRIDAL *attire* information

BRIDAL SALON _____   Phone _____

   Address _____

   Salesperson _____   Date Ordered _____

   Payment Terms _____   Date Required _____

	Description	*Cost*	*Deposit*	*Balance Due*
WEDDING GOWN				
Manufacturer				
Style #				
HEADPIECE				
Manufacturer				
Style #				
VEIL				
Manufacturer				
Style #				

ACCESSORIES

   Slip _____ ❏ *(Picked up)* _____

   Bra _____ ❏ *(Picked up)* _____

   Hosiery _____ ❏ *(Picked up)* _____

   Shoes _____ ❏ *(Picked up)* _____

   Garter _____ ❏ *(Picked up)* _____

   Gloves _____ ❏ *(Picked up)* _____

   Jewelry _____ ❏ *(Picked up)* _____

   Hair Accessories _____ ❏ *(Picked up)* _____

   Other _____ ❏ *(Picked up)* _____

TOTAL COST _____

ALTERATIONS

   Fitting Dates/Times: _____ / _____ / _____   Final _____ / _____

   Alteration Person _____   Phone _____

   Location _____   Cost _____

   Delivery _____

   Date _____   Time _____ ❏ Home   ❏ Church   ❏ Pick-up

   Pressing Instructions _____

_____

_____

BRIDAL *attire* worksheet

	Option #1		Option #2	
	Bridal Salon _____		Bridal Salon _____	
	_____		_____	
	Phone _____		Phone _____	
	Description	*Cost*	*Description*	*Cost*
BRIDAL GOWN Designer Size Color/Fabric Train Length				
HEADDRESS/VEIL Style Color Veil Length				
UNDERGARMENTS Bra Slip Stockings				
SHOES Size Style Color Dyeing Charge				
ACCESSORIES Gloves Garter Hankie				
FITTINGS/ALTERATIONS				
TOTAL				

BRIDAL SALON CHOICE

Name _____   Order Date/Deposit _____

Address _____   Fitting Date _____

Phone/Salesperson _____   Pickup Date _____

Total Cost _____   Balance Due _____

BRIDAL *attendants* worksheet

	Estimate #1		Estimate #2	
	Salon Name _____		Salon Name _____	
	_____		_____	
	Phone _____		Phone _____	
	Description	*Cost*	*Description*	*Cost*
MAID/MATRON OF HONOR DRESS Color/Fabric Size Manufacturer				
BRIDESMAIDS' DRESSES Color/Fabric Sizes Manufacturer Style #				
FLOWER GIRL'S DRESS Color/ Fabric Size Manufacturer Style #				
SHOES/STOCKINGS Style Sizes Dyeing Charge				
ACCESSORIES Hat Gloves Other				
FITTINGS/ALTERATIONS				
TOTAL				

BRIDAL SALON CHOICE

Name	_____	Order Date/Deposit	_____
Address	_____	Fitting Date	_____
Phone/Salesperson	_____	Pickup Date	_____
Cost of Each Outfit	_____	Balance Due	_____

GROOM'S *attendants* worksheet

	Estimate #1		Estimate #2	
	Salon Name _____		Salon Name _____	
	_____		_____	
	Phone _____		Phone _____	
	Description	*Cost*	*Description*	*Cost*
GROOM Style Color Size				
ATTENDANTS Style Color Size				
RING/TRAIN BEARER Style Color Size				
FATHERS Style Color Sizes				
SHOES				
ACCESSORIES Hat Gloves Other				
TOTAL				

FORMALWEAR SHOP CHOICE

Name _____

Address _____

Phone _____   Salesperson _____

Deposit _____   Balance Due _____

Fitting Date _____   Pickup Date _____   Return Date _____

Groom _____   Each Attendant _____

Each Father _____   Child Attendant _____

Attendants' *sizes and* measurements

Bridal Attendants' Sizes and Measurements

Attendant's Name	Dress	Shoe	Hose	Slip	Glove	Head

Groom's Attendants' Measurements

Attendant's Name	Coat	Sleeve	Neck	Waist	Inseam	Shoe

The *Write* stuff

YOUR *guide* to INVITATIONS and STATIONERY

*I*f a wedding is a production worthy of Hollywood — and it is — then consider invitations to be your guests' sneak preview of coming attractions. It is their initial, tantalizing glimpse of what you have in store for them, conveying both the tone of the event and your personal vision.

In the not too distant past, invitation selections were limited to one "correct" choice, ecru card stock or paper with black ink. Not so anymore. Just as wedding styles have become more varied and unique, so too have the invitations that couples can now choose from. Even when it comes to having a formal wedding, there's quite a variety available for classic, yet personal, invitations. Consider an embossed design or edge, which gives dimension and texture to the paper, but no color to distract the eye. Or if color is what you're looking for, add it in a clean, architectural, beveled edge with a touch of unexpected color.

If your wedding style is semi-formal or informal, you have even more options. Consider handmade papers, vellum or parchment overlays, embellished with ribbon, floral motifs, and color. Some couples even go so far as to have a graphic designer create a personal logo for them, then use it on the invitations as well as throughout the whole celebration as a recurring element.

Color can be added in many unique ways, with paper and ink colors running the gamut, from pale pastels to strong rich hues. If you don't want the entire invitation printed in colored ink, or your wedding colors are so pale as to make the text too hard to read, consider adding a design element to the invitation. This can be in the color of your choice, leaving the text in basic black, navy, or dark gray. You can also use color in the form of a ribbon you add to the invitation or in the paper on which you print it. There are many lovely patterned papers available, from pale marble washes to elegant Florentine designs. Or perhaps you'd prefer just a touch of color by way of an envelope liner, a thin tissue, or a rice paper insert.

If your wedding has a theme — garden, beach, winery, or any of the seasons — consider incorporating that theme into your invitations with a design element or motif such as sea shells, flowers, boats, wineglasses, or by using colors associated with that theme or season. Many invitations are available with meaningful religious symbols, or consider an ethnic detail or two to celebrate your culture. Whatever you choose, couples can now select invitations that are as unique as they are.

HOW MANY INVITATIONS DO YOU NEED?

When you shop for your invitations, it'll help to know how much you've budgeted and how many invitations you'll be sending. That will give you a good idea of your price range per invitation. As you tally up your guest list, keep the following in mind:

→ Each couple, whether married or living together, will need only one invitation.

•) If you're inviting two people who are a "couple" but not living together, they may receive one invitation.

→ A child over sixteen, even if still living with their family, receives a separate invitation. If more than one child over sixteen lives in a household, they may receive joint invitations, with the name of the eldest being listed first.

→ Don't forget to order invitations for yourself, your parents, your bridal party, and your officiant. You'll definitely want keepsakes.

So, for a guest list of 200, you may need as few as 120 invitations, especially if most of your guests are couples, and you're not inviting many children over the age of sixteen. If you've allowed an invitation budget of $450, then you can spend approximately $3.75 per invitation, but remember, that includes envelopes and any inserts you order.

Now that you know how much you can spend, you can begin the selection process. Be prepared to spend some time with this, because there are truly hundreds and hundreds of options available.

ELEMENTS OF STYLE

The finest quality invitations are printed on 100 percent cotton rag paper, although other elegant choices would be linen or vellum. More individualized choices might utilize parchment, rice paper, or handmade papers with a rich, textured feel.

Cotton fiber – 100 percent cotton paper. THE classic traditional choice for elegant, formal wedding invitations.

Linen – slightly grainier than cotton, but still quite elegant. Think of linen as elegance with texture.

Vellum – a translucent, smoothly finished paper made from a cotton blend. Sturdy enough to be printed on, this makes a beautiful overlay.

Parchment – an antique looking paper, it can be either translucent or opaque.

Jacquard – paper on which a design has been printed, such as a pattern of lace or leaves, giving the illusion of layers.

Corrugated – paper that has thick wrinkles, grooves, or textures. Lends itself well to edgy, urban chic, or elemental Zen designs.

Handmade paper – made from natural fibers, which may or may not have botanicals embedded. It's heavily textured and can run the gamut from slightly uneven to coarse and irregular. Is difficult to print on using traditional methods. Letterpress works best.

Glassine – a thin, transparent paper with a smooth surface. Most commonly used in envelopes.

Rice paper – thin and supple, yet nicely textured. An unusual yet elegant choice. Like handmade paper, it's difficult to print on using traditional methods and is best suited to letterpress printing.

Special Effects and Finishes

Deckle edge – regular and symmetrical or irregular with a torn-edge look and feel.

Die cut – a sharp metal piece is used to "cut" a shape or pattern, usually along the outer edge of the paper, such as invitations with scalloped edges or shaped like a wedding cake.

Marbled – paper that has a swirled, multicolored design and mimics the feel of the natural patterns found in marble.

Matte – A flat finish that doesn't reflect light.

Sizing It Up

While there's a wide selection of sizes to choose from, there are two sizes that remain the standard: Embassy, which is 5 x 7, and Classic, which is 4 x 6 (inches). The invitation can be a single sheet of three-ply card stock in this size or a sheet of heavy paper (32 – 42 pound bond is the standard for wedding invitations) that's folded to this finished size. The wording can run either vertically or horizontally.

Part of what determines the size you select is how much wording you need to put on your invitation. If both sets of parents are hosting the wedding, or there is a fair amount of wording for other reasons, the smaller size invitation may not work for you. Another consideration is cost. If you opt for an oversized or unusually sized invitation, or one that has other special mailing needs, you'll need to take into consideration the extra postage required.

Embellishments

These elements are added when the couple is looking for a special, unique touch to make their invitation really stand out.

> Architectural borders
> Botanical elements
> Custom designed logos
> Layered invitations
> Motifs
> Pen and ink drawings
> Sealing wax
> Sheer ribbons
> Wrapped invitations that open like a present

Printing

There are various printing processes available for your invitations, and you can ask your stationer to show you a sampling of them. They vary in price, so let a combination of your budget and style become the determining factor.

Engraved invitations are the most traditional and formal of all, but also the most expensive. This is an old process, whereby the paper is pressed onto a metal plate, causing the letters to be slightly raised on the paper.

Thermography, the most popular choice for invitations today, is a less expensive method that gives the same look and feel of engraving, but at about half the cost. This process fuses ink and powder together on the paper to create the raised letters, which resemble engraving.

Offset printing is the least expensive of the three processes. This is the standard printing process where the ink lays flat on the paper. This is a less formal look, but there are many ink colors and type styles to select from.

Letterpress invitations are made on an old fashioned, moveable type machine or press. Raised type is then inked and pressed, or stamped, into the invitation. This works exceptionally well on delicate papers and gives a wonderful, antique effect. The difficulty often lies in finding someone who knows how to do it. It can also be costly.

Calligraphy has become increasingly popular over the last few years, due both to the new computerized machines that can produce it, and the growing formality of weddings. Calligraphy is an elegant old italic script, used primarily in the past to address envelopes. Now, with the new computerized calligraphy machines, which create a perfect script each time, invitations can easily be done as well.

LETTERING

Don't forget that as stunningly beautiful as you want your invitations to be, they still must legibly convey some basic nuts-and-bolts details of the wedding. When selecting your ink color and font type, it's wise to keep this in mind.

Ink colors vary from the standard black and navy all the way through the rainbow: cranberry, forest green, dove gray, indigo, violet, burgundy, chocolate brown, purple, gold, or silver. Font styles are practically unlimited, from traditional nuptial scripts to standard Romanesque fonts, and everything fun and funky in between. The hardest part will be choosing which one you think says YOU.

INVITATION WORDING

Now that you've selected the perfect invitation that personifies your wedding celebration, what do you put on it? The classic wording is that of the hosts announcing the marriage of the couple, then requesting the honour of the guest's presence, and then giving the details.

TRADITIONAL WORDING

Since weddings are usually the most formal of our celebrations, there are some definite rules about wedding invitation wording.

* Use full names, no nicknames or initials. If you don't know the full middle name, skip it.

* The only accepted abbreviations are Mr., Mrs., Ms., and Jr. (make sure to use the period). Everything else needs to be spelled out, including titles and words like Street, Road, and Boulevard, as well as the names of states. Use a comma between the city name and the state (i.e., Chicago, Illinois).

* Dates and the time are written out in full; the year may be omitted if preferred. Use a comma between the day and the date. (Sunday, the twentieth of October)

* Street addresses may be in numerical form.

* The correct wording for the half-hour would be half after, not half past. AM and PM are not used.

* The traditional wording for a religious ceremony taking place in a house of worship would be "the honour of your presence." (Note the British spelling of the word honour. You would also use the British spelling of the word favour.)

* In secular locations, such as a club, home, or ballroom, or on an invitation for the reception only, the wording would be "the pleasure of your company."

* The bride's name always comes before the groom's.

* Professional titles are used for grooms and fathers, but not for brides, unless the bride and groom issue the invitations instead of their parents.

* When requesting a response, it may be written in any of the following ways: "R.S.V.P.," "Please respond," "Kindly respond," or "The favour of a reply is requested."

* The one sponsoring the wedding is not necessarily the one paying for it.

* The placement of the wording on invitations is critical in communicating the relationships involved, as well as conveying who is hosting the event.

CONTEMPORARY WORDING

Let's say you've decided to forgo the trappings of tradition and formality and have chosen a more modern and creative celebration. Then you can adapt the traditional wording to suit your own style. Consider:

* Omitting all social titles, using first names instead.

* Using professional titles for the women as well as the men.

* Using first or second person such as, You are cordially invited or We invite you to join us in celebrating . . .

* Examples:

  Would love for you to join us . . .

  Invite you to celebrate . . .

  Invite you to witness our vows . . .

WORDING NO-NOS

Never indicate where you're registered for gifts, not on the invitation itself or on an enclosure card.

Never indicate that children aren't allowed or welcomed. The way the invitation is addressed (to the parents only) will make this perfectly clear.

MILITARY *Note*

Perhaps even more steeped in tradition and formality than weddings, military titles have their own rules.

On the invitation itself:
Brides and grooms on active duty would use their military titles. Fathers, whether retired or active, may use their military titles. The military branch is listed below the names of enlisted personnel and non-commissioned officers. Senior officers' rank appears before their name, and the branch after.

John Anthony Worthington
United States Navy

General Patrick Hampton
United States Army

Addressing the Invitations
When inviting a military guest, the invitation should be addressed using the military title, using the same protocol as above.

Sample Wording

Traditional Invitation

> Mr. and Mrs. Charles Smith
> request the honour of your presence
> at the marriage of their daughter
> Donna Marie
> to
> Mr. William Hunt Crain
> Saturday, the seventh of September
> Two thousand and two
> at four o'clock
> First Presbyterian Church
> Santa Barbara, California

Combined Ceremony and Reception Invitation

This example also includes the response or R.S.V.P. at the bottom. A separate response card could be sent in place of this, if you prefer.

> Mr. and Mrs. Charles Smith
> request the honour of your presence
> at the marriage of their daughter
> Donna Marie
> to
> Mr. William Hunt Crain
> Saturday, the eighth of June
> Two thousand and two
> at four o'clock
> First Presbyterian Church
> Santa Barbara, California
> Reception
> immediately following the ceremony
> Biltmore Hotel
> R.S.V.P.
> 89 Lilac Lane
> Santa Barbara, California 93108

One Remarried Parent Hosts

When the bride's remarried mother is the host. (This is an example without the year.)

> Mr. and Mrs. Donald Ryan
> Request the honour of your presence
> at the marriage of her daughter
> Donna Marie Smith
> to
> Mr. William Hunt Crain
> Saturday, the fifth of June
> at four o'clock
> First Presbyterian Church
> Santa Barbara, California

When the bride's remarried father hosts, it would read:

> Mr. and Mrs. Charles Lee Smith
> request the honour of your presence
> at the marriage of his daughter

One Divorced Unmarried Parent Hosts

When the bride's unmarried mother hosts, she uses her maiden and married name.

> Mrs. Helen Johnson Smith
> requests the honour of your presence
> at the marriage of her daughter
> Donna Marie
> to
> Mr. William Hunt Crain
> Saturday, the fifth of June
> at four o'clock
> First Presbyterian Church
> Santa Barbara, California

When the bride's unmarried father hosts:

> Mr. Charles Lee Smith
> requests the honour of your presence
> at the marriage of his daughter

Two Remarried Parents Host

If the bride's parents are divorced, and both remarried, but wish to co-host the wedding, the names should appear with the mother's name first.

> Mr. and Mrs. Donald Ryan
> and
> Mr. and Mrs. Charles Smith
> request the honour of your presence
> at the marriage of
> Donna Marie Smith
> to
> Mr. William Hunt Crain
> Saturday, the fifth of June
> at four o'clock
> First Presbyterian Church
> Santa Barbara, California

A Stepmother Hosts

When the bride's stepmother and father sponsor the wedding, the invitation can read as below. This example would most commonly only be used if the stepmother raised the bride, or the bride's mother is deceased.

> Mr. and Mrs. Charles Lee Smith
> request the honour of your presence
> at the marriage of Mrs. Smith's
> stepdaughter
> Donna Marie
> to
> Mr. William Hunt Crain
> Saturday, the fifth of June
> at four o'clock
> First Presbyterian Church
> Santa Barbara, California

Divorced Unmarried Parents Co-Host

If the bride's parents are divorced and neither has remarried, the invitation may read:

> Mrs. Helen Johnson Smith
> and
> Mr. Charles Lee Smith
> request the honour of your presence
> at the marriage of their daughter
> Donna Marie
> to
> Mr. William Hunt Crain
> Saturday, the fifth of June
> at four o'clock
> First Presbyterian Church
> Santa Barbara, California

On an informal invitation, you may delete Mr. and Mrs.

> Helen Johnson Smith
> and
> Charles Lee Smith
> request the honour of your presence
> at the marriage of their daughter

Another option, depending on their relationship is:

> Mr. and Mrs. Charles Lee Smith
> request the honour of your presence
> at the marriage of their daughter

Groom's Parents Host

When the groom's family sponsors the wedding the invitation may read:

> Mr. and Mrs. Richard Crain
> request the honour of your presence
> at the marriage of
> Donna Marie Smith
> to their son
> William Hunt Crain
> Saturday, the fifth of June
> at four o'clock
> First Presbyterian Church
> Santa Barbara, California

Bride's and Groom's Parents Co-Host

> Mr. and Mrs. Charles Smith
> and
> Mr. and Mrs. Richard Crain
> request the honour of your presence
> at the marriage of their children
> Donna Marie Smith
> and William Hunt Crain
> Saturday, the fifth of June
> at four o'clock
> First Presbyterian Church
> Santa Barbara, California

Bride and Groom Host

When the bride and groom are sponsoring their own wedding, the traditional wording would be:

> The honour of your presence
> is requested at the marriage of
> Donna Marie Smith
> to
> William Hunt Crain
> Saturday, the fifth of June
> at four o'clock
> First Presbyterian Church
> Santa Barbara, California

SAMPLE CONTEMPORARY WORDING

The following are examples of some contemporary wording:

Bride's Parents Host

A less formal invitation sponsored by the bride's parents:

> We ask those dearest in our hearts
> to join us in celebrating the marriage
> of our daughter Donna to Bill Crain
> at four o'clock
> July fifth, two thousand and two
> First Presbyterian Church
> Santa Barbara, California
> Helen and Charles Smith

Bride and Groom Host

> We invite you to join us
> in celebrating our love.
> On this day we will marry the one
> we laugh with, live for, dream with, love.
> We have chosen to continue our growth
> through marriage. Please join
> Donna Smith
> and
> Bill Crain
> at four o'clock
> Saturday, the fifth of July
> First Presbyterian Church
> Santa Barbara, California

INVITATIONS FOR SECOND WEDDINGS

Bride's Parents Host

> Mr. and Mrs. Charles Smith
> request the honour of your presence
> at the marriage of their daughter
> Donna Smith Wilson
> to
> Mr. William Hunt Crain
> Saturday, the eighth of September
> at four o'clock
> First Presbyterian Church
> Santa Barbara, California

Bride and Groom Host

> The honour of your presence
> is requested at the marriage of
> Donna Smith Wilson
> to
> Mr. William Hunt Crain
> Saturday, the eighth of September
> at four o'clock
> First Presbyterian Church
> Santa Barbara, California

Children Invite Guest to the Marriage of Their Parents

> Jamie and Jeff Adams
> and
> Lauren, Todd, and Ashely Johnson
> Request the honour of your presence
> At the marriage of their parents
> Janice Stewart Adams
> to
> Robert Lee Johnson
> Saturday, the fifth of June
> at four o'clock
> First Presbyterian Church
> Santa Barbara, California

INVITATION INSERTS

These are the components that are inserted into the invitation when it is mailed. They should be printed at the same time as the invitations, and in the same paper and print style. You may need many of these, or none, depending on your situation.

RECEPTION CARDS

When the ceremony and reception are held in different locations, or when only certain guests are invited to the reception, a separate reception card is enclosed. The card indicates the name and address of the reception location and the time. It should be in the same style and format as your invitations, but about half their size. You may want to include directions or a small map on the back. It is also perfectly acceptable to include the reception site at the bottom of the wedding invitation, provided everyone is invited to both.

HERE ARE SOME EXAMPLES OF RECEPTION CARD WORDING

An Informal Reception Card

Reception
immediately following the ceremony
Biltmore Hotel
13495 Cabrillo Boulevard
Santa Barbara

A Formal Reception Card

A formal reception card to accompany a formal invitation:

Mr. and Mrs. Charles Smith
request the pleasure of your company
Saturday, the eighth of September
at half after four o'clock
Biltmore Hotel

R.S.V.P.
1438 Edgecliff Lane
Santa Barbara, California

RESPONSE CARD

You don't have to send out a response card, but you'll get more people to R.S.V.P. if you do. If you're having only a ceremony and not planning a reception, there's no need to send them at all. If you do choose to send a response card (also known as a reply card), it should be accompanied by a self-addressed stamped envelope.

The favour of a reply is requested
by the twenty-first day of May
M_____
will_____attend

or

Please respond on or before
the twenty-first of May
M_____
will _____attend

PEW CARDS

Pew cards are often used in very large weddings when you want to seat close friends and relatives in reserved sections, usually designated by ribbons. The pew card is mailed after the guest has accepted the invitation and should be handed to the usher before seating when the guest arrives.

Catherine and Robert
First Presbyterian Church
Bride's Section
Pew Number _____

or

M _____
First Presbyterian Church
Bride's Section
Pew Number _____

MAP AND DIRECTIONS

If your wedding is in an out-of-the-way location, or if you're inviting a number of guests from out of town, it's a nice gesture to enclose a map or directions with your invitation. It's also possible to print the directions on the back of the reception card, if you're having one. Again, these should match the look and feel of your invitations.

ACCOMMODATION CARD

Accommodation cards are for out-of-town guests who might need some ideas of where to stay if they attend the wedding. They generally list the names and numbers of local hotels, as well as any airport or other transportation information you deem relevant.

INVITATION TO THE RECEPTION

If the ceremony is small or just for family members, and the reception guest list is larger, invitations are issued to the reception, with ceremony cards enclosed for those who are also invited to the ceremony. The invitation would read:

> Mr. and Mrs. Charles Smith
> request the pleasure of your company
> at the wedding reception of their daughter
> Donna Marie
> and
> Mr. William Hunt Crain
> Saturday, the eighth of September
> at half after four o'clock
> Biltmore Hotel
> Santa Barbara, California
>
> Please respond
> 1438 Edgecliff Lane
> Santa Barbara, California

Formal ceremony card

> Mr. and Mrs. Charles Smith
> request the honour of your presence
> Saturday, the eighth of September
> at four o'clock
> First Presbyterian Church
> Santa Barbara, California

Informal ceremony card

> Ceremony
> at four o'clock
> First Presbyterian Church

AT-HOME CARDS

A nice, traditional way to inform your friends of your new address and let them know which name you'll be using. These are optional cards, but if you're going to use them, they should be ordered at the same time as the invitations or announcements. At-home cards are usually included with the announcement or sent out separately after the wedding.

ANNOUNCEMENTS

Of course, you want to invite everyone you have ever met to your wedding, but you can't. Logistics and budgetary constraints tend to get in the way. For those people who were not invited to the wedding due to distance, or others who you weren't quite that close to, the wedding announcement is the perfect way to let them know of your new marriage. Announcements do not require a gift, so it's a nice way for people to find out without feeling obligated to send something.

Announcements may be sent by either set of parents, or by the couple themselves. They are mailed the day of, or the day after the ceremony, but not before. The date is included, but not the time or location.

TRADITIONAL ANNOUNCEMENT

> Mr. and Mrs. Charles Smith
> have the honour of announcing
> the marriage of their daughter
> Donna Marie
> and
> Mr. William Hunt Crain
> on Saturday, the seventh of September
> Two thousand and two
> Santa Barbara, California

ADDRESSING THE ENVELOPES

Much of the same formality and tradition that appears in the invitation is also used on the envelopes. Basically, the guest's full formal name including any title — social, professional, or otherwise — is included on the outer envelope. On the inner envelope you would list their names with no title or address, use only the first names for children, and, if you choose, address intimate relatives by their title — grandfather, aunt, uncle, etc.

Addressing Do's and Don'ts

➡ Do address all wedding invitation envelopes by hand or have them done by a calligrapher or calligraphy machine. Never use a computer to print your labels.

➡ Do spell out all street names and states.

➡ Do address the invitation to both members of a married couple, such as Mr. and Mrs. Reginald Lawrence. Political correctness and preferences aside, traditional etiquette claims that Mrs. Penelope Lawrence is incorrect.

➡ Do send one invitation to couples living together, and address it to both of them with each name appearing on a separate line.

> Mr. Reginald Lawrence
> Ms. Penelope Howington

➡ Do list a woman with a military or professional title on a separate line, above her husband's name, on the outer envelope. The ranking title — professional, military, or social — always goes first. On the inner envelope, you would still use her title, but she and her husband would be listed on the same line, her name first.

> Outer: Doctor Diane Bartlett
>   Mr. David Bartlett
> Inner: Doctor Bartlett and Mr. Bartlett

➡ Do send a separate invitation to children over sixteen years of age. If there is more than one child over sixteen years of age, one invitation may be sent to the two of them, listing their names alphabetically.

➡ Do list the names of children who are invited to the wedding under their parents names on the inner envelope.

> Mr. and Mrs. Jones
> Carol and Michael

➡ Don't write "and family."

➡ Don't write "and guest." Take the time to find out the name of the guest's significant other, or don't invite them.

➡ Don't abbreviate.

CALLING *all* titles

Here *are* some common titles and how they should be handled on the invitation envelope.

Lawyer =
Esq. Or Esquire

Doctor =
Doctor

Professor =
Professor John W. Callahan
or John W. Callahan, Ph.D.

Judge =
The Honorable
James Callahan

Mayor =
The Honorable Alfred Dibble,
Mayor of Greenstown

Captain =
Captain Miles Standish,
United States Army

Minister =
The Reverend Sam Roberson

Priest =
Father Gerald McGuire

Rabbi =
Rabbi Samuel Nadel

anywhere from
six to nine
months in advance. **6-9** *months*

By the sixth month,
you should decide
on your choice **6** *months*
and firm up your guest list.
Begin compiling any
information you'll need for the
enclosures, such as maps,
parking information, reception
details, etc. Get a firm,
itemized quote and cost
breakdown, then place your
invitation order.

Anywhere from **4-5** *months*
four to five months
before the wedding
is good for addressing the
invitations and assembling them.

Mail all the
invitations at once, **6-8** *weeks*
about six to eight
weeks before the wedding.
This will give you time to mail
additional invitations to guests
on your stand-by list should
any of the first batch of guests
decline.

ASSEMBLING THE INVITATIONS

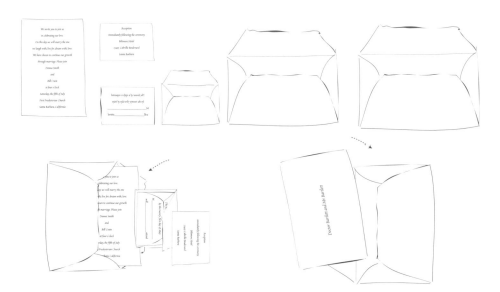

It can get confusing on how to put all the pieces of the wedding invitation together, and in what order and facing which direction, so here's the scoop.

The invitation should be placed in the envelope with the engraved or printed side facing up. Extra enclosures such as pew cards, reception cards, or at-home cards, may be placed next to the engraved side or be inserted in the fold, if any. The unsealed inner envelope is then placed in the outer envelope so that the guests' names are seen first when the envelope is opened. Weigh the invitation before mailing it to ensure proper postage.

OTHER STATIONERY NEEDS

Many couples take this opportunity to order other stationery they'll need in their lives together, such as thank you notes or informals, a sort of all-purpose stationery card. Sometimes there is a discount for purchasing everything together in bulk like that, so talk to your stationer and check on their policy.

WEDDING PROGRAMS: THE INS AND OUTS

You've spent a lot of time planning a ceremony that is meaningful to you. How do you make sure its meaning isn't lost on your guests? While you might know you picked roses, freesia, and stephanotis because they mean love, fidelity, and forever, will anyone else know what they represent? Or what the significance of the Unity Candle ceremony is? Or who the woman is doing the special reading? And why is that particular reading so meaningful to you? Well, you get the idea. A wedding program might just be the perfect answer.

The good news is that wedding programs, falling somewhat outside the traditional classicism of weddings, are subject to no particular formats or guidelines. In fact, they're not even required, just a thoughtful touch. This means that you are completely free to design an individual, unique program that fits your needs.

If you feel that you're already spread too thin planning the rest of the wedding, the program might be a great project for the groom or one of the parents to take on, or perhaps a particularly computer or design savvy wedding attendant. That way you can delegate the bulk of the task and merely oversee the production. Another possibility is to hand the entire project off to your printer or stationer. Whatever works best for you.

The program should be handed to the guests when they arrive at the ceremony, or put on a table for them to pick up themselves. If you choose the latter, be aware that some guests will probably miss them, either for being in a hurry or not realizing what they are. Another nice touch is to roll up the programs like a scroll, and tie them with an elegant bit of ribbon and maybe a flower or two. Then place them on the pews or seats for the guests to find when they sit down.

THE INS

The contents of the program should be listed in order. This will assist the guests as they try to follow along. Most often, the name of the bride and groom, along with the date and place, are used as the title. Begin with your cast of characters, making sure to list a few brief words describing each person's relationship to the bride or groom. Include anyone who is helping to make your ceremony special and meaningful to you. This could include attendants, officiants, musicians, people doing readings or saying a prayer. If you want, you can even list the special prayer or reading in order to allow its meaning to linger with your guests in a way that quickly spoken or recited words cannot.

List the titles of any scheduled readings or prayers, as well as the titles of the musical selections you've made. If you've written your own vows or are using unusual ones for the ceremony, consider adding them as well, so your guests can remember the beautiful words you've chosen. Any special religious or cultural elements or rites can also be explained in the program.

If you wish to memorialize someone special who is not able to attend your ceremony, such as a grandparent or close friend who has passed away, the program is the perfect place to do it. It also makes a wonderful place to publicly thank your parents and friends for all the loving support they've given you throughout the last few months.

THE OUTS

Here's where you can give free reign to your inner graphic designer. While the programs should coordinate with the overall look and feel of your wedding and invitations, you can let yourself go a little more wild here, especially since programs really have no protocol or formality attached to them.

Was there a paper that you absolutely fell in love with, but wouldn't work for your invitations? Consider using that as the cover for your program. Did you see a particularly witty and engaging emblem or motif that you weren't quite daring enough to use on your invitations? The program might be the perfect place for that.

Your program can be a small booklet or a single page. It can be printed at a fine stationer's or done on your computer's desktop publishing program. Handmade papers, transparent vellum, or other embellished papers make beautiful program covers, as do special details such as ribbons, elegant rubber stamping, gold ink, tasseled cords, or dried, pressed flowers. Whatever you do, remember that your program will be a lasting keepsake for many, and a lovely reminder of your nuptial celebration. ✳

Please Join Us
in
Celebrating The Marriage
of
Susannah Parker Stewart
and
Ethan Ellis Peters

September 14, 2002 5:00 PM

Baptist Unity Church
Chicago, Illinois

THE GROOM	Ethan Ellis Peters
THE BEST MAN	Jonathan Peters, *Brother of the Groom*
OFFICIANT	Reverend Albert Stueben
THE READER	Laura Graham Baker, *Friend of the Bride*
MOTHER OF THE BRIDE	Margaret Parker Stewart
MOTHER OF THE GROOM	Helen Louis Peters
FATHER OF THE GROOM	Samuel Peters
BRIDESMAID #1	Caroline Mahoney, *Cousin of the Bride*
BRIDESMAID #2	Lorraine Clark, *Friend of the Bride*
GROOMSMAN #1	Martin Mcallister, *Friend of the Groom*
GROOMSMAN #2	Justin Wyatt, *Friend of the Groom*
MAID OF HONOR	Ashleigh Parker Stewart, *Sister of the Bride*
FATHER OF THE BRIDE	William Aames Stewart
THE BRIDE	Susannah Parker Stewart

PRELUDE
Pachabel Canon in D

PROCESSIONAL
Trumpet Tune
Bridal Chorus

OPENING WORDS
Reverend Albert Stueben

READING
"To Be One With Each Other"
George Eliot (1819-1880)

What greater thing is there for two human souls
than to feel that they are joined
together to strengthen each other in all labor,
to minister to each other in all sorrow,
to share with each other in all gladness,
to be one with each other in the
silent unspoken memories?

READ BY
Laura Graham Baker
FRIEND OF THE BRIDE AND GROOM

RECITATION OF VOWS
Written by
Susannah Parker Stewart and Ethan Ellis Peters

I promise to love you and cherish you, and to most tenderly care
for you in both sickness and in health, when life is peaceful and
when it is in disorder. I will love you always, when we are
together and when we are apart, when life is peaceful and in
times of pain. I will honor our goals and dreams. I pledge to
share my life with you through the best and worst of what is to
come and I pray that our love flourishes and grows through all
the trials and triumphs that life has in store for us.

EXCHANGE OF RINGS

UNITY CANDLE CEREMONY

Susannah Parker Stewart and Ethan Ellis Peters, the two lighted
candles symbolize your separate lives, your separate families, and your
separate sets of friends. I ask that you each take one candle and that
together you light the center candle. The individual candles represent
your individual lives before today. Lighting the center candle represents
that your two lives are now joined to one light, and represents the
joining together of your two families and sets of friends to one.

RECESSIONAL
Ode to Joy, Beethoven

SUSANNAH AND ETHAN PETERS WISH TO THANK THEIR PARENTS,
WILLIAM AND MARGARET STEWART AND
SAMUEL AND HELEN PETERS
FOR THEIR LOVE AND SUPPORT THROUGHOUT THE YEARS
AND FOR MAKING THIS WEDDING POSSIBLE.

Lindsay Paulette Wagner and Gregory Lowell Quinn

June Twentieth, Two Thousand Two
First Episcopalian Church
Santa Monica, California

PRELUDE
"All I Ask of You"
from Phantom of the Opera
Andrew Lloyd Webber

PROCESSIONAL
"Wedding March"
from A Midsummer's Night Dream
— Mendelssohn

OPENING WORDS
Reverend James McKinley

READING
"Never Marry But for Love"
William Penn (1644-1718)

READ BY
Lauren Beth Wagner
SISTER OF THE BRIDE

RECITATION OF VOWS
Written by Lindsay Wagner and Gregory Quinn

EXCHANGE OF RINGS

RECESSIONAL
"What a Wonderful World"
— Louis Armstrong

STATIONERY *wording* worksheet

Type Style _____   *Color Ink* _____

INVITATION:

_____
_____
_____
_____
_____
_____
_____
_____
_____
_____
_____
_____
_____
_____
_____
_____

RETURN ADDRESS FOR ENVELOPE:

_____
_____
_____

RECEPTION OR CEREMONY CARDS:

_____
_____
_____
_____
_____

RESPONSE CARDS:

_____
_____
_____
_____

STATIONERY *wording* worksheet

ADDRESS FOR RESPONSE CARDS:

_____

_____

_____

_____

PEW CARDS:

_____

_____

_____

_____

_____

ANNOUNCEMENTS:

_____

_____

_____

_____

_____

_____

_____

_____

_____

NAPKINS/MATCHBOOKS:

_____

_____

THANK YOU NOTE:

_____

_____

ADDRESS FOR THANK YOU NOTE ENVELOPE:

_____

_____

_____

STATIONERY worksheet

	Estimate #1		Estimate #2	
	Name_____		Name_____	
	_____		_____	
	Phone_____		Phone_____	
	Description	*Cost*	*Description*	*Cost*
WEDDING INVITATIONS Quantity Printed Envelopes Envelope Liners Calligraphy				
RESPONSE CARDS Quantity Printed Envelopes				
ANNOUNCEMENT CARDS Quantity Printed Envelopes				
AT-HOME CARDS Quantity Printed Envelopes				
THANK YOU NOTES Quantity Printed Envelopes				
MISCELLANEOUS Napkins Matchbooks Seating Place Cards Programs				
TOTAL				

STATIONER CHOICE

Name _____

Address _____

Phone _____ Salesperson _____

Deposit _____ Balance Due _____

Order Date _____ Pickup Date _____

GUEST *Accomodation* list

Guest Name

Date Arriving	Time Arriving
Date Departing	Time Departing

Name of Hotel

Hotel Address

Hotel Phone	Hotel Rate

Type of Room

Reservation Date	Deposit

Guest Name

Date Arriving	Time Arriving
Date Departing	Time Departing

Name of Hotel

Hotel Address

Hotel Phone	Hotel Rate

Type of Room

Reservation Date	Deposit

Guest Name

Date Arriving	Time Arriving
Date Departing	Time Departing

Name of Hotel

Hotel Address

Hotel Phone	Hotel Rate

Type of Room

Reservation Date	Deposit

Guest Name

Date Arriving	Time Arriving
Date Departing	Time Departing

Name of Hotel

Hotel Address

Hotel Phone	Hotel Rate

Type of Room

Reservation Date	Deposit

Guest Name

Date Arriving	Time Arriving
Date Departing	Time Departing

Name of Hotel

Hotel Address

Hotel Phone	Hotel Rate

Type of Room

Reservation Date	Deposit

Guest Name

Date Arriving	Time Arriving
Date Departing	Time Departing

Name of Hotel

Hotel Address

Hotel Phone	Hotel Rate

Type of Room

Reservation Date	Deposit

GUEST *Accomodation* list

Guest Name

Date Arriving	Time Arriving
Date Departing	Time Departing
Name of Hotel	
Hotel Address	
Hotel Phone	Hotel Rate
Type of Room	
Reservation Date	Deposit

Guest Name

Date Arriving	Time Arriving
Date Departing	Time Departing
Name of Hotel	
Hotel Address	
Hotel Phone	Hotel Rate
Type of Room	
Reservation Date	Deposit

Guest Name

Date Arriving	Time Arriving
Date Departing	Time Departing
Name of Hotel	
Hotel Address	
Hotel Phone	Hotel Rate
Type of Room	
Reservation Date	Deposit

Guest Name

Date Arriving	Time Arriving
Date Departing	Time Departing
Name of Hotel	
Hotel Address	
Hotel Phone	Hotel Rate
Type of Room	
Reservation Date	Deposit

Guest Name

Date Arriving	Time Arriving
Date Departing	Time Departing
Name of Hotel	
Hotel Address	
Hotel Phone	Hotel Rate
Type of Room	
Reservation Date	Deposit

Guest Name

Date Arriving	Time Arriving
Date Departing	Time Departing
Name of Hotel	
Hotel Address	
Hotel Phone	Hotel Rate
Type of Room	
Reservation Date	Deposit

Guest Name

Date Arriving	Time Arriving
Date Departing	Time Departing
Name of Hotel	
Hotel Address	
Hotel Phone	Hotel Rate
Type of Room	
Reservation Date	Deposit

Guest Name

Date Arriving	Time Arriving
Date Departing	Time Departing
Name of Hotel	
Hotel Address	
Hotel Phone	Hotel Rate
Type of Room	
Reservation Date	Deposit

WEDDING *Guest* list

Name	Street, City, State, Zip	Invited to Ceremony	Reception	R.S.V.P. Number Attending
1.				
2.				
3.				
4.				
5.				
6.				
7.				
8.				
9.				
10.				
11.				
12.				
13.				
14.				
15.				
16.				
17.				
18.				
19.				
20.				
21.				
22.				
23.				
24.				
25.				

WEDDING *Guest* list

Name	Street, City, State, Zip	Invited to Ceremony	Reception	R.S.V.P. Number Attending
26.				
27.				
28.				
29.				
30.				
31.				
32.				
33.				
34.				
35.				
36.				
37.				
38.				
39.				
40.				
41.				
42.				
43.				
44.				
45.				
46.				
47.				
48.				
49.				
50.				

WEDDING *Guest* list

Name	Street, City, State, Zip	Invited to Ceremony	Reception	R.S.V.P. Number Attending
51.				
52.				
53.				
54.				
55.				
56.				
57.				
58.				
59.				
60.				
61.				
62.				
63.				
64.				
65.				
66.				
67.				
68.				
69.				
70.				
71.				
72.				
73.				
74.				
75.				

WEDDING *Guest* list

Name	Street, City, State, Zip	Invited to Ceremony	Reception	R.S.V.P. Number Attending
76.				
77.				
78.				
79.				
80.				
81.				
82.				
83.				
84.				
85.				
86.				
87.				
88.				
89.				
90.				
91.				
92.				
93.				
94.				
95.				
96.				
97.				
98.				
99.				
100.				

Wedding *Guest* list

Name	Street, City, State, Zip	Invited to Ceremony	Reception	R.S.V.P. Number Attending
101.				
102.				
103.				
104.				
105.				
106.				
107.				
108.				
109.				
110.				
111.				
112.				
113.				
114.				
115.				
116.				
117.				
118.				
119.				
120.				
121.				
122.				
123.				
124.				
125.				

WEDDING *Guest* list

Name	Street, City, State, Zip	Invited to Ceremony	Reception	R.S.V.P. Number Attending
126.				
127.				
128.				
129.				
130.				
131.				
132.				
133.				
134.				
135.				
136.				
137.				
138.				
139.				
140.				
141.				
142.				
143.				
144.				
145.				
146.				
147.				
148.				
149.				
150.				

ANNOUNCEMENT *list*

Name	Street, City, State, Zip	Gift	Thank You Sent

Weekend WEDDING itinerary

Fill out, photocopy and send to each guest invited to the activites

DAY _____   Date _____

   Activity _____   Time _____

   Location _____

   Dress _____

   Comment _____

DAY _____   Date _____

   Activity _____   Time _____

   Location _____

   Dress _____

   Comment _____

DAY _____   Date _____

   Activity _____   Time _____

   Location _____

   Dress _____

   Comment _____

DAY _____   Date _____

   Activity _____   Time _____

   Location _____

   Dress _____

   Comment _____

DAY _____   Date _____

   Activity _____   Time _____

   Location _____

   Dress _____

   Comment _____

DAY _____   Date _____

   Activity _____   Time _____

   Location _____

   Dress _____

   Comment _____

GUEST *List for* WEEKEND Activities

Day/Date	Time	Activity	Guest Attending

A GRAND Affair

PLANNING your reception

Have you always dreamed of sipping champagne under the stars at your reception? Dancing in your husband's arms to a twenty-piece orchestra? Do you envision an elegant seated meal with muted classical music in the background, or the boisterous crush of a buffet party with guests laughing and talking over the lively music you've selected? How about a beautiful, romantic wedding brunch set in a lavish garden surrounded by nature's bounty? Or perhaps you'd prefer a sophisticated cocktail party, topped off with an elegant cake, passing on many of the more traditional elements of the wedding reception.

The reception is probably the biggest and most lavish party you'll throw in your lifetime. It is certainly the most emotionally meaningful. Give yourself plenty of time to think and plan, to daydream and fantasize about this once-in-a-lifetime event. Your wedding style, degree of formality, size of your guest list, and budget all play a part in helping you decide what type of reception suits your needs. Keep in mind that the time of day is a critical factor in determining your reception, with receptions later in the day usually being more expensive.

A reception early in the day will probably include a breakfast or brunch, with food that is lighter in substance. You could also consider a buffet or seated luncheon reception. Again, the food served at this time of day is lighter and usually less costly.

Late in the afternoon lends itself well to a cake and champagne only reception, a high tea reception, or a cocktail and hors d'oeuvre reception. Whenever hosting a reception of this nature, one that doesn't include a full meal, find a tasteful way to mention it on your invitation so that your guests aren't left wondering. If your invitation says: Please join us for cocktails and hors d'oeuvres or Please join us for cake and champagne, then your guests know to make arrangements for their own meal.

A reception held at dinnertime is usually an all-out affair that includes cocktails, dinner, whether seated or buffet, and dancing. It is also the most expensive type of reception to have.

Planning the Reception

A number of your planning decisions will be determined by the location you select, as well as the type of catering you choose. For example, if your reception will take place at a banquet hall with an on-site catering staff, your planning tasks will mostly be to select from an offering of menu and decoration choices, then follow up on the details. If you're staging a wedding reception at a location whose main function is not that of receptions, or have chosen a location that is a completely blank canvas — a backyard, beach, or private home — then your planning will be much more involved and cover everything from the rentals to the caterers to the decorations and everything in between.

The basic elements of reception planning are the space itself, physical comfort, decorations, catering, music, and dancing, if applicable.

The space you have chosen will undoubtedly have its own ambience, whether it needs to be transformed into something wonderful, or you merely need to complement an already spectacular room, such as a ballroom or deluxe banquet hall. Either way, you'll need to take into account the space itself and any architectural or structural pluses or minuses. You'll need to allow for the guests' physical comfort, in way of adequate parking, restroom facilities, temperature control, and seating capacity. Adequate heating and air conditioning are a must, as is a backup plan in case of rain, hail, or snow.

Decorations

Lighting

While a large portion of the decorating will be the flowers and floral arrangements that you choose, there is more to consider. Lighting, place settings, and table settings are also important to the overall look and feel of your reception. In fact, lighting can run a close second to flowers for overall impact. Used correctly, it can transform a room into something magical. Overhead lighting, colored lighting, projected images on dance floors, and white curtained walls, spotlights, and twinkle lights can all have a place in your reception scheme.

Other lighting elements to consider are moonlight, sunsets, paper lanterns, and torches. And don't forget candles. From votives to tapers to pillars, all add a spark of drama and a definite romantic glow.

→ Arrange high and low pillar candles on a mirror to reflect more light.

→ Fill shallow bowls with water and floating candles.

→ Groupings of mismatched wineglasses or water goblets picked up at flea markets or antique stores make striking votive holders.

→ Small clear or frosted votive holders wrapped with a beautifully colored ribbon or unique paper.

Special Touches

Other added touches that can transform a reception room, home, or garden into a warm romantic setting for an evening reception.

→ Use the votive candles in other places, such as along walkways, around a pool, or in the bathrooms.

→ Use twinkle lights to add a magical feeling to a room, or especially to a garden. If small trees are brought in to warm up a reception hall, add some twinkle lights to them.

→ Consider luminara, garden torches, old fashioned tin lanterns, or paper lanterns for fun lighting effects.

OTHER DECORATIVE TOUCHES

Other elements can include draped fabrics, fountains, small potted trees, and shrubbery. Consider using ribbon or bows for bits of colorful decoration. From big wide satins to sheer delicate organza or cheerful plaid grosgrains, all make fabulous accents for the reception. Wrap them around pillar candles, tie them on doorknobs, and drape them across the backs of chairs. A simple, beautiful ribbon, artfully tied, makes an easy but striking napkin holder.

Tulle or netting can be draped over chairs, pooled on tables, or floated from the ceiling in ethereal cascades for a highly romantic decoration.

Balloons can add a fun celebratory touch, especially floating in a room with a high ceiling. Check out the newer metallic and pearlescent colors or opt for the more traditional pastels. Ribbon streamers trailing down add to the effect. You might even consider a balloon arch.

TABLE SETTINGS

Table linens come in an enormous assortment of colors, fabrics, textures, and styles. From classic and traditional fine white linens with elegant silver to warm lush color combinations of peach, rose, celadon green, lilacs, and blues. Whatever your wedding style and theme, there are linens out there to complement it. Check with party rental companies in your area, or on the Internet.

Along with the china and linens, the table numbers, place cards, and favors you choose will be a part of your table decorating scheme.

Table numbers are a necessary logistic if you are arranging seating for your guests. How else will they know which table to sit at? Below are some wonderful ways to turn your table numbers into a personal design statement:

❋ Silver frames

❋ Crystal frames

❋ Thick cards decorated with spun sugar or royal icing numbers

❋ A charming pot of flowers as a centerpiece, with the number painted on the pot itself

❋ Beautiful ceramic tiles with numbers painted on them (these are often used for addresses)

❋ Elegant calligraphy banners or large cards

❋ A banner with the number on it, wrapped around a large pillar or votive

❋ An attractive garden stake with the table number written on it and placed in a flower pot centerpiece

Money
SAVING
tip

If you enjoy doing things with your hands, consider taking calligraphy classes soon after your engagement. You'll save yourself a lot of money and provide a wonderful personal touch, if you can do some simple calligraphy on your own.

Rim your champagne flutes with pink sugar and float edible flower petals in the champagne.

Personalize wedding flutes or goblets with stencils and etchings.

The most elegant calligraphy can turn a simple card into a work of art.

Pen a personal message to each guest on a piece of high quality paper. Roll it up like a scroll and tie with a beautiful ribbon, or insert into a specially designed envelope.

Consider having bathroom emergency kits on hand for guests. They could include aspirin, antacid, mints, mouthwash, small sewing kit, and other necessities.

Flea markets, antique shops, swap meets, and thrift stores are wonderful sources for inexpensive wedding decorations: handkerchiefs, tea towels, old glass bottles, wine goblets, champagne glasses, platters, old china, all of which can be incorporated into an elegant mix and match look.

Place cards don't just tell your guests where to sit; they can be a cornerstone of your table decorations and often do double duty as a favor for your guests to take home. Here are some unique ideas for place cards:

❋ Small silver or jeweled frames

❋ An elegant calligraphic card tucked into a folded napkin

❋ Small name flags in petit fours or chocolate candies

❋ Tie small nametags on favors that sit on the plate and let these nametags double as place cards

❋ A small pinecone awash with silver, gold, or white paint

❋ Names written on a beautiful paper doily

FAVORS

Many brides and grooms choose to give their wedding guests a favor, a small gift that tells the guest thank you for joining in our celebration. Favors don't have to be expensive, but they can be if you have the budget for it. They can be personal, traditional, or whimsical. They can even be edible! Here are some great ideas.

❋ Beautifully decorated sugar cookies or petit fours

❋ Small candles in the shape of apples or pears, tucked in burlap bags

❋ Tiny shopping bags made of elegant paper and filled with small candy kisses, sugar coated almonds, or fragrant soaps

❋ Small votives wrapped with beautiful, decorated paper and tied with a ribbon.

❋ Little silver or jeweled frames

❋ Beautifully decorated packets of seeds for planting

❋ Fortune cookies with wedding fortunes in them

❋ Small bunches of flowers for each guest to take home

❋ Fragrant soaps in unusual wrappings

❋ Drawstring organza bags filled with soaps, candles, candies, or colored almonds

❋ Porcelain or white paper boxes filled with cookies, candies, or other treats

❋ Colorful floral boxes filled with almonds, truffles, or other candies

❋ Paper cones filled with sugar coated almonds, jelly beans, or other candies, perhaps even flower petals

For more great ideas on wedding favors see my book, *Favorable Occasions*.

TAKE A SEAT

Reception seating arrangements can vary, depending on the type and formality of the reception or the layout of the location. It's always best to select a head or centrally located table for the bride's table. After all, it's you they came to see; you should be the center of activity. For a buffet with open seating, be sure to reserve a head table; you want to avoid embarrassing a guest who might happen to sit there unknowingly.

The bridal table may include only the parents with the bride and groom, or you may want only the attendants, with or without spouses or dates. A third alternative would be to combine the first two. This decision may depend on several things: the size of the bridal party, the amount of space, the size of the table, and whether the parents are divorced.

Usually, very formal luncheon or dinner receptions require a seating plan designated by a seating chart or place cards. For formal or semi-formal receptions, place cards are optional, and informal receptions, in most cases, have open seating or standing, depending on the type of reception.

Young children should always be seated with parents. Use your discretion when it comes to teenagers; seat them with parents or place them at a table together.

The guests' seating arrangements are up to you. However, you may request the help of your mother and the groom's mother when it comes to assigned seating, especially if many of the guests are their friends who you are only slightly acquainted with. You want to seat people so they are comfortable and encouraged to mingle with their neighbors. The other alternative is to let them choose their own seats.

GUEST SEATING TIPS

→ Seat people with similar interests together.

→ Try to seat people at a table where they know at least one person.

→ Similar aged people often find they have things in common.

→ Put long lost family members or distant relations together at a table since they don't get to see each other that often.

→ If the bride or groom's parents are divorced, consider allowing them to host their own table or handpick special guests and family members to sit with them.

→ Try alternating the sex of your seated guests to stir things up a bit.

→ Do try to keep an even number of guests at each table so no one ends up feeling like a fifth (or seventh, or eleventh) wheel.

→ Place the guests that you know love to dance near the dance floor so they'll be sure to get things moving early on.

IT IS BETTER TO RECEIVE

Whichever type of reception you decide on, the first order of business will be to greet your guests. The receiving line is a formal greeting process that ensures the bride and groom, as well as their parents and any other hosts, have the opportunity to welcome each and every guest and thank them for coming. Some couples feel a receiving line is too formal and rigid for their tastes and would prefer to mingle among their guests, greeting everyone that way. Stop and consider just how easy it will be to miss someone in a crowd of one hundred or two hundred people. What if someone is dancing when you stop at their table? Or has stepped out for a bit of fresh air or a visit to the restroom? You really don't want to risk missing a single guest, and without the receiving line, it's a definite possibility.

INTRODUCING ...

If you don't have the receiving line immediately following the ceremony, then the reception usually starts with a receiving line. Select a location ahead of time, one that allows for good traffic flow in order to avoid congestion.

The bride's parents usually head the line and are the first to greet guests. The bride and groom are next, with the groom's parents after them. Any honor attendants and bridesmaids you wish to include would stand after the groom's parents. Another option is to have the mother of the bride head the line, then the bride and groom, followed by the mother of the groom. The bride's father and the groom's father can then circulate among the guests. The decision of who stands in the line is up to you. However, the best man, ushers, flower girl, and ring bearer normally do not participate. With a larger reception, you may want to eliminate the maid of honor and bridesmaids from the line, in order to help it move more quickly.

Keep the conversation short — you don't want guests to have to stand in line too long. This is a good time to get them to sign the guest book; it can be placed either before or after the line.

RECEIVING LINE TIPS

→ The bride and groom should review the guest list with both families to refresh their memories on names a day or two prior to the wedding.

→ Introduce yourself to guests you don't know.

→ If you forget a name — which is easy to do — smile, thank the person for coming, or apologize and ask to be reminded.

→ Smile at everyone, shake hands, or give a hug and kiss to those you know better.

→ Gloves should not be worn.

→ You may have ushers or waitresses bring something for the guests to drink in line.

→ Go to the restroom or get a drink, if needed, before forming the line, but do it quickly.

→ Designate a place to put the bouquets or arrange for someone to take them.

PLANNING YOUR TIME

 Below is a general timetable. Most receptions last from three to five hours, so you will need to do some personal adjusting. For a more complete schedule, please refer to Chapter 25, Your Wedding Day.

FIRST HALF-HOUR

Wedding pictures are taken, if they weren't taken before the ceremony. The cocktail hour begins, and guests start arriving at the reception site. They mingle and get something to drink. Music has already begun.

SECOND HALF-HOUR

Receiving line is formed and guests pass through. Guest book is signed and place cards picked up. Cocktail hour continues and any planned hors d'oeuvres are served.

SECOND HOUR

The emcee or catering manager announces the meal. Guests begin to form a line at the buffet table or they circulate among the food stations. If you are having a sit-down meal, the guests are seated. Wedding party is seated and served, and then food is served to the guests. Blessings are said. The best man proposes the first toast, followed by any other toasts. The bride and groom have the first dance, followed by any other special dances. Guests may follow on the dance floor.

THIRD HOUR AND FOURTH HOUR

Tables are cleared. Guests may mingle or dance. Musicians announce cake-cutting ceremony. Cake is cut and served. Dance music resumes.

LAST HALF-HOUR

Bride throws the bouquet. Groom throws the garter. Bride and groom change into going-away clothes. Rice, birdseed, or dried rose petals are given to guests and then tossed on the bride and groom as they run to their car. If you prefer, wedding bubbles may be used instead for a fun, whimsical send off. The bar closes, music stops, and guests start to leave. Parents gather personal belongings and gifts before leaving.

GIFTS brought TO THE *Reception*

Some of your guests will bring gifts to the reception. Many hotels and restaurants will take the gifts and look after them for you, but it's a good idea to assign a trusted friend, family member, or bridal attendant to oversee the gift table. Arm them with tape so they can secure the cards to the gifts to avoid any confusion. Another good system is to have each guest sign his/her name on a list next to a number. That same number is then written on the gift. When the reception is over, have the designated gift checker make sure that every gift signed for is there, and this person can make arrangements to have them taken to your home for you to open after the honeymoon.

RECEPTION TRADITIONS

Much of the reception is taken up with the enactment of well-loved, time-proven wedding traditions. Here is the scoop on the most popular.

TOASTING

Wedding toasts are a way to call everyone's attention to, and give thanks for, the good fortune that brought them there. It's a way to stop and enjoy the here and now and give everyone an opportunity to savor it.

Traditionally, the best man gives the first toast. It's given any time after the guests have been seated, or have found their seats after moving through the buffet line. (Toasting can also take place during cocktails, after everyone has been served a flute of champagne.) The best man's toast reflects on his relationship with the couple, then proceeds to wishing them a long and happy life together.

In the past, guests were expected to stand once the toast was made. Today, raising glasses is considered sufficient, especially if more than one toast will be offered, otherwise everyone may end up feeling rather like formally dressed jack-in-the-boxes.

The traditional beverage for toasting or special celebrations is champagne; however, white wine or punch can be used. There are also many brands of non-alcoholic champagne available that can be used. The bride and groom do not stand or drink when being toasted.

The best man doesn't get to have all the fun. Other members of the bridal party can join in with a toast of their own, with the maid of honor being next in line, if she so chooses. The groom may toast his bride and then thank his parents and his new in-laws as well as his guests. While you don't want to stifle anybody, try to keep the toasting to a minimum.

DANCE THE NIGHT AWAY

The leader of the band or master of ceremonies should signal the beginning of the dancing formalities. This usually occurs just before, or immediately after, the main course is served. The dance floor should be located near, or in front of, the bride's table. The bride and groom lead off the first dance, typically with a song they've selected especially for this occasion. This is their first dance as man and wife, not necessarily the first dance of the reception. If the reception is large, with open seating or standing, you may choose to have the guests start dancing after they go through the receiving line. This gives them something to do while you finish greeting guests and catch your breath. The dance floor can then be cleared, and all eyes focused on the bride and groom as they begin their first dance as husband and wife. You can dance together for the entire length of the song and then open up the dance floor to everyone, or you can choose to have a traditional first dance sequence as listed below.

→ The bride's father cuts in and dances with his daughter while the groom asks the bride's mother to dance.

→ The groom's father cuts in and dances with the bride, while the bride's father cuts in on the groom to dance with his wife.

→ The groom then asks his mother to dance.

→ The bride dances with the best man and the groom dances with the maid of honor.

→ Attendants and guests join in. The bride and groom should try to make time for another dance or two together before the evening is over. After all, it is your romantic moment!

CUTTING THE CAKE

The cake cutting takes place near the end of the reception, usually signaling that the festivities will be drawing to a close soon. For an afternoon tea, or cocktail reception, the cake is usually served after the receiving line and once guests have their drinks.

The bandleader or master of ceremonies announces the event. The groom places his right hand over the bride's and together they cut the first slice. They then offer one another a bite, which signifies a willingness and a pledge to share life together. For a nice touch, the bride may then offer a piece of cake to her new in-laws and the groom should do the same. The rest of the cake is then cut by a friend or waitress and served to the guests.

TOSSING THE BOUQUET AND GARTER

This is an old tradition that hearkens back to the days of yesteryear and is meant as a way to pass the "luck" of marriage on to unwed men and women attending the bride and groom. The bouquet and garter toss can take place either just before or just after your cake cutting, usually toward the very end of the reception. Be sure your photographer is prepared as these are prime photo ops that you'll want to catch on film.

Have all the single women gather on the dance floor or in a central location. The bride then turns her back on them and lobs her bouquet back over her head. Tradition has it that whoever is lucky enough to catch the bouquet will be the next to marry.

If you *choose* to preserve your bouquet, or if a prayer book was carried instead, buy a smaller, "tossing" bouquet for this ritual.

Since old traditions seem to be convinced that marriage is the answer for everyone, the garter toss is the men's equivalent of the bouquet toss. This time the single men gather in hopes of catching the garter. With the bride sitting on a chair, the groom slips the garter off her leg (which is why it's a good idea not to place the garter too high on the leg — just above or below the knee is perfect). He then hauls off and pitches it toward the single men, with the one who catches it being the next to wed. ✻

RECEPTION *information* sheet

RECEPTION SITE _____

Address _____

Site Coordinator _____ Phone _____

Confirmed Date _____ Time _____ to _____

Room Reserved _____

Deposit Amount _____ Date Due _____

Balance Amount _____ Date Due _____

Cancellation Policy _____

Last Date to Give Final Head Count _____

NUMBER OF GUESTS _____ *Invited* _____ *Confirmed* _____

TYPE OF RECEPTION ❏ Sit-Down ❏ Buffet ❏ Cocktails/Hor d'oeuvres

CATERER *(when different from reception site)* _____

Contact Person _____ Phone _____

Confirmed Date/time _____ Last Date for Final Head Count _____

RECEPTION COST

Cost Per Person: Food _____ Beverage _____ *Total* _____

Number of confirmed guests	_____
Cost per person	_____
(Number of guests x cost per person) Subtotal	_____
Sales tax	_____
Gratuity	_____
(Site or equipment) Rental fee	_____
Other	_____
Total Cost	_____
Less Deposit	_____
Balance Due	_____

EQUIPMENT *check* list

RENTAL COMPANY _____   Date Ordered _____

Address _____

Contact Person _____   Phone _____

Delivery Date/Time _____ / _____   Pick-up Date/Time _____ / _____

Cancellation Policy _____   Damaged/Broken Policy _____

Item	Quantity	Cost
CEREMONY EQUIPMENT		
Aisle Runner (length)	_____	_____
Aisle Stanchions	_____	_____
Aisle Candelabra		
Free-standing	_____	_____
Clamp style	_____	_____
Altar Candelabra	_____	_____
No. of lights	_____	_____
No. of lights	_____	_____
Candles	_____	_____
Size _____	_____	_____
Candle Lighter	_____	_____
Canopy/Chuppah	_____	_____
Flower Stands	_____	_____
Style_____ Size_____	_____	_____
Style_____ Size_____	_____	_____
Guest Book Stand	_____	_____
Kneeling Bench	_____	_____
Lattice Backdrops	_____	_____
Lattice Arch	_____	_____
Microphone	_____	_____
Other _____	_____	_____
CHAIRS		
Style _____	_____	_____

Item	Quantity	Cost
TABLES		
Round tables		
36" seats 4 people	_____	_____
48" seats 6 people	_____	_____
60" seats 8 people	_____	_____
72" seats 10 - 12 people	_____	_____
Oblong tables	_____	_____
6' seats 6 - 8 people	_____	_____
8' seats 8 - 10 people	_____	_____
Square tables	_____	_____
34" square	_____	_____
LINENS		
Round cloths - Color	_____	_____
60" fits 24"- 36" table	_____	_____
72" fits 24" to floor or	_____	_____
36"- 48" table	_____	_____
90" fits 36" to floor or	_____	_____
48"- 60" table	_____	_____
100" fits 48" to floor or	_____	_____
60"- 72" table	_____	_____
Long cloth	_____	_____
54" x 54" fits cardtable	_____	_____
60" x 60" fits cardtable	_____	_____
60" x 120" fits 6' and 8' tables	_____	_____

Item	Color	
NAPKINS		
Cocktail size	_____	_____
Dinner size ❑ Paper ❑ Cloth	_____	_____

Equipment *check* list

Item	Quantity	Cost
DINNERWARE ❏ China ❏ Paper		
Dinner plates	_____	_____
Salad plates	_____	_____
Bread plates	_____	_____
Luncheon plates	_____	_____
Soup bowls	_____	_____
Cake plates	_____	_____
Coffee cups/saucers	_____	_____
Demitasse cups/saucers	_____	_____
FLATWARE ❏ Stainless ❏ Silverplate		
Dinner knives	_____	_____
Steak knives	_____	_____
Butter knives	_____	_____
Dinner forks	_____	_____
Salad forks	_____	_____
Dessert forks	_____	_____
Teaspoons	_____	_____
Soup spoons	_____	_____
Demitasse spoons	_____	_____
Serving spoons	_____	_____
Meat forks	_____	_____
Cake knife/server	_____	_____
GLASSWARE ❏ Glass ❏ Plastic		
Wine glasses	_____	_____
Champagne glasses	_____	_____
Water goblets	_____	_____
Highballs	_____	_____
Double rocks	_____	_____
Snifters	_____	_____
Water glasses	_____	_____
Punch cups	_____	_____

Item	Quantity	Cost
TRAYS ❏ Stainless ❏ Silverplate		
Round 12"	_____	_____
Round 14"	_____	_____
Round 16"	_____	_____
Round 20"	_____	_____
Oval 13" x 21"	_____	_____
Oval 15" x 24"	_____	_____
Oblong 10" x 17"	_____	_____
Oblong 14" x 22"	_____	_____
Oblong 17" x 23"	_____	_____
Meat platters	_____	_____
Waiters' trays/stands	_____	_____
SERVING PIECES		
Chafing dish, 2 qt.	_____	_____
Chafing dish, 4 qt.	_____	_____
Chafing dish, 8 qt.	_____	_____
Bowls, 12"	_____	_____
Bowls, 16"	_____	_____
Bowls, 20"	_____	_____
Punch fountain, 3 gal.	_____	_____
Punch fountain, 7 gal.	_____	_____
Punch bowl, ladle	_____	_____
Coffee maker, 35 cup	_____	_____
Coffee maker, 50 cup	_____	_____
Coffee maker, 100 cup	_____	_____
Silver coffee and tea set	_____	_____
Insulated coffee pitcher	_____	_____
Creamer & sugar set	_____	_____
Sugar tongs	_____	_____
Salt & pepper set	_____	_____
Water pitchers	_____	_____
Ashtrays	_____	_____
Table candles	_____	_____

EQUIPMENT *check* list

Item	Quantity	Cost
MISCELLANEOUS EQUIPMENT		
Barbeque grill	_____	_____
Electric hotplate	_____	_____
Microwave	_____	_____
Portable bar	_____	_____
Ice chest	_____	_____
Coolers	_____	_____
Dance Floor	_____	_____
Size _____	_____	_____
Stage Platform	_____	_____
Lighting	_____	_____
Twinkle lights	_____	_____
Tiki torches	_____	_____
Spot lights	_____	_____
Pole lights	_____	_____
Hurricane lights	_____	_____
Heaters	_____	_____
Fans	_____	_____
Extension cords	_____	_____
Tents/canopies	_____	_____
Size _____	_____	_____
Umbrellas	_____	_____
Indoor/outdoor carpet	_____	_____
Size _____	_____	_____
Trash cans/liners	_____	_____

Item	Quantity	Cost
Coat rack	_____	_____
Portable toilets	_____	_____
Electric bug zapper	_____	_____
Stands for table #s	_____	_____
Bar	_____	_____
Bottle/can openers	_____	_____
Corkscrews	_____	_____
Cocktail shakers	_____	_____
Strainers	_____	_____
Electric blender	_____	_____
Ice buckets	_____	_____
Ice tubs	_____	_____
Sharp knives	_____	_____
Tall spoons	_____	_____
Condiments tray	_____	_____
Other	_____	_____
_____	_____	_____
_____	_____	_____
_____	_____	_____
_____	_____	_____

TOTAL RENTAL COST _____

DEPOSIT _____

BALANCE DUE _____

RECEPTION *seating* chart

Type and size of table _____   *Number of chairs per table* _____

Table # _____   Table # _____   Table # _____   Table # _____

_____   _____   _____   _____
_____   _____   _____   _____
_____   _____   _____   _____
_____   _____   _____   _____
_____   _____   _____   _____
_____   _____   _____   _____
_____   _____   _____   _____
_____   _____   _____   _____
_____   _____   _____   _____
_____   _____   _____   _____

Table # _____   Table # _____   Table # _____   Table # _____

_____   _____   _____   _____
_____   _____   _____   _____
_____   _____   _____   _____
_____   _____   _____   _____
_____   _____   _____   _____
_____   _____   _____   _____
_____   _____   _____   _____
_____   _____   _____   _____
_____   _____   _____   _____
_____   _____   _____   _____

Table # _____   Table # _____   Table # _____   Table # _____

_____   _____   _____   _____
_____   _____   _____   _____
_____   _____   _____   _____
_____   _____   _____   _____
_____   _____   _____   _____
_____   _____   _____   _____
_____   _____   _____   _____
_____   _____   _____   _____
_____   _____   _____   _____

RECEPTION *seating* chart

Type and size of table _____   *Number of chairs per table* _____

Table # _____   Table # _____   Table # _____   Table # _____

_____   _____   _____   _____
_____   _____   _____   _____
_____   _____   _____   _____
_____   _____   _____   _____
_____   _____   _____   _____
_____   _____   _____   _____
_____   _____   _____   _____
_____   _____   _____   _____
_____   _____   _____   _____

Table # _____   Table # _____   Table # _____   Table # _____

_____   _____   _____   _____
_____   _____   _____   _____
_____   _____   _____   _____
_____   _____   _____   _____
_____   _____   _____   _____
_____   _____   _____   _____
_____   _____   _____   _____
_____   _____   _____   _____
_____   _____   _____   _____

Table # _____   Table # _____   Table # _____   Table # _____

_____   _____   _____   _____
_____   _____   _____   _____
_____   _____   _____   _____
_____   _____   _____   _____
_____   _____   _____   _____
_____   _____   _____   _____
_____   _____   _____   _____
_____   _____   _____   _____

Feeding the *masses*

CATERING *options* for YOUR RECEPTION

*T*he biggest slice of your budgeting pie will most likely go toward feeding your guests. Their memories of the food you serve will be second only to how beautiful you look and how moving your ceremony is. Fortunately for you, gone are the days of Rubber Chicken Supreme and Mystery Meat Especiale. An exquisite array of culinary masterpieces await the discerning couple and their guests. At a price. Your assignment, should you choose to accept it, is to select a wedding menu that reflects your personal taste and style, titillates the taste buds of your guests, and doesn't send you into debt for the next five years.

The time of day, and in turn, which meal you serve at that time of day, will greatly impact your budget, with cost usually escalating along with the lateness of the hour. A light brunch will be less expensive than a luncheon, which will in turn be less costly than a full sit-down dinner. Traditionally, those weddings and receptions that take place earlier in the day tend to be of the informal and semi-formal variety, but you can have a formal wedding breakfast or luncheon. Very formal, by its definition, occurs later in the day.

EARLY IN THE DAY

A breakfast makes for a fresh, festive reception following a morning wedding at 9 or 10 o'clock. This may be served buffet style, or the guests may be seated at specified tables.

There are lots of fresh, light-yet-satisfying choices for a wedding breakfast or brunch: Fresh juice, fruit, quiches, omelets, Belgian waffles, crepes, flaky croissants, or richly textured brioche. (Is your mouth watering yet?) Hot coffee and tea are a must, while serving alcoholic beverages is optional. If desired, you could serve champagne, champagne punch, wine, screwdrivers, or Bloody Marys. Pastries or a wedding cake should also be served.

A brunch could be served anywhere from 11:00 to 2:00. Food is similar to breakfast and consists of egg dishes, fruit salads, cold salads, pasta salads, a selection of sweet and savory crepes, frittatas, cold cut platters, fresh vegetable salads, or full meal salads such as Cobb, Chef, or Chinese Chicken. You may also want to include a collection of breads, juices, punch, and coffee. Again, you could offer alcoholic drinks, but they are optional. Consider serving non-alcoholic drinks, except for champagne for the wedding toast, to significantly cut your beverage costs.

Luncheons may be either sit-down or buffet style. They generally follow a late morning or high noon ceremony and are served between 12 and 3 PM.

Buffet luncheons, like brunch, may include a wide variety of salads, such as potato, fruit, Cobb, chicken, pasta, or vegetables with dip. Poached salmon and shrimp are popular, but also expensive. Sandwiches, cold cuts, and cheeses are often served, and are relatively inexpensive. Consider some of your favorite ethnic foods — Mexican, Thai, Chinese, Sushi, Italian — for a fun twist to the menu. Your reception coordinator or caterer will have suggestions, according to your budget.

Sit-down luncheons may be started by serving champagne, cocktails, and hors d'oeuvres while guests go through the receiving line. Once the guests are seated, a white wine may be served with soup or salad to start. How about chicken skewers with grilled vegetables, Chicken Satay, or Cajun style blackened chicken? Beef, while popular, can be pricey, but consider something like beef fajitas or beef shish kabobs. Your caterer is sure to have some tempting suggestions. Serve coffee or tea with the wedding cake. Having an espresso/cappuccino bar or offering chocolate cups filled with cordials adds a nice touch.

LATER IN THE DAY

Tea receptions are generally held between 2:00 and 5:00, usually starting no later than 3:30. A smorgasbord of teas, both iced and hot, coffee, and punch, both with and without champagne or wine, is generally served. Lots of elegant tea sandwiches and sumptuous dessert bites, along with wedding cake, is the basic requirement. This type of reception is the least expensive to have, and perfect when there's a large guest list and a small budget. If

held in a home or garden, this type of reception will cut down on rentals.

This time of day is also perfect for a cake and champagne only reception, so you may choose to forego a meal altogether. It's still fairly early in the day for alcoholic beverages, so you would have minimal costs there. If you decide on a cake and champagne reception, have the cake be as absolutely stunning as possible. Pay extra attention to presentation — linens, crystal, and china — to give this type of reception an elegant feel. Another alternative would be to have a small offering of hors d'oeuvres before the cake is served. It's a nice idea to mention this on your invitation so that your guests won't be expecting a meal.

Please join us for cake and champagne . . .

Cocktail receptions are held between 4:00 and 7:30 PM. If only cocktails are being served, with no dinner to follow, the reception should start by 5:30 or 6:00 at the latest.

Usually champagne, wine, punch, or beer is served and in many cases there's an open bar, depending on the budget. A mouth watering array of both hot and cold hors d'oeuvres may be served or set out on buffet tables. If you're planning a cocktail-only reception, it's thoughtful to mention this on your invitation, *Please join us for cocktails*, so that no one shows up looking for a feeding trough. Two to three hours for a cocktail reception is about right, because you don't want the event to feel either rushed or drawn out.

EVENING

As a rule, an evening reception indicates a full dinner meal, so this is generally the most expensive time of day to plan for. The dinner can be a buffet or sit-down affair, and usually includes cocktails. A dinner reception starts sometime between 6:00 and 9:00 PM. In many cases, cocktails and hors d'oeuvres are served in the first hour, with a sit-down or buffet dinner following. With a dinner menu, the sky's the limit. If your cocktails last more than about twenty to thirty minutes, you will need to serve some food with them, but bear in mind that this will add to your expenses. To keep expenses down, offer wine and beer rather than a full bar. A cocktail hour of some kind gives people time to go through the receiving line and mingle with friends, especially when a sit-down dinner follows.

It's perfectly acceptable to have a late night wedding with only cake and champagne being served at the reception. Again, do think to mention this on your invitation.

Once you've decided on the time of day, you'll need to decide on the types of food you'll want to serve. Choose food not only for its mouth-watering taste, but also for its color and texture. You'll want to put together an interesting and appealing variety for a stunning presentation. When designing your menu, also keep in mind that your goal is not to stuff your guests so full of food that they can do nothing but sit around and groan for the rest of the reception. You want them to have a pleasant sufficiency, but not end up feeling like stuffed trout.

HORS D'OEUVRES

These can almost be a light meal unto themselves, if you offer enough of a variety. Or, they can precede a more significant dinner or luncheon. Because of their labor-intensive nature, they can be expensive, running anywhere from $1.50 to $8.00 per piece. For a cocktail hour before a dinner party, allow six to ten pieces per person. For a cocktail only party, allow eighteen to twenty-four pieces per person.

Your selection of of hors d'oeuvres might consist of: fruit and cheese platter, sausage in pastry, stuffed mushrooms, mini quiches, chicken kabobs, chicken wings, patés and spreads, jumbo shrimp, crab cakes, mini tostadas, sushi, and quesadillas. Your caterer will have many other ideas to tantalize your taste buds. Just remember to pick hors d'oeuvres that aren't too messy. No one in their wedding finery wants to eat chicken wings dripping in barbecue sauce and risk a spill.

FOOD STATIONS

Food stations, where small buffet tables are set up around the room, or in different areas of a garden, are an increasingly popular option. The spread-out location of the food helps encourage the guests to mingle. You want the stations to be accessible from all angles, and make sure there's someplace for each guest to sit.

For a fun, lively touch, you can give each food station a different theme and type of food. Decorate them with floral displays and unique serving pieces for a truly eye-catching effect. Food stations might include: a beautiful display of cheeses with breads and fresh fruits displayed in baskets, an ice-carved boat filled with jumbo shrimp and crab legs, a chef carving a roast, serving hot won tons from a wok, or a chicken crepe made right in front of the guests' eyes. Also consider cold cuts, patés and spreads, sushi, pastas, a burrito or tostada bar where guests can choose their fillings, a small grill, and an espresso bar. You might also consider having a particular signature beverage station. For example, a margarita, daiquiri, or martini station where guests can design their own drinks.

BUFFET RECEPTIONS

At a buffet reception, all the food is laid out on a large buffet table, like a feast spread out before royalty. Guests are then invited to serve themselves. After filling their plates, they can choose to sit at a table of their choice, or you can assign seats ahead of time. The buffet table is arranged with a variety of food, and can be either round or oblong, with the food placed around the edge. It may also be rectangular with food served from behind one side, or with food displayed along both sides. The area available and the number of guests will determine the way the tables are arranged. Try to avoid making the guests wait in a long line. For a larger number of guests have two buffet tables, one at each end of the room.

Buffets are not necessarily cheaper than a sit-down meal. Much depends on the food you choose. Also, when guests are allowed to serve themselves, there's no portion control and they may end up taking far more than would have been brought to them on a plate. One way around this is to have servers operating the buffet table, placing portions on your guests' plates.

Buffet selections are endless. Warm or cold meat entrees, pastas, either hot or cold, side dishes such as risotto, potatoes au gratin, rice pilaf, salads, hot vegetable side dishes, as well as assorted breads and rolls. If you're having a semi-formal or informal wedding, consider one of your favorite ethnic cuisines: Mexican, Thai, Chinese, Indian, or Italian. Contact your favorite ethnic restaurant and see if they might be willing to cater it for you.

Sit-Down Receptions

Seating guests at pre-arranged tables and serving them a meal is certainly the most formal way to dine. If dinner is the meal being served, it's most often preceded by a cocktail hour so the guests can mingle. A sit-down reception provides for more organization. It is easier to get the guests' attention when the traditional ceremonies, such as cutting the cake, are to begin. On the other hand, some people feel the sit-down service tends to quiet a party down, and discourages people from mingling.

If you have this type of reception, you will incur the additional expense of wait staff, which you or your caterer will have to arrange. Usually the sit-down dinner menu includes a soup or salad, an entrée, side dish, vegetable dish, and bread of some kind. You may or may not want to serve dessert. It is perfectly acceptable to have the wedding cake

be the dessert, and this is a great way to cut meal costs. Some dinner menu suggestions would be:

Caesar Salad
Roast Filet of Beef au Poivre
Roasted Red Potatoes
Garlic Sautéed Green Beans
French Bread

Stuffed Artichokes
Grilled Swordfish with Mango Salsa
Assorted Grilled Vegetables
Rice Pilaf
Rosemary & Dill Bread

Romaine, Pear, & Walnut Salad
with Blue Cheese Vinaigrette
Poached Salmon
New Peas
Confetti Rice
Hot Rolls

Who's Doing the Cooking?

There are three basic choices when it comes to who's doing the cooking. It can be an on-site chef, a catering company or restaurant, or you can do it yourself.

On-Site Chef

If you're having your reception at a hotel, club, banquet hall, or restaurant, they will most likely be doing the catering for you. You will probably not have any choice in this matter, but hopefully their catering reputation is one of the reasons you chose the location in the first place. (See Chapter Nine, Setting Your Sites) They will have a wide variety of menu selections, hopefully in a wide variety of budget ranges. The chef may or may not be open to trying something new or adapting menu ideas the two of you may have. It never hurts to ask.

INDEPENDENT CATERER

When your reception is being held in a home, garden, or location that allows you to book your own cooking staff, then you can select your own caterer. Good caterers are reserved months in advance so begin your search early. Start interviewing as soon as you've decided on your location, and be ready to put down a deposit to reserve the caterer of your choice. Caterers may have a wide variety of menus that they do well, or they may specialize. Find out what their menu specialties are and see if there is a way to sample their wares. Oftentimes, restaurants will also do catering. Check with a few of your favorites to see if they offer this service.

When interviewing prospective caterers, find out exactly what they will provide in the way of service, equipment, and food. Some will only prepare the food, deliver it, and serve it. Others will arrange for every aspect of the reception, including the food prep, serving, arranging the rental of all equipment, set up, clean up, liquor, beverages, and linens. Some will even be able to provide the cake, or at the very least recommend a baker. Most caterers will have pictures of weddings they've done. Look at them, check their references, and taste their food before signing that contract. Read the contract carefully to be sure it includes everything you agreed on and states the total price. Check the cancellation policies. The catering fee is usually a flat fee based on the number of guests, or a fee per person, depending on the type and amount of food provided. A 15 percent service charge plus sales tax is usually added to the total. Be sure to check. You wouldn't want any surprises. Most require a 50 to 75 percent deposit and a total guest count a week or two before the ceremony. Don't pay the balance until after the reception, and only if you are satisfied that you received what was agreed upon.

Your caterer will make menu suggestions to fit the style, budget, and number of guests of your particular wedding. A good caterer will be flexible and offer a variety of items with varying prices to enable you to serve something appropriate and stay within your budget. Serve chicken breast rather than filet mignon, or have a beautiful display of fruit or cheese rather than one of expensive shrimp and crab. Try to offer a variety so there will be something suitable for everyone's taste.

When *giving* the final *head* count to your caterer or banquet facilities, don't forget to include wedding vendors such as your photographer, band members, officiant, videographer, or wedding planner, who will be on site during your reception. These people will also need to be fed.

Doing It Yourself

Perhaps you're a fabulous cook, or your whole family gets together to cook as part of your favorite things to do together. Maybe your wedding will be small, or informal, and you have lots of time on your hands, or you are just a very motivated do-it-yourselfer. Whatever the reason, catering your own reception can be done, but consider carefully before committing to this course of action.

It will be a lot of work.

It will take a lot of organization.

It will be a lot of work. (This bears repeating!)

Don't forget that if you do the cooking or have other friends do it, you'll be responsible for making sure all the rentals, tables, chairs, linens, china, etc. are reserved and set up.

Wait Staff

If your restaurant, hotel, or caterer provides this service, then you're in luck. If not, you'll need to locate some wait staff on your own. If your caterer doesn't provide wait people, then they should have some recommendations as to where to look. Even if you do it yourself, consider hiring people to help set up, serve, clear, and clean up. Wait staff can run anywhere from $10.00 to $15.00 per hour.

Important Contract Notes

→ Determine the last date on which you can give the caterer or banquet manager your final guest count. Have them base the costs on a per-person basis, and charge you only for those guests who will be attending, not for the number of guests you originally invited.

→ With your caterer, specify in writing the exact menu items that are to be served. Some caterers have been known to substitute less expensive food items than those you originally contracted for. Don't pay 100 percent of the bill in advance; hold something out until the reception is over.

Liquor and Beverages

Which beverages you decide to serve at your reception will be influenced by a number of factors — the time of day, the type of reception, your wedding style, and the personal preferences of the two of you, as well as your family. You can opt for full bar service, with wine at dinner and champagne for the wedding toast. You can also choose soft bar service, which includes beer, wine, and other non-alcoholic beverages, along with champagne. You may decide you want champagne available throughout the entire reception or poured only when it's time for the wedding toast. Other options are to have a soft bar, along with a limited offering of other alcoholic beverages, say a margarita, daiquiri, or martini bar set up, which will limit the variety of alcohol you will need to stock. About the only option you should not consider is having a cash bar. That is a no-no. Offer what works for your budget and preferences, and don't charge any guest for anything, just as you wouldn't hand them a scotch on the rocks at home, then sweetly request $5.00, please.

On Premises Bar Service

Most restaurants, hotels, banquet facilities, and private clubs have a liquor license, which allows them to serve and sell alcoholic beverages. While, yes, this does make life easier for you, it's also a tremendous money maker for them. At these facilities, your pricing options will be per consumption or a flat per person fee.

Pricing per consumption means that you are charged only for what your guests actually consume, usually measured by the amount left in the bottle. This applies to hard liquor only. Beer and wine are charged per open bottle. Some places will try to charge per open bottle of hard liquor, which is not as desirable because if only your dear Great Uncle Ben drinks scotch, you will be charged for the whole bottle, not just the two drinks he consumed. If your guests don't drink much, or are moderate drinkers, this is a good choice. If going this route, it's a good idea to advise the wait staff and maître d' NOT to clear away half empty glasses, thereby forcing guests to go to the bar to get another drink. Another option is, instead of a bar set up, to have wait staff circulating and taking drink orders and bringing them back to your guests. This slows down the process a little bit, thereby reducing the overall alcohol consumed.

A flat rate per person, anywhere from $10.00 to $15.00 per guest, is just what it states. For every guest you have, you will be assessed a flat fee, whether or not those guests drink alcoholic beverages. If you know your guests like to celebrate a good time with lots of drinking, this is a more economical choice.

PROVIDING YOUR OWN BEVERAGES

Some hotels and facilities will allow you to provide your own alcohol. This can be one way to effectively control your liquor costs, but keep in mind that most places will charge a corkage fee for opening each bottle of wine or champagne, which can add up. Check their policy. They will also probably charge you a flat fee per person bar set up charge, in order to bring in a bar with glasses, mixers, garnishes, etc. Good places to shop for liquor deals are discount warehouses, superstores, wine shops, liquor stores, and local wineries.

One important thing to be aware of is that in most states, party givers are held personally liable for any accidents that ensue from the alcohol served at their parties. So it's a good idea to check with your insurance agent as well as the Alcoholic Beverage Control Department to see what liability coverage they recommend.

If supplying your own liquor, here are some things to keep in mind.

→ Buy more than you think you'll need.

→ See if you can return unopened bottles.

→ Make sure someone has allowed and arranged for bar miscellany, glasses, stirrers, cocktail napkins, ice, garnishes, mixers, etc.

→ Try to have your white wine and champagne delivered chilled.

Your caterer may provide the alcohol, or may refer you to a reputable liquor dealer. Most liquor dealers can provide any brand you request, along with appropriate mixes. Dealers who provide this service are well worth using. Most will deliver, and bring more than what is usually consumed, so you won't run short. You are only charged for the bottles that are opened. Make sure to take an inventory of what was delivered, have someone keep an eye on the bartenders, and count both the opened and unopened bottles

going *the*
NON-ALCOHOLIC
route

Now, more than ever, there are lots of non-alcoholic options available. Many wineries are producing non-alcoholic versions of their wine and champagne, and most major breweries have non-alcoholic beer available. You should at least offer some of these, even when having a full bar service at your reception. Many people choose not to consume alcohol, and it is a nice gesture to allow for this.

PUT
it *on*
ICE

You will need one-and-a-half pounds of ice per person, two-and-a-half if you are chilling bottles.

Bottles need to be set in ice for at least two hours, and crushed ice works better than cubes.

How much Is Enough?

People generally drink more in the evening, with the first hour being the heaviest in terms of alcohol consumption. Allow two to three cocktails per person.

A one-liter bottle of hard liquor makes approximately fifteen to eighteen drinks.

Popular liquor you should consider stocking: vodka, gin, sweet vermouth, dry vermouth, scotch bourbon, whiskey, rum, and tequila.

You should allow one bartender for every fifty guests.

Allow two to three drinking glasses per person.

One case of champagne equals seventy-five drinks.

Allow one and a half cases per one hundred guests for toast only or three cases per one hundred guests for continuous service.

One bottle of wine equals six drinks.

Generally the white wine to red wine ratio is two to one.

Beer drinkers will consume four bottles on average.

to make certain none have disappeared. Liquor dealers can also provide wine, beer, and champagne. Their prices are considerably less than buying through a retail liquor store. They are experienced and can provide advice as to brands and quantities within your budget.

Be sure to provide non-alcoholic beverages, soft drinks, or punch. The caterer can prepare champagne punch or non-alcoholic punch, unless you're doing the reception yourself.

PUNCH RECIPES

CHAMPAGNE PUNCH

1 gal. Sauterne wine

4 quarts champagne

2 quarts ginger ale

l/2 pt. sherbet

Chill wine, champagne, and ginger ale. Pour into large punch bowl, then add sherbet, ice cubes, or ice ring just before serving.

NON-ALCOHOLIC PUNCH

2-12 oz. cans frozen orange juice

2-12 oz. cans frozen lemonade

8 cans of cold water

2 cups Grenadine

Juice of three fresh lemons

3 qts. ginger ale, chilled

Mix together in large punch bowl just before serving. Float orange slices and cherries on top. Add ice cubes or ice ring.

PARTY PUNCH

1 fifth bourbon

8 oz. unsweetened pineapple juice

8 oz. unsweetened grapefruit juice

4 oz. fresh lemon juice

2 bottles (qt.) 7-Up

Pre-chill all the ingredients. Mix together right before serving. Add 7-Up last. Decorate with fruit and ice ring.

HOSPITALITY PUNCH

1/2 gal. orange juice

1/2 gal. pineapple juice

l/2 gal. lime juice

2 quarts ginger ale

2 quarts light or dark rum

l/2 lb. sugar

Pre-chill all ingredients. Mix together right before serving. Add ginger ale last. Garnish with fresh fruit. Add ice cubes or ice ring.

MONEY SAVING TIPS

- Buy liquor from a wholesaler who will let you return unopened bottles.

- Keep beverage costs down. Serve a punch, wine only, or non-alcoholic drinks, like sparkling cider or grape juice.

- Handle rentals yourself. Get rentals directly from a rental company rather than through your caterer. You can avoid the middleman.

- Decide on a morning or an afternoon reception. A breakfast or brunch is less expensive than a dinner. For an afternoon reception, serve cake and hors d'oeuvres rather than a full meal. Also, people tend to drink less early in the afternoon.

- If having an open bar, limit the cocktail hour, and then serve only wine after that allotted time. Consider having someone pass drinks on a tray — this can help deter people from setting drinks down, then going to the bar to order another one.

- Avoid selecting the most expensive menu item. Shrimp, lobster, crab, and beef are more expensive than chicken or pasta.

- Serve less expensive hors d'oeuvres. Avoid serving hors d'oeuvres that are labor intensive or use expensive ingredients.

- Have buffet food served by the caterer's staff, rather than have guests pile food, much of which will remain uneaten, on their plates themselves. This will also help avoid the embarrassment of running out of food — the nightmare of every hostess.

- Reduce the size of your guest list. Consider eliminating dates and children of friends, business associates and casual acquaintances.

- Check hotel reception packages. Some hotels have special reception packages, which include a discount on a bridal suite when the reception is held there, or when you book a block of rooms for out-of-town guests.

- Plan a home wedding. Have your reception in your or a friend's home or garden.

Use the following worksheets to help you select a caterer and record the menu you plan to serve. ✳

QUESTIONS *to* ASK *your* CATERER

Photocopy and use one for each caterer interviewed.

CATERER _____

What type of food items do
you recommend for my budget
and the number of guests? _____

What type of service,
sit-down dinner, or buffet,
would be best? _____

Discuss menu selections,
ask the cost per person. _____

Do you provide linens? _____

Is there an additional fee? _____

Is there a color selection? _____

Do you supply glasses,
plates, and silverware? _____

Is there an additional charge? _____

Do you handle all rental
equipment such as tables,
chairs, serving pieces? _____

Would it cost less if I
handle the rentals myself? _____

How much time will
you need to set up? _____

Can we go over the table
locations and seating
arrangements ahead of time? _____

Do you handle the clean up? _____

Rental returns? _____

Will you personally handle
and attend my reception? _____

If not, what is the name of
the person who will? _____

Do you make arrangements
for flowers, decorations,
and music? _____

Do you provide the
wedding cake? _____

If not, is there a cake
cutting fee? _____

Do you charge extra to
pour coffee? _____

Will you provide the groom's
cake, if we want one? _____

Do you provide the liquor? _____

What is the cost per drink? _____

Is it cheaper if we provide
our own liquor? _____

Do you charge a corkage fee
per bottle if we provide our
own wine and champagne? _____

Do you require a guaranteed
number of guests? _____

What is the last date I can
give you a final guest count? _____

Do you have a contract? _____

When will you provide the
final per person cost? _____

What is the payment policy? _____

What is the deposit to
hold the date? _____

What is your refund or
cancellation policy? _____

Are gratuities already figured
in the total price? _____

If so, what percent is
being charged? _____

Do you provide food for
the photographer,
videographer, or musicians? _____

Is this an extra per person fee? _____

Will you pack a to-go snack
for the bride and groom? _____

Will you pack the top tier
of the wedding cake? _____

CATERER *worksheet*

	Estimate #1 Name_____ _____ Phone_____	**Estimate #2** Name_____ _____ Phone_____	**Estimate #3** Name_____ _____ Phone_____
	Description　　　　*Cost*	*Description*　　　　*Cost*	*Description*　　　　*Cost*
FOOD 　Hors d'oeuvres 　Buffet 　Sit-down 　Wedding Cake			
BEVERAGES 　Open Bar 　Champagne/Wine 　Non-alcoholic			
SERVICE 　Waiters 　Bartenders 　Valet			
EQUIPMENT 　Tables 　Chairs 　Linens 　Tent			
DECORATIONS 　Flowers 　Candles 　Other			
SERVICE 　Waiters 　Bartenders 　Valet			
MISCELLANEOUS			
TOTAL			
GRATUITIES 　INCLUDED	❑ Yes　　　❑ No	❑ Yes　　　❑ No	❑ Yes　　　❑ No
SALES TAX 　INCLUDED	❑ Yes　　　❑ No	❑ Yes　　　❑ No	❑ Yes　　　❑ No
NUMBER OF HOURS			
OVERTIME COST 　per hour			
CANCELLATION 　Policy 　Fee			
DEPOSIT REQUIRED	*Amount*　　*Date required*	*Amount*　　*Date required*	*Amount*　　*Date required*

NOTES

Let them Eat *Cake!*

FINDING the *perfect* wedding CAKE

*T*he wedding cake is the crown jewel in your wedding feast, so you'll want it to be not only awe inspiring but incredibly tasty as well. While there is room for the traditional white layer cake with white frosting rosettes, today's spectacular new cake designers have turned wedding cakes into an art form, adding architectural elements, all manner of textures, embellishments, and decorations. When selecting your wedding cake, you will want to take into account the visual appeal of the cake as well as its flavor. The two elements combined will ensure a perfectly unique cake that will cause breathless admiration from both you and your guests.

THE GREAT CAKE HUNT

You should begin researching wedding cakes at least five to six months ahead of your wedding date if you have your heart set on a spectacular one. If you have a simpler cake in mind, you can begin your search three to four months ahead of time.

Get recommendations from friends, wedding consultants, caterers, reception site coordinators, bridal fairs, and regional bridal magazines. Review the baker's portfolio so you can see pictures of the cakes they've created. Most bakeries have opportunities for you to come in and have a tasting, so take full advantage of this service. When you're ready to order your cake, make sure you cover the specific terms such as size, tiers, flavors, fillings, colors, decorations, presentation, delivery, date, time, and location.

Your baker will need to know:

* Number of guests
* Season or room temperature
* Overall room size
* Final decorations
* Any other desserts being served
* Room décor, decorations, and colors
* Kitchen logistics (refrigeration)
* Name of reception site coordinator, florist, and caterer
* Address of reception site to which cake is to be delivered, along with clear, concise directions and any specific instructions regarding delivery

Wedding cakes have a wide cost range, beginning at around $200 and going up to $1,000 plus. Many of the absolutely stunning ones that you see in national magazines can be upward of $1,200. Cakes are also priced by serving, with the range being from $2.00 per serving on up to $20.00 per serving.

TYPES OF WEDDING CAKE BAKERS

Many times your caterer or reception location will provide the wedding cake. Since wedding cakes may not be their expertise, ask to see pictures and taste a sampling of their baking skills. They may be limited in design ability, but then again, they may be great. By having your caterer or reception site provide the cake, the fee for cutting the cake is usually included in the price. It will probably be an extra charge of $1.00 to $2.00 per slice if you choose to purchase a cake from another source.

Commercial, specialized bakeries are the most common source for wedding cakes. Many specialize in nothing but wedding or special occasion cakes. These bakeries produce a large quantity of cakes, and generally have a variety of cake styles and designs from which to choose.

Non-commercial wedding cake bakers usually work out of their home (or rent a small kitchen somewhere) and specialize in unique, creative wedding cakes. Each cake is individually designed to your specifications. Many of these bakers are true artists, and their love is to create spectacular cakes. The trend to use this type of baker has grown over the past few years, and prices vary widely. In some cases they can be less expensive than a commercial baker because of lower overhead; in other cases they are more expensive because of the elaborate detail and personalized design they offer. Also, finding this type of baker may not be as easy as finding a commercial baker.

WEDDING CAKE COMPONENTS
STYLE

You will want to take into account your overall wedding style, colors, and degree of formality when considering cake designs. Another important element will be the reception site and how it lends itself to the cake's presentation. A starkly modern wedding style will lend itself to a grand structure of a cake, complete with elements pulled from architecture and unusual textures. Romantic or traditional themes will benefit from beautiful flowers, pastel colors, and ribbon or lace motifs. Round layers are the most common, but many cakes are made with square, rectangular, or heart shaped layers as well.

Another style element is how the cake is assembled. Most wedding cakes are tiered, with the three to four inch high tiers being either stacked or separated. Stacked cakes have the layers placed on top of each other, usually with foam rounds in between to protect and reinforce the layers. Separated cakes have some sort of arch, column, or other architectural element, which keeps the layers separated. This requires some heavy reinforcement, with both foam rounds and wooden dowels to support the cake's weight and to keep it from being crushed.

OTHER CREATIVE WAYS TO PERSONALIZE YOUR WEDDING CAKE

* Coordinate the decorations on your cake with an element on your wedding gown, such as the lace, buttons, swags, bows, and bustles.

* Decorate the cake with flowers (fresh or icing) that match your bouquet.

* If you're using a wedding theme, pull that element into your cake as well, either in coloring or overall style. A pastel pink, or light celadon green frosting, for example, or

fall fruit and foliage on an autumn themed cake. Use (sugar) seashells for a wedding by the seashore, a basket weave design for an outdoor garden wedding.

✳ Match the cake color and design to your new wedding china. Use the new china when you cut your first slice.

✳ Incorporate a personal hobby or interest onto your cake, such as a nautical theme, a fairytale theme, or a historical theme.

LOVE IS A MANY FLAVORED THING

In addition to which flavors set your mouth watering, you'll need to consider a few logistics when selecting flavors and icings. For example, season and temperature will be critical to the success of your cake. Some cakes can't be refrigerated, or it will ruin their frosting. Some cakes must be refrigerated, or it will ruin their frosting. How hardy is the filling you've chosen and will it stand up to your location?

Chocolate is overtaking the more traditional white and yellow cake in popularity, but there's also a whole new crop of cake flavors showing up on the scene as well.

CAKE FLAVORS	FILLING FLAVORS
Carrot	Amaretto mousse
Chocolate	Chocolate mousse
Chocolate mousse	Cream cheese
Coconut	Hazelnut
Lemon chiffon	Lemon cream or mousse
Mocha	Mocha cream
Raspberry truffle	Orange cream
Spice	Pineapple
Tiramisu	Raspberry
	Strawberry cream

THE ICING ON THE CAKE

Butter cream frosting is smooth and creamy with a delicate buttery flavor that isn't too sweet. The soft texture is easy to cut, but needs to be kept refrigerated until just a few hours before serving, otherwise it can bead, run, drip, or melt its way into a mess. The texture also lends itself well to decorations such as basket weaves, swags, swirls, fleur de lis, and flowers. It offers one of the best values in terms of price.

Whipped cream is a very delicate and, unfortunately, temperamental frosting that doesn't like heat or humidity one bit. It MUST be kept refrigerated until it

HOT *Trends* in wedding CAKES

✳ More sophisticated, less overly sweet flavors such as coconut, cheesecake, tiramisu, fruitcake, sponge cake, or angel food cake.

✳ Frostings infused with delicate, unusual flavors such as champagne, Kahlua, Grand Marnier, ginger, or mocha.

✳ White cakes (There are still many brides who choose these) with lots of visual interest in the way of texture, design, fine detailing, or mixed white-on-white tones.

✳ Frostings that have a lustrous, opalescent, or pearlescent finish, which is achieved by a special luster wash. Think shimmering make-up trends.

✳ Dr. Seuss or Alice in Wonderland cakes that sport a charming whimsy of wild, vivid colors and off-kilter and out-of-the-ordinary shapes.

✳ Smaller individual cakes for each table of guests, sometimes in differing flavors, fillings, and frosting decorations.

✳ Miniature individual cakes at each place setting. This takes the concept of cupcakes to a whole new level.

✳ Fresh flowers used to decorate cakes.

is served. Its lighter, fluffier texture tends to limit its decorating options.

Fondant is usually rolled out like a piecrust, smooth and flat. Made primarily of sugar and corn syrup, it should not be refrigerated, so make sure that you select a filling that is equally sturdy. The rolled sheets of fondant are wrapped around the cake, creating a smooth, flat surface on which to pipe icing decorations or place flowers. Looks gorgeous, but is not particularly tasty and can be hard to cut.

Royal icing dries to a very hard finish after being piped onto the cake in a variety of shapes and patterns, and it is used for creating many of the decorative touches you see on cakes. Finishing touches may also be added with marzipan (almond paste), spun sugar, and pastillage.

CAKE TOPPERS

Cake toppers are a fun way to personalize your cake and they come in a wide variety of styles, materials, and sizes. Be sure that your cake is strong enough to support whatever cake topper you've chosen. If you want to be unique and creative, use something that reflects your personalities and interests. In addition to the traditional bridal couple statuette, you might consider:

✳ Kissing cherubs

✳ A beautiful music box

✳ A tiny car that is the replica of the one you used on your first date

✳ Blown glass, either a swan or a castle or a sailing schooner — something that reflects you

✳ Sports themes

✳ Flowers

✳ Marzipan fruit

✳ Candles

✳ Mini flags

✳ Sparklers

✳ Ornaments

✳ Ethnic themes

THE SETTING

No jewel is complete without its setting, and the wedding cake is no exception. The cake table should be carefully thought out since it will be a focal point at the reception. Using lovely linens and flowers, along with a special cake knife and server, will really set the stage for the cake cutting.

The size of the cake will determine the size of the table, and make sure it's sturdy! If you'll be having a toast along with the cake cutting, set out a spectacular pair of toasting flutes as well. The bride and attendants' bouquets can also be placed on the table to give the feeling of flowers spilling about everywhere.

THE CUTTING OF THE CAKE

A popular tradition and reception staple, everyone loves to gather to watch the bride and groom cut into this stunning creation. The groom places his hand over the bride's as it rests on the knife. Together, they slice into the bottom layer, carefully making three cuts, and removing a small piece onto a cake plate. Then, gently or enthusiastically — it's their choice — they feed each other a bite.

A nice touch is for the bride and groom to cut additional pieces and serve the cake to their parents. After the bride and groom have cut the first piece or two, they turn the rest of the cake cutting over to the caterer or servers.

THE GROOM'S CAKE

The groom's cake has traditionally been a dark fruitcake or decadent chocolate cake that's cut into pieces and placed in boxes for the guests to take home. With the revival of this old tradition, many brides are adding a creative touch by opting for a chocolate-layered cake in a variety of shapes representing the groom's favorite sport or hobby. These cakes are either being served at the rehearsal dinner or the reception, along with the wedding cake, or, following the old tradition, placed in a box for the guests to take home. Legend has it that a girl who places this cake under her pillow at night will dream of the man she will marry.   However, considering the high cost of weddings these days, many brides choose to omit this tradition. This is perfectly acceptable.

MONEY SAVING TIPS

Find a non-commercial baker who works out of his or her home, and whose overhead is lower.

Keep decorations simple. Don't select a cake with extremely elaborate decorations, such as hand-made sugar lilies that look as if they've just been picked.

Add height by using Styrofoam tiers. If you love the look of a tall cake, but don't need to feed a lot of people, cut your cost by decorating Styrofoam shapes and using them for two of the tiers.

Order an elaborate, smaller cake for the ceremonial cake cutting. Then have sheet cakes of the same recipe made to serve the guests.

Don't save the top tier. Many couples save the top of their cake to eat on their first anniversary, and then take one look at the cake a year later and, sad to say, toss it into the garbage. Time doesn't do much to improve the quality or appearance of wedding cake. If, for reasons of tradition, you want to save something, consider keeping just one or two pieces of the top tier. Or, for your anniversary, have a duplicate of the top tier made.

Order less cake. If you're serving another dessert in addition to the wedding cake, or having a sweets table, plan on fewer servings of your cake and having smaller portions served.

Skip the groom's cake. If you're working on a tight budget, eliminate the groom's cake. It's an old tradition, but probably won't be missed. ✳

BAKERY *worksheet*

	Estimate #1 Name _____ _____ Phone _____	*Estimate #2* Name _____ _____ Phone _____	*Estimate #3* Name _____ _____ Phone _____
	Description *Cost*	*Description* *Cost*	*Description* *Cost*
CAKE Size Shape Number of Tiers			
CAKE FLAVORS			
FILLING FLAVORS			
ICING FLAVORS			
DECORATIONS			
GROOM'S CAKE			
TOTAL			

BAKERY SELECTED

Name _____ Order Date/Deposit _____

Address _____ Balance Due _____

Phone/Contact _____ Delivery Date/Time _____

A Rose by any OTHER name

YOUR guide to WEDDING flowers

Flowers have been associated with weddings since the beginning of time — for their lively, colorful beauty, their fragrance (thought in earlier times to have the ability to ward off evil, or at the very least, evil smells), or as a symbol of purity and fertility. Not only are flowers fraught with all this symbolic history, but they are the perfect, breathtakingly romantic backdrop to your nuptial celebration. Whether you select flowers for their personal significance, fragrance, color, or theme, they will provide the perfect touch to your big day. In fact, the majority of your decorating budget will most likely go toward floral arrangements.

It's possible that you already know the exact type of flowers you want at your wedding. Or perhaps you want to consider all the options available to you — and there are many. Either way, here are a few things to keep in mind as you choose your flowers.

Durability and Hardiness – Some flowers tire more easily than others. Consult with your florist and try to avoid those that are the quickest to wilt, especially in warm temperatures or direct sun. If you're absolutely set on these types of fragile flowers for your wedding, use them in small doses where their beauty will not fade. For the balance, select blooms with staying power, those that will outlast the final couple on the dance floor and keep looking good the following morning, especially if you're planning a morning-after brunch or a weekend wedding.

Color – Pick a color, any color. One that coordinates, contrasts, or blends, whichever you choose. Pale pastels, brilliant jewel tones, rich, deep-hued colors, or the clean pureness of white. Coordinate with your wedding colors and theme for a breathtaking effect. And don't forget greenery, which gives a rich, lush feel without breaking your budget.

Fragrance and Scent – One of flowers' greatest assets can also be somewhat of a liability, if not thoroughly thought out. Wildly fragrant blossoms such as gardenia, jasmine, or freesia, which are absolutely lovely for bouquets, are probably not the best choice for centerpieces at the dining tables. Their scents can overwhelm if they're not used judiciously. Also, keep in mind that some strong scented flowers can stir up allergies

GREAT color *Combos* to CONSIDER

✳ Soft lavender with darker purple or magenta, to really pop

✳ Soft sage or celadon green with deep or pale yellow, coral for extra zip

✳ Robin's egg blue with a cheerful yellow or cream

✳ Pale blush pink with celadon green

✳ Platinum with almost any shade of lavender or purple

✳ Pink with darker pink, magenta, or purple accents

REALITY *check*

Most florists are design-oriented and love to create beautiful things. If your florist tells you that a particular idea you have won't work or can't be done, it probably can't, otherwise they would be eager to give it a try. Many times, what you see in books or magazines doesn't have to stand up to the rigors of an actual wedding day, so listen to your florist's suggestions.

or other reactions in your guests. In those cases, the softer, more delicately scented varieties will be a better choice.

Availability – It's best to go with flowers that are in season, for freshness, logistics, and cost savings. If you're dead set on peonies for your wedding, plan your celebration during the six to eight weeks a year that peonies are available. Make sure to check the availability of other flowers that may have limited availability. While it's true that in this day and age you can probably get anything you want, it's equally true that it will cost you. Bundles.

Uniqueness – While the traditional wedding flower classics are beautiful, consider incorporating another element into the arrangements to give your own individual stamp. It can be as whimsical as a scattering of feathers, or strategically placed crystals, or as elegant as a unique satin ribbon embroidered with gold threads and pearls. Whatever flower you select, consider taking it just a step further to make them uniquely your own.

Here's a list of some popular wedding flowers and their meanings.

✳ Apple blossoms - *good fortune*

✳ Bluebells - *constancy*

✳ Blue violets - *faithfulness*

✳ Carnations - *distinction*

✳ Forget-me-nots - *true love*

✳ Gardenias - *joy*

✳ Lilies - *purity and innocence*

✳ Lilies of the valley - *happiness*

✳ Orange blossoms - *purity and fertility*

✳ Orchids - *beauty*

✳ Roses - *love*

✳ Stephanotis - *marital harmony*

✳ Tulips - *love and passion*

✳ White daisies - *innocence*

FINDING A FLORIST

Since flowers are such a focal point of the wedding, it's critical to find a florist who you feel "gets" your vision, is willing to carry it out, and who's capable of doing so. Your goal is to find a florist with creative vision as well as a healthy dose of common sense so you can stay within your meticulously planned budget.

FLOWER description *Chart*

Amaryllis	Usually deep red, also available in white. Shaped similar to a lily with a long stem.	Spring, Winter May be hard to get
Anemones	Available in white, blue, red violet, yellow. Shaped similar to poppies.	Spring through Fall
Asters	Usually available in white, pink, rose, and purple.	Summer
Baby's Breath	Usually white. Fine delicate, tiny flowers.	Available year round through florist
Bachelor Buttons	Available in white, pink, red, blue. They look like tiny carnations.	Summer
Calla Lily	White with yellow center. Unusual shape with long stems.	Spring through Fall
Canterbury Bells	Usually blue, purple, or pink. Shaped like little bells.	Summer
Carnations	Available in many colors. Very fragrant. A commonly known flower.	Available year round Usually inexpensive
Catlaya Orchids	Usually white with shades of pink or lavender in the center of each petal. Larger than other orchids.	Available through florist year round Very expensive
Chrysanthemum	Available in white, yellow, red. They come in many shapes and sizes.	Summer to Winter
Daffodils	Available in many colors. A pretty flower that is very common.	Spring
Daisies	Usually white or yellow with yellow center. A popular flower similar, but smaller than a chrysanthemum.	Summer through Fall Inexpensive in season
Day Lily	Usually in shades of cream, orange, red, yellow with a variety of stem lengths.	Spring through Fall
Delphinium	Usually in white, rose, lavender, blue. Long spikes of flowers with lacy foliage.	Spring through Fall
Forget-me-not	Dainty blue flower with yellow or white centers. Very pretty.	Spring
Gardenias	Pretty white flower with dark green leaves. Very fragrant.	Spring
Iris	Available in white, blue, violet, yellow, and orange. Long stalks, large petals with two that drop down a little.	Spring through Summer
Lilac	Usually white or lavender. Stalks with many tiny flowers. Very fragrant.	Spring
Lily	Usually white or cream with tinges of pink or lavender.	Spring through Summer
Lily of the Valley	White flowers. Bell-shaped and clustered on a long spike stem. Very fragrant and delicate.	Spring
Orchid	Usually white, or in shades of pink or lavender. Popular and common flower.	Available year round through florist
Roses	Available in a number of colors. A bud at the end of a long, thorned stem. Buds vary in size down to a miniature rose with a bud of less than one inch. Very popular and fragrant.	Summer is their season, but available year-round through florist
Spray Orchid	Long spikes covered with tiny orchid-like flowers.	Winter. Very expensive
Stephanotis	These are white trumpet-shaped flowers which grow on vines. Popular in bouquets and have a sweet fragrance.	Summer
Strawflowers	Available in white, yellow, orange, red. Straw-like petals shaped like daisies.	Summer
Violets	Available in white, blue, purple. Tiny flowers with a nice fragrance.	Spring
Zephyr Lily	Available in white, yellow, and shades of pink. Smaller than most lilies.	Summer through Fall

A Rose by Any Other Name

KITCHEN *table* advice

When shopping for your florist, here are some good questions to ask.

Have they done many weddings?

Do they have photographs of past work? References?

Does their overall floral style appeal to you?

Are they a good listener, and do they tune into your ideas and build on them?

Who will be the one handling your floral arrangements?

How many other weddings will they be handling that week?

Get recommendations from friends, your caterer, the hotel, or restaurant, and start interviewing florists at least six to eight months in advance. Ask to see pictures of other weddings they've done. Discuss with them the type of wedding you plan to have. It's a big help if they're familiar with the location you'll be using.

Once you've decided on a florist, go over the details with them. Be prepared. For your first meeting with your prospective florist, have your budget in one hand, swatches of fabric you're planning to use in the other, and a list (or better yet, pictures) of your favorite flowers clamped firmly between your teeth. This will go a long way towards making sure you and your florist are on the same wavelength. Never has the saying a picture's worth a thousand words been truer than in the case of discussing floral arrangements.

In the meeting, discuss your overall wedding style, colors, and any themes you may be incorporating. Tell them where your ceremony and reception will be, or even better, bring them pictures. Now would be the time to mention your "must have" flowers so you can discover any difficulties or obstacles to using them. Have the florist discuss all the options available to you, and clearly communicate your budgetary limitations. Discuss everything that's on your mind — from the boutonnieres to the centerpieces, from the floral arches and chair swags to the bridal bouquet. Get the exact number of each item and include the exact flowers to be used in each.

When drawing up the contract with your florist, keep the following in mind:

→ Avoid disappointment; in your contract specify the type and number of flowers to be used in the bouquets and table arrangements. List flowers that can be substituted in the event your first choice is not available. Specify price adjustments if less expensive flowers are substituted. For example, don't just indicate, Bridal Bouquet – Tulips. Give the exact number and color of tulips you expect to receive, such as, Bridal Bouquet – ten pink tulips, four pale cream peonies, and twelve white old fashioned roses.

→ Give your florist pictures of bouquets and arrangements similar to what you want. In your contract, also specify details like the sizes and colors of the arrangements and bouquets. The pictures will ensure that florist has an idea of what you want. Make provisions to adjust the balance due if the arrangements are smaller than you contracted for, or if they are not fresh.

- → Be sure to designate the time, place, and date the flowers are to be delivered, as well as to what set up help, if any, the florist will be providing.

- → The contract should also include the cost, deposit amount, payment schedule, and when the balance is due, as well as any cancellation policy.

Flowers for the Bridal Party

The flowers the bride and her attendants carry can vary from a large bouquet to a single flower. And here's a little secret. Not only does carrying flowers or a bouquet add to the overall beauty of the event, it also gives nervous brides and bridesmaids something to do with their hands, other than wringing them.

Bridal Bouquets

This will be the crème de la floral crème, coordinating perfectly with the bridal gown, the size of the bride, and the overall look and feel of the wedding. If you wish to keep and preserve your bouquet, ask your florist to give you a smaller "throwing" bouquet.

Maid of Honor and Bridesmaids' Flowers

Generally smaller than the bride's, the bridesmaids' bouquets should coordinate with the bridal bouquet. Size and color should complement their dresses as well as the overall look of the wedding. The maid's or matron's of honor bouquet may be slightly different, whether in color or size, in order to set her apart from the others.

Flower Girl

Most flower girls wear a delicate wreath and carry a nosegay or small basket decorated with flowers and colored ribbons. The basket is filled with rose petals to be scattered in the path of the bride. If this is prohibited in your place of worship, have her hand a single rose to guests as she walks down the aisle.

Hairpieces

Many brides choose to wear flowers in their hair rather than another type of headpiece. Flowers may be worn alone or as a delicate wreath with a veil attached to the back. Make sure they are securely fastened!

Hot trends in *bridal* BOUQUETS

Bouquets made up of only one kind of flower. This showcases the flower's individual beauty.

Monochromatic color schemes.

Letting the stems show instead of having them completely wrapped and hidden.

Adding unusual elements to the bouquet such as feathers, crystals on a wire, or leaves washed in silver or gold.

Wrapping the entire bouquet (not just the stem!) in a layer of soft tulle for an ethereal, romantic effect.

CONSIDER *this*

If you're not wild about the idea of carrying flowers (allergic, maybe?) then consider carrying an heirloom fan or family Bible decorated with a flower or two (silk, if need be) and satin ribbons.

Bouquets should be carried with your lower arm resting on the top of the hipbones.

CONSIDER *this*

In place of a corsage, you may want to add more sentiment by giving each of your mothers a rose from your bouquet once you have reached the end of the aisle.

HOT *trends* in
BOUTONNIERES

In addition to the traditional single sprig of flowers (usually coordinating with the bridal bouquet), lots of other elements with a nature theme are being showcased. In winter, consider a small sprig of white snowberries or a stem of cheerful red holly with its shiny green leaves. An autumn groom and his ushers could sport beautifully colored fall leaves enhanced with an acorn. Variegated ivy, decoratively wrapped pine needles, rosemary tied with a tiny blue ribbon, and natural grasses are all finding their way into absolutely stunning boutonnieres.

MOTHERS AND GRANDMOTHERS

Both of your mothers and grandmothers should be presented a corsage to either pin on their dress or handbag. If preferred, they may wear the corsage around their wrist. Check to see which style they would prefer or if a special color is needed to coordinate with their dresses.

GROOM, FATHERS, AND USHERS

All of the men traditionally wear boutonnieres, generally a single blossom such as a rosebud or shaft of lilies of the valley. A new trend in boutonnieres is the use of greenery, grasses, and other botanical elements that are not floral. All of the men's boutonnieres are alike except for the groom's. He wears something a little special. The boutonnieres should be pinned on the left side of the jacket, with the pins hidden.

RING BEARER

The ring bearer may or may not wear a boutonniere. It depends on his outfit. With a tuxedo, you may want him to wear a boutonniere, whereas with knickers and knee socks, it may not be appropriate.

FLOWERS FOR THE CEREMONY

The first step in deciding on flowers for your ceremony is to check if your church or synagogue has any regulations or restrictions regarding them.

The types of arrangements you choose should be influenced by the size and lighting of the church, the season, and the colors of your wedding. Keep in mind that the purpose of flowers at a church ceremony is to direct visual attention toward the front of the church and to the bridal couple. Therefore, they also need to be seen by the guests seated in the back.

In elaborate, formal weddings with larger budgets, flowers and ribbons are draped down the aisle to mark the pews and add color. When cost is a concern, this is one place you can cut back. Instead, use live flowers in decorative baskets at the altar, or line the aisle with them. Another cost-saving idea, which can be done if the ceremony and reception are held in the same location, is to use table centerpieces on both sides of the altar and then bring them to the tables.

In a Jewish ceremony, the vows are said under a chuppah, which is placed at the altar and covered with greens and fresh flowers. For outdoor ceremonies, decorated arches are always popular. Your florist will have some great ideas!

FLOWERS FOR THE RECEPTION

Never underestimate the ability of the right floral arrangements to help transform a stark reception hall into a warm, colorful room. In addition, consider renting indoor plants or small trees to achieve a garden effect.

When selecting flowers for your reception, keep your wedding theme in mind, as well as the size of the room, tables, and budget. The height of the centerpieces can also be an issue for some. Generally speaking, keep them below eye level, around fourteen inches from the table surface. If you prefer elevated floral arrangements — meaning your reception is taking place in a room with a high ceiling, for example — have the floral arrangements start at eye level and keep them light and airy, not dense, so they don't block people's view of each other.

Don't limit your centerpiece vision to cut flowers in matching vases. Consider an eclectic mix of floral containers, ranging from cut crystal to glass bowls and porcelain vases. You can use your own or borrow from a friend's collection. Some antique stores are willing to rent such things, so do a little research in your area. Take it a step further and create different (but coordinating!) centerpieces for each table.

Individualize your floral decorations using the following fun tips and ideas:

❋ Topiaries of either live ivy grown around simple wire forms or shapes, or topiaries consisting of dried or silk flowers you make (or have made) yourself.

❋ Incorporate beautiful fruits, either plain or sugared and frosted, into your floral arrangements or centerpieces. Vegetables also work well for this purpose. Consider apples, pears, grapes, colorful squashes, gourds, artichokes, or whatever coordinates with your look and is seasonally available. This works especially well for buffet tables.

❋ A mini garden basket with a profusion of flowers and foliage tumbling merrily out of the container and trailing onto the table.

❋ Round, fish bowl styled vases filled with a single type of cut flower. Or fill the bowls with water and float flower blossoms and petals on the water's surface.

❋ Forced bulbs that are just beginning to bloom, potted in shallow flower containers.

❋ Small live flowering plants or succulents in small pots, painted white, silver or gold, or any color that matches your theme. For a winter wedding, you could use small evergreens, junipers, or poinsettias in silver tin buckets. Small cheerful baskets or a collection of pitchers can also work well.

❋ If you have cut flowers in water at your reception, consider softly coloring the water to match your wedding colors.

KITCHEN *table* advice

With the wonders of modern technology, many flowers are available outside of their traditional season. However, consult the list below to see which flowers will be the most available and at their least expensive during their natural seasons.

Spring
Daffodil
Freesia
Iris
Jonquil
Lilac
Lily
Lily of the
   valley
Larkspur
Peony
Ranunculus
Sweet pea
Tulip
Violet

Summer
Aster
Calla lily
Canterbury
   bells
Dahlia
Daisy
Geranium
Hydrangea
Larkspur
Roses
Stephanotis
Strawflowers
Stock

Autumn
Aster
Chrysanthemum
Dahlia
Shasta daisy
Zinnia

Winter
Amaryllis
Spray orchids
Star of
   Bethlehem

Year Round
Baby's breath
Bachelor button
Carnation
Delphinium
Gardenia
Lily
Rose

DRYING
rose
Petals

If rice is not allowed (or maybe you have an aversion to it), have some friends help you collect rose petals a few months before the wedding. Dry the petals individually by placing them on a cookie sheet at a warm temperature in your oven. Store them in plastic bags until the wedding day (you may add a few drops of jasmine, rose, or geranium oil for fragrance). On the day of the wedding, they can be placed in silver bowls and passed out to the guests. Or you may want to wrap the petals in six-inch circles of nylon netting gathered with a satin ribbon, which may be placed at each table setting or passed to guests just before the bridal couple's departure.

OTHER WAYS TO USE FLOWERS

Chair backs – Use a special floral swag to decorate the bridal chair. It can be an elaborate drape of clustered roses or a single hydrangea bloom tied with a bit of beautiful ribbon.

Napkins – A stunning table decoration is a single bloom — daisy, rose, lily of the valley, spring of lavender, or rannunculus — tucked into a folded napkin.

PRESERVING YOUR BOUQUET

If you're a bride who wants to keep your bouquet for sentimental reasons, make sure you order a "throwing" bouquet.

Ask your florist about preserving the bridal bouquet for you. To do this, the moisture is removed, then it's sprayed with a protective solution. It can be displayed in a shadow box or put under a glass case.

The preserving process may also be done yourself by placing your bouquet in a box and completely covering it with borax or silica gel. This process usually takes about a week.

PRESSING

This is another method of preserving your bouquet. It takes about six weeks and is commonly done if the bouquet is to be framed. Separate the bouquet, place the flowers between newspapers, and cover them with books or heavy objects.

POTPOURRI

This preservation method is a great idea. Preserve the bouquet and place it in a glass jar or box and have the wedding date inscribed on it, or put it in a sachet pouch. Once the petals have been removed and individually dried, which can be done by placing them on a cookie sheet at a warm temperature in your oven, mix in the following herbs and spices for a nice fragrance: mint, bay leaves, lemon balm, or cinnamon and fruit peels. Then add a few drops of jasmine, rose, or geranium oil (can be purchased in drugstores). The fragrance will intensify over time.

Money Saving Tips

- Share floral costs with another bride. Find out if there will be another wedding at your church or synagogue on the same day. Possibly you can arrange to share the cost of floral decorations.

- Use flowers in season. Avoid exotic, expensive flowers that may have to be imported, or flowers that are not in season.

- Decorate with greenery. Use greenery such as trees and garlands of ivy to fill large areas. It can give a dramatic impact for relatively little money. Small trees can usually be rented.

- Have a garden wedding. Consider having the ceremony and/or the reception in a beautiful garden, surrounded by natural flowers.

- Don't plan your wedding to be held near a holiday. Flower prices escalate dramatically around Valentine's Day and Mother's Day. Planning your wedding around Christmas, on the other hand, might save you some money because many reception locations will already be decorated for the holiday season.

- Limit your attendants, therefore limiting the number of bouquets you'll need to buy.

- Use balloons. Balloons are an inexpensive way of adding color to a reception site, and they are especially effective for a larger room with high ceilings.

- Use the same floral arrangements for both the ceremony and reception; this is easy to do when they are both in the same location. Floral table arrangements can be used to line the aisle, or may be grouped together and placed on each side of the altar. Bouquets can also be used to decorate the cake and guest book table.

- Rather than having the bride and bridesmaids carry large, expensive bouquets, choose to carry small, elegant ones. ✳

Other *Fun* flower IDEAS

✳ Flower petal confetti

✳ Decorated arches

✳ Petals strewn about the floor and tables for a romantic whimsical look

✳ Artistic floral arrangements on your cake

✳ Petals floating in the punch

FLORAL *checklist*

FLORIST **FLORIST** _____ Date Ordered _____

Contact Person _____ Phone _____

Quantity	Item	Description (style, color, flowers)	Cost

BRIDE

_____ Bouquet _____

_____ Bride's Throwing Bouquet _____

_____ Floral Headdress for Reception _____

_____ Going-away Corsage _____

_____ Delivered to _____ Time _____

BRIDAL ATTENDANTS

_____ Matron of Honor _____

_____ Maid of Honor _____

_____ Bridesmaids _____

_____ Flower Girl _____

_____ Floral Headdresses _____

_____ Delivered to _____ Time _____

GROOM AND ATTENDANTS

_____ Groom's Boutonniere _____

_____ Best Man's Boutonniere _____

_____ Ushers' Boutonnieres _____

_____ Ring Bearer's Boutonniere _____

_____ Delivered to _____ Time _____

Bridal Party Total _____

FAMILY

_____ Corsage for Bride's Mother _____

_____ Corsage for Groom's Mother _____

_____ Corsages for Grandmothers _____

_____ Mothers' Roses _____

_____ Other Corsages (Stepmothers, Aunts) _____

_____ Boutonniere for Bride's Father _____

_____ Boutonniere for Groom's Father _____

_____ Other Boutonnieres (Stepfathers, Grandfathers) _____

_____ Delivered to _____ Time _____

Family Total _____

FLORAL *checklist*

Quantity	Item	Description (style, color, flowers)	Cost

FLOWERS FOR HELPERS:

_____ Bridal Consultant _____

_____ Officiant _____

_____ Soloist _____

_____ Instrumentalist(s) _____

_____ Guest Book Attendant _____

_____ Gift Attendant _____

_____ Others _____

Helpers Total _____

CEREMONY SITE

_____ Arch/Canopy _____

_____ Candelabra _____

_____ Candelighters _____

_____ Altar Floral Sprays _____

_____ Pews _____

_____ Aisles _____

_____ Other _____

Ceremony Site Total _____

RECEPTION SITE

_____ Bride's Table _____

_____ Parents' Table _____

_____ Attendants' Tables _____

_____ Guests' Tables _____

_____ Cake Table _____

_____ Top of Cake _____

_____ Guest Book Table _____

_____ Gift Table _____

_____ Ladies' Powder Room _____

_____ Other _____

Reception Site Total _____

(Total of all Categories) Subtotal _____

Sales Tax _____

Grand Total _____

Deposit _____

Balance Due _____

FLORAL *checklist*

DUTIES

Person responsible for distributing flowers to bridal party _____

Person responsible for taking ceremony flowers to reception site _____

Person responsible for taking reception flowers after reception _____

Flowers to be taken to _____

Person responsible for having bouquet preserved _____

Rental equipment to be returned to florist by _____

or, _____

picked-up on *(date)* _____

at *(time)* _____

seventeen

Rhapsody in *B* major

YOUR *guide* to WEDDING MUSIC

*I*f music has the power to soothe the savage beast, just think what it can do for your wedding! And while no one's suggesting your guests are savage beasts (honest), you can still be reasonably assured that whatever music you choose will have a profound impact on your ceremony and reception and, therefore, your guests. The music and songs you select will help make the wedding uniquely your own.

There are usually two different types of music desired: softer, more romantic music sung or played during the ceremony, and entertaining or dancing music played for the reception. In some cases, the same musicians will play both, although this is more common when the wedding and reception are held in the same location. An alternative is to have one set of musicians or the church organist and soloist for the ceremony, and a band or DJ for the reception.

CEREMONY MUSIC

First off, make sure to check with your site coordinator or officiant regarding any restrictions or limitations they might have on music selections. Some places of worship limit the music selections to whatever their own organist can play. However, there are many other options for your ceremony music, when allowed.

Harpist	Violinist	Classical guitarist	Flutist
String quartet	Trumpeter	Keyboardist	Vocals/Choir

THE PRELUDE

Music is often played well before the ceremony begins. This music is instrumental in establishing an atmosphere for your guests and may include mood-setting pieces that your early-to-arrive guests can enjoy as they wait for the show to begin. From classical selections to R&B, mellow jazz, soft folk music, or New Age selections, let your music punctuate the whole tone of your celebration. If you'd like, you can also play special songs just as the last members of the family are seated, for added emphasis.

SOME SELECTIONS TO CONSIDER:

"All I Ask Of You" (from Phantom of the
    Opera),— Andrew Lloyd Webber

"As Time Goes By" ("A Kiss Is Just a Kiss")
    — Tony Bennett

"Brandenburg Concertos" — Bach

"Evergreen" — Barbra Streisand

"First Time Ever I Saw Your Face"
    — Roberta Flack

"God Only Knows" — The Beach Boys

"Greensleeves" — Traditional

"Isn't It Romantic" — Glenn Miller

"Jesu, Joy of Man's Desiring" — Bach

"Lady" — Kenny Rogers

"Longer" — Dan Fogelberg

"Moonlight Sonata" — Beethoven

"Ode to Joy" — Beethoven

"Pachelbel's Canon" — Pachelbel

"Prelude to the Afternoon of a Faun"
    — Claude Debussy

"Rhapsody In Blue" — Gershwin

"The Four Seasons" — Vivaldi

"Truly" — Lionel Richie

"Violin Concerto in A" — Haydn

"Water Music" — Handel

"Wedding Song" — The Band

THE PROCESSIONAL

Collective breaths are held as guests anticipate the moment when the bride makes her grand entrance. This is the part everyone's been waiting for. Drama is good here. So is pomp and pageantry. In order to accentuate your entrance, you'll probably want to select a different piece for the bridal party's procession. Some great selections are:

"Bridal Chorus" ("Here Comes The Bride")
    from Lohengrin — Wagner

"Canon in D Minor" — Pachelbel

"Evergreen" — Barbra Streisand

"Four Seasons, Spring" — Vivaldi

"Jesu, Joy of Man's Desiring" — Bach

"Ode to Joy" — Beethoven

"Sunrise, Sunset" from Fiddler on the Roof

"The Prince of Denmark's March" — Clarke

"Trumpet Tune" — Purcell

"Trumpet Voluntary in D ("The Prince of
    Denmark's March")" — Clarke

"Unforgettable" — Nat King Cole

"Water Music" — Handel

"Wedding March" from The Marriage of
    Figaro — Mozart

"What a Wonderful World" — Louis
    Armstrong

"Wedding March" from A Midsummer's Night
    Dream — Mendelssohn

THE RECESSIONAL

This is the music played when the ceremony is over and the bridal party leaves the altar area. Think joyous here. Almost giddy with delight. You've done it! You're truly man and wife now, and you want this music to lift that happy fact clear up to the rafters!

"Hallelujah Chorus" from The Messiah — Handel

"How Sweet It Is" — James Taylor

"I Got You" ("I Feel Good") — James Brown

"Magnificat In D" — Bach

"Maybe I'm Amazed" — Paul McCartney

"Ode To Joy" from *The Ninth Symphony*
    — Beethoven

"Sunshine of My Life" — Stevie Wonder

"The Long and Winding Road" — The Beatles

"Trumpet Tune" — Purcell

The Postlude

A concluding piece that plays as your guests leave the ceremony site, this music is still happy and joyous, but with a little less drama than the recessional. If you have a large number of guests, this can take anywhere from ten to twenty minutes.

"A Whole New World" — Peabo Bryson and Regine Belle

"Annie's Song" — John Denver

"Can't Help Falling in Love" — Elvis Presley

"Feelin' Alright" — Joe Cocker

"I Won't Last a Day Without You" — Andy Williams

"Layla" — Eric Clapton

"New York, New York" — Frank Sinatra

"On the Wings of Love" — Jeffrey Osborne

"The Song Is Love" — Peter, Paul and Mary

"Top of the World" — Carpenters

"Up Where We Belong" — Joe Cocker

"When the Saints Come Marchin' In" —Traditional

"What a Wonderful World" — Louis Armstrong

"What Are You Doing the Rest of Your Life" — Michel LaGrand

"When I'm 64" — The Beatles

"You're My Best Friend" — Queen

Reception Music

Reception music can be either a refined background element or a main focal point that all your guests will enjoy dancing to. You get to pick. And the choices are wide and varied. A string quartet, violin, or harp make for a very muted yet polished backdrop for your celebration, while a rock band or twelve-piece orchestra will provide a wide range of lively tunes to get your guests up out of their seats and onto the dance floor. Obviously,

to dance or not to dance will greatly influence your decision. Good bands and DJs book up way in advance. Start looking early, anywhere from nine to twelve months in advance, depending on how essential music is to your celebration.

And the Band Played On

The band can be as traditional and refined as a twenty-piece orchestra or simply a small group of local rock and rollers from your favorite club. (Think personal wedding style here.) Probably more important than the type of band they are, or the selection of music they play, is whether or not they are talented performers who are skilled in getting the crowd to have a good time. In a nutshell, good ones will carry the reception, bad ones can ruin it outright. Do your homework.

Whether you want a jazzy band, a string quartet, or a small combo, be sure to hear them in action before you decide to sign on that dotted line!

While a live band might seem like the ultimate in wedding reception entertainment, keep in mind that most won't have the same range of selection that DJs will. There will also be "dead air" when the band takes their scheduled breaks, unless you make arrangements for something to be played during that time. And while they can cost a pretty penny, they do make for a rousing reception.

Spin City

DJs are popular because their range is virtually unlimited. While they come in all shapes, sizes, and levels of good taste, it bears repeating — a good one can be great, almost acting as the master of ceremonies for the evening, while a bad one can end up feeling like a flat comedy routine set to music. Make sure the one you choose isn't of the latter variety. The DJs role is about the music you want for your wedding, not about their gaudiest stand up act, complete with disco glitter ball (unless that's what you asked for in your contract).

THE Music
YOU
Want –
when YOU want IT

Remember, the musicians aren't booked until you've signed the contract and paid the deposit. If you need a few days to think about it, see if the band or DJ will check with you before booking any other gigs for that date. Make your musical arrangements as far in advance as possible. Give the musician a deposit to secure the date, and get everything agreed upon in a written contract.

Also, confirm that the DJ is willing to play the songs you have in mind. There are a number of horror stories regarding DJs who were stuck on their own kind of music (from the '60s, say) and couldn't be budged into playing something else. (Another reason why you only pay a portion of their fee beforehand and put those tune selections in their contract if you can.)

You can find musicians by asking friends or relatives, caterers, wedding consultants, or clergyman, or by checking the yellow pages or musicians' union in your area. If the reception is held in a hotel or restaurant, the manager may be helpful with music suggestions.

Interview a few groups before making a final decision. Ask to hear them play. You may do that at one of their events, or most bands today have a video of themselves, which is helpful.

Don't forget that your guests come in all shapes, sizes, and ages; try to select musicians that can play a variety of songs, from slower traditional to '50s and rock and roll to faster contemporary music for dancing. Unless you truly don't care what you get, it's critical that you make a list of songs you would like played and give it to the bandleader. Try to have a good mix of fast and slow songs. The bandleader or DJ will be able to help you with your selections, if needed. Also, go over with him (or her) the timing of important announcements, such as the grand entrance, the first dance, cutting the cake, and throwing the bouquet and garter.

POINTS TO DISCUSS
BEFORE SIGNING ON THE DOTTED LINE

♪ How many hours they will play?

♪ How many and how long will their breaks be?

♪ Check to see if they have recorded music that can be played during the breaks.

♪ What will they wear?

♪ Will they also act as emcee?

♪ Do they need special equipment? Chairs, tables, risers?

♪ Do they require special lighting? And if so, does it blend with your overall reception theme and feel?

♪ Does your reception site have the required electrical outlets?

♪ How early will the band or DJ need to set up?

♪ Who will be doing the setting up?

♪ Can they play into overtime, if needed?

OTHER CONTRACT POINTS

Be aware that many bands either break up or change musicians, so the band you heard and booked eight months ago may not be the same group of musicians that will show up on your wedding day.

→ Deal with an agent or the bandleader. Specify the names of individual musicians you want to play or sing, and have their names written on the contract stating that they'll appear in person on that date. To be safe, have them sign it personally, when possible.

→ Always get a contract that specifies the date, the location, the time that the band or disc jockey should arrive, the number of hours they will play, the number of breaks they'll take, the cost, and overtime charges. List the names of the individual band members and specify the appropriate attire for the musicians or disc jockey.

MONEY SAVING TIPS

🪙 Hire a professional disc jockey. You can usually get continuous music for less than the cost of a band.

💿 Use prerecorded music. Prerecorded music for the ceremony can also be purchased. Check the restrictions and equipment available with your church or synagogue ahead of time.

💿 Have a friend sing. If you have friends who sing or play instruments such as organ, guitar, or harp, ask them to play or sing at your ceremony.

🪙 Hire fewer musicians. To keep costs down when you want live music at the reception, choose a band with fewer musicians or hire a single performer.

MUSIC IDEAS

The following are favorite songs that may help you to make your selections for the receiving line, reception, and first dance. List these or others of your choice. Write your selections on the music list provided. A copy should be given to the bandleader.

"A Love Song" — Kenny Loggins

"A Time For Us" — Snyder

"A Whole New World"
    — Peabo Bryson and Regine Belle

"All I Ask of You" — The Phantom of the Opera

"And I Love You So" — McLean

"Annie's Song" — John Denver

"Arthur's Theme" — Christopher Cross

"As Time Goes By" — Casablanca

"Beautiful" — Gordon Lightfoot

"Beauty and the Beast"
    — Peabo Bryson and Celine Dion

"Because of You" — Tony Bennett

"Beginnings" — Chicago

"Breathe" — Faith Hill

"Can You Feel the Love Tonight" — Elton John

"Can't Help Falling in Love" — Elvis Presley

"Chances Are" — Johnny Mathis

"Don't Want to Miss a Thing" — Aerosmith

"Endless Love" — Diana Ross and Lionel Ritchie

"Endless Love"
    — Luther Vandross and Mariah Carey

"Everything I Do, I Do It for You" — Bryan Adams

"Feelings" — Morris Albert

"From This Moment On" — Shania Twain

"Have I Told You Lately" — Rod Stewart

"Hero" — Enrique Iglesias

"Hopelessly Devoted to You" — Olivia Newton John

"How Sweet It Is (To Be Loved by You)"
    — James Taylor

"I Could Have Danced All Night" — Anne Murray

"I Just Want to be Your Everything" — Andy Gibb

"I Love You Just the Way You Are" — Billy Joel

"I Love You So" — McDonald and Chevalier

"I Only Have Eyes for You" — Art Garfunkle

"I Will Always Love You" — Whitney Houston

"I Won't Last a Day Without You" — Andy Williams

"If Tomorrow Never Comes" — Garth Brooks

"In My Life" — Beatles

"In the Mood" — Glenn Miller

"In Your Eyes" — Peter Gabriel

"It Had to Be You" — Harry Connick, Jr.

"Longer" — Dan Fogelberg

"Love Is a Many Splendored Thing" — Percy Faith

"Love Song" — Anne Murray

"Love Theme from the Godfather" — Andy Williams

"Love Won't Let Me Wait" — Luther Vandross

"Masterpiece" — Atlantic Star

"Maybe I'm Amazed" — Paul McCartney

"Misty" — Johnny Mathis

"My Girl" — The Temptations

"New York, New York" — Frank Sinatra

"On the Wings of Love" — Jeffrey Osborne

"Only You" — The Platters

"Our Love" — Carpenters

"Our Love Is Here to Stay" — Harry Connick, Jr.

"People" — Barbra Streisand

"Save the Best for Last" — Vanessa Williams

"Sometimes" — Henry Mancini

"Sometimes When We Touch" — Dan Hill

"Sound of Music" — Rodgers and Hammerstein

"Sunshine on My Shoulders" — John Denver

"That's All" — Johnny Mathis

"The Hands of Time" (Brian's Song)
    — Michel LaGrand

"The Song Is Love" — Peter, Paul and Mary

"The Way You Look Tonight" — Frank Sinatra

"This Love" — Don Henley

"Through the Eyes of Love" — Sager/Hamlisch

"Till There Was You" — Beatles

"Time in a Bottle" — Jim Croce

"Top of the World" — Carpenters

"Truly" — Lionel Ritchie

"Try to Remember" — Harry Belafonte

"Unforgettable" — Nat King Cole

"Unforgettable" — Natalie Cole

"Up Where We Belong" — Joe Cocker

"Waiting for a Girl Like You" — Foreigner

"We've Only Just Begun" — Carpenters

"What Are You Doing the Rest of Your Life"
    — Michel LaGrand

"When a Man Loves a Woman" — Michael Bolton

"When I Fall in Love" — Lettermen

"Wonderful Tonight" — Eric Clapton

"You Are So Beautiful to Me" — Joe Cocker

"You Are the Sunshine of My Life" — Stevie Wonder

"Your Song" — Elton John

"You're My Best Friend" — Queen

"You're the One" — Shania Twain

"You've Got a Friend" — James Taylor

WHEN TO PLAY WHAT

You will most likely want to play something soft, relaxing, and conducive to conversation for the first hour or two of your reception during the receiving line, cocktails, and dinner. After that, the tempo can pick up, especially if you've planned for dancing. Be sure to go over the timing of important announcements, such as the grand entrance, first dance, cake cutting, and bouquet toss, with the bandleader ahead of time. ✳

CEREMONY *Music* information

CEREMONY MUSICIANS SELECTED

Ceremony Location _____

Contact Person _____ Phone _____

Wedding Date _____ Arrival Time _____

Appropriate Dress _____

Rehearsal Date _____ Time _____ Location _____

INSTRUMENTALISTS

_____ Phone _____ Fee _____

_____ _____ _____

_____ _____ _____

_____ _____ _____

_____ _____ _____

SOLOISTS

_____ Phone _____ Fee _____

_____ _____ _____

_____ _____ _____

_____ _____ _____

_____ _____ _____

_____ _____ _____

Cancellation Policy _____   *Total Cost* _____

_____   *Deposit Paid* _____

_____   *Balance Due* _____

CEREMONY MUSIC SELECTIONS

Prelude _____   During Ceremony _____

_____   _____

First Solo _____   Recessional _____

_____   _____

Second Solo _____   Postlude _____

_____   _____

Processional _____   Notes _____

_____   _____

RECEPTION *Music* information

RECEPTION MUSICIANS SELECTED

Reception Musicians Selected _____ _____

Reception Location _____

Contact Person _____ Phone _____

Reception Date _____ Arrival Time _____ _____

Appropriate Dress _____ _____

Rehearsal Date _____ Time _____ Location _____

Phone _____ *Fee* _____

Disc Jockey _____ _____ _____

Agent/bandleader _____ _____ _____

Name Of Band _____ _____ _____

Key Band Members _____ _____

_____ _____

_____ _____

_____ _____

Cancellation Policy _____ *Total Cost* _____

_____ *Deposit Paid* _____

_____ *Balance Due* _____

RECEPTION MUSIC SELECTIONS

Newlyweds' Arrival _____ Ethnic Dances _____

_____ _____

Receiving Line _____ _____

_____

First Dance _____ Bouquet Toss _____

Garter Toss _____

Dancing or Background Music _____ Newlyweds' Get-Away _____

Last Dance _____

Other _____

_____ _____

_____ _____

_____ _____

_____ _____

Pretty as a *Picture*

HOW *to* get GREAT Wedding *Pictures*

*I*f a picture paints a thousand words — and it does — then you'll want to make sure you have a true artist with a full palette of colors and nuances at their disposal to capture this incredible day you've planned.

The average bride and groom spend approximately twelve months planning an event that will last four hours, or, as many brides and grooms claim afterwards, is over in the blink of an eye. Quite often, they are so consumed in the here and now of it all that they don't get to savor their hard planned details. Well, in the wedding photos you get to do exactly that. You get to relive the moment as often as you like for the rest of your life.

That leads us to Wedding Photography Brutal Truth #1: You have exactly four hours to get it right. Forever. No retakes. No, "Oh wait! I forgot …"

Which takes us directly to Wedding Photography Brutal Truth #2: This is NOT an area to scrimp, penny-pinch, cut back, or otherwise engage in endangering misplaced cost cutting steps. Yes, of course, you'll want to get the most value for your dollar. Who doesn't? But too much rests on this Keepsake for Posterity for you to risk having substandard wedding photographs.

It's so easy, in the hurly-burly of it all, to miss the emotions of the day. Certainly you'll feel emotional, giddy even, as you laugh and cry your way through your wedding and the reception. Then there are the additional, more subtle moments and details that can pack an intense emotional wallop: The ring bearer and flower girl, conked out, side by side, gently snoring away on a little sofa. Your grandparents out on the dance floor, the love shining in their eyes an emotional knockout, as you see the promise of what lies ahead as you begin your life together. However, these gems are easy to miss, and this is where great photography can be an incredibly powerful tool. Don't cheat yourself out of discovering the lovely hidden nuances of your wedding day and how truly memorable it was by scrimping on the photography.

Don't forget to talk to your reception site and wedding site coordinator and find out if there are any restrictions regarding photography. Also, find out how early the photographer can begin setting up his equipment. If there's any possibility of inclement weather, have a backup location in mind for any group portraits you plan to take outside.

Okay, we've convinced you. Now how do you go about ensuring picture perfect memories of this day?

→ Decide on a photography style you like.

→ Set a budget (or refer back to the one you set in Chapter Six).

→ Get referrals.

→ Ask questions (lots and lots of them).

It's critical to find a photographer who has a style you admire and who's willing to help you obtain the wedding pictures of your dreams. The very best photographers realize that every wedding couple is unique and will have their own individual perspective to bring to the body of work that's going to represent their lifelong commitment. If you feel the photographer has too much of his/her own agenda, or applies an identical template to all the weddings they shoot, then move on down the list. It's also a good idea to look for a photographer who doesn't schedule more than one wedding per day. That way, there won't be any time constraints or sense of needing to rush.

PHOTOGRAPHY STYLES

Traditional – The standard wedding photos we've all seen throughout the years, the classics and standbys. These are artfully posed shots, either individual or in groups: the wedding party at the ceremony site, bride and groom at the ceremony site, etc. Also included in this category would be the informals, which are basically a kind of posed candid shot. Think feeding each other a piece of cake, tossing the bouquet, checking watches, or pinning on of boutonnieres. While the format is standard, in the hands of a good photographer the results will be anything but.

Candid – These types of photographs are taken without people posing for them — which has its pros and cons. Candid shots can catch more of the dreary little details of real life, wadded up cocktail napkins, overflowing ashtrays, and cake crumbs on the table, but people also look more relaxed and as if they're actually having a good time. Photographers should shoot extra film to make sure there are enough great shots left once you eliminate the everyday reality from some of the shots.

Romantic – These are usually couple shots or bride-only shots and are taken with a soft focus lens and special lighting. While you may want a few shots in this style, you wouldn't want to shoot your whole wedding this way.

Portraiture – These are formal portraits, usually best taken in a photographer's studio with the right lighting. Competently photographed formal shots can take on the same qualities as portraits.

Photojournalism – A hot new trend with today's couples, this style documents the day without resorting to posed shots. One of the huge benefits of this style is that a good photojournalist pretty much fades into the background, making you forget they are even there.

Color or Black and White – Another of today's trends is the upswing in black and white photography. Black and white prints don't fade with time and interesting effects can be achieved by printing on different textured papers. Also, everything looks very artistic in black and white. However, most people spend far too much time and money on their wedding decorations to not want to capture some of the sense of color of the big day. While it's true that color prints can fade over time, you'll also want at least some pictures in color.

NOTE: While black and white prints can be made from color film, they can often look gray and grainy. It is better to have your photographer shoot black and white film for your black and white photos.

Infrared – This is black and white film that reacts to heat, not light. There's a dramatic, luminescent quality to these shots that make them pop off the page. However, it's a highly stylized look and you may want them in addition to as opposed to the only photograph style you shoot.

SETTING A BUDGET

Most brides and grooms spend at least $1,000 on their wedding photos and many spend $4,000 and upwards. Again, this isn't an area in which to go the discount bargain route. While wedding photos may seem pricey, don't forget that we're talking priceless artifacts here. To make things even more confusing, photographers charge in different ways for their services.

When interviewing a photographer, discuss the number of pictures he takes, the cost of each print, the style and cost of the albums he offers, and whether there are travel costs or extra fees included. Photographers' fees can vary tremendously. Use the forms included in the back of this section to make accurate comparisons.

Most photographers that do a number of weddings offer a package, which is a predetermined number of pictures in various sizes for a set fee that includes the prints and the album. Generally, pictures are less expensive when ordered this way. Check to see if packages are available for parents' albums.

FLAT FEE – BARE MINIMUM

Here you pay a single amount for the photographer's time, film, and expenses. This amount is usually based on an estimate of the number of shots expected. You will get proofs and negatives, but printing the photos and any cropping or retouching will be done on your own nickel. Most often, in these cases, you'll take possession of the negatives. Be aware that this can become a big project, turning these proofs into professional quality photo albums.

In other instances, the flat fee will include the photographer supplying a photo album and handling the printing of the photographs for you. Usually, they'll then retain ownership (and possession) of the negatives, although they may sell you the negatives more cheaply later on.

PHOTO PACKAGES

Most photo packages specify a limited amount of time, usually from two to eight hours, with the price going up accordingly. After that, hourly overtime rates would apply, which can range from $85 to $250/hour. These packages may also include a set number of prints of various sizes, say twenty-five 5 x 7s and ten 8 x 10s in a particular type of photo album. You might consider asking them if removing the album from the package will allow you to receive an additional discount. It's very likely that you'll receive one as a wedding gift or, at the very least, find one more to your own liking.

HOURLY FEE

Here, photographers charge a flat hourly fee, which may or may not include film and expenses. It's important to find out what the additional charges will be for getting proofs and ordering the photos.

LOCATION CHARGES

Some photographers charge more for changes of location. Others offer no location limit and are willing to shoot in as many locations as you've selected. If you're dressing where the ceremony will be held, and the ceremony and reception will be at the same location, then this won't be an issue. If, however, there's no dressing room at the ceremony site, or your ceremony and reception will be held at different places, you might have as many as three locations for the photographer to travel to, so you'll need to discuss this with him.

HOW TO FIND A PHOTOGRAPHER

Most good photographers are heavily in demand, especially during the popular wedding months, so book early. Start interviewing nine to eleven months before your wedding date.

If you're lucky, you'll have friends or acquaintances that have married in the recent past. Ask to see their wedding albums and inquire if they were happy with their photographers. You can also get recommendations from your caterer, florist, site coordinator, or officiant. Bridal fairs are a great place to see the work of various photographers; get the names of those whose style you like. Many times, photographers will advertise in the back of regional wedding magazines or the regional editions of national bridal magazines. Often the picture they selected for the ad is their best work or a signature of what they feel they do best. There are many professional groups and organizations that will refer you to wedding photographers in the area.

When you've got a list of recommendations, you'll need to make appointments to interview them. Here are some points to cover.

- Be sure the photographers you contact specialize in weddings. Don't hire a commercial or part-time photographer who occasionally handles weddings.

- Ask to see sample wedding albums or a set of proofs from a recent wedding. In addition to showcasing the photographer's work, they may give you ideas for your own wedding.

- As you're looking at the sample albums, note if the photographer used different types of lighting and whether he varied the backgrounds. Are the albums well balanced, with traditional and candid shots covering both wedding and reception?

- Look for diversity in the poses. Does he seem to capture the personality of the bride and groom and the mood of their wedding?

- Do the pictures have good color and clarity?

- Did he pay attention to detail?

- Does he capture the emotions and expressions of the day?

- Is he creative with various poses?

- Does he use soft lenses and lighting?

- Can he do multiple exposures and split framing, which make interesting pictures?

- Consider the personality of each photographer; choose the one you feel is most competent and whose personality will make you and your guests feel most comfortable.

- Get every aspect of the agreement with the photographer in a written contract. The contract should include: the date, arrival time, length of shooting time, fees, and overtime charges, if any. List all locations — the bride's home, ceremony, and reception, giving addresses and directions. Include the cost and details of a photo package selection, and the cost of additional photos you may want to order.

- Don't forget: If you're planning to send an announcement of your wedding to the newspaper, be sure your photographer knows, and takes a black and white portrait of the two of you as husband and wife. Order an 8 x 10-inch black and white glossy print to send to the paper.

- If you're contracting a studio, make sure you'll be happy with whatever photographer they send out, or be sure to specify in your contract which studio photographer you will want to use.

- Ask if he keeps the negatives and for how long. See if they can be purchased now or in the future. They should be kept in a fireproof safe, in the event your pictures are ever destroyed.

When to Take the Photographs

It's a subject of some furious debate as to whether or not to take wedding photos before the ceremony or after the ceremony. Before the ceremony ruins the whole, "don't let the groom see the bride until she appears in the church" idea, but waiting until afterwards tends to make for a long wait for your guests between the ceremony and reception. Here are some pros and cons of taking photographs before the ceremony.

Pros

→ Photographers prefer to take the photos before because they don't have the pressure of two hundred guests tapping their collective toes waiting to visit with the bride and groom. They feel as if they can take their time.

→ You will look as close to perfect as you ever will that day, with no time for tears or beverages spilled to mar your perfection.

Cons

→ Can be draining.

→ Takes away that one singular moment when the groom spies his beloved walking toward him during the ceremony.

→ If you take your pictures before the ceremony, allow one and a half to two hours for the photographs.

→ If you have your photographs taken after the ceremony, you'll need to allow for the same amount of time between the ceremony and reception. One compromise if you don't want the groom to see you until the ceremony, is to have the photographer take as many pictures as he can without the two of you together before, and finish the remainder after the ceremony.

It's wise to take any pictures involving small children or elderly relatives as early in the day as possible before they become too tired or wilted.

If you're *considering* TAKING formal portraits a few weeks before the ceremony, discuss this option at the same time you're discussing the day-of-the-wedding photos. These are generally taken in the photographer's studio where he has necessary lighting, backdrops, and equipment. Wear your hair and accessories the same way you will on your wedding day.

➡ After the ceremony, take pictures working from the largest groups down to the smallest groups. This frees up more people quickly, so they can join the guests when they're done.

ITEMS FOR THE PORTRAIT SESSION

❋ Wedding dress

❋ Hat, headpiece and veil

❋ Gloves, if any

❋ Wedding shoes and stockings

❋ Appropriate undergarments

❋ Jewelry to be worn

❋ Bible, hanky, garter, and bouquet, if not furnished by photographer, but desired

BEWARE OF!!

➡ A friend or photographer may tell you that they've done other people's weddings and assure you they can handle yours. Be cautious; ask to see pictures from those weddings. Even if the price is "great," even free, think twice about it. Pictures may not seem so important now, but not having good wedding pictures may be something you may regret for years to come.

➡ Some photographers who have a studio with other photographers working for them book your wedding and lead you to believe that they'll be the one taking the pictures. The day arrives, and so does another photographer, someone you've never met. Specify in your contract the name of the person who will be taking the pictures. Look at pictures of the weddings that person has shot (not the ones of the other studio photographers).

➡ Meet with the actual photographer who will be taking your pictures — at the wedding site, if possible. Discuss the type and number of shots, the length of time the photographer will be taking pictures and the appropriate dress.

➡ In the event that for some reason your photographs don't turn out, state in your contract that you're not obligated to purchase them and that all deposits be refunded.

➡ Don't be lured into what you think is a great deal by committing to the lowest priced package, and then end up having to pay heavy prices for additional photos. Some photographers make the package deal sound cheap until they've completed the job. Ask ahead of time what the additional picture charge will be for 5 x 7s and 8 x 10s. If considering a package, really study the options to select the package that will most realistically cover all the shots you want of your wedding and avoid the extra expensive "additional photos."

→ If your contract with the photographer is for a specified number of hours, be sure to make prior agreement of what overtime charges will be in the event the reception runs longer than anticipated. You don't want the photographer to leave at the end of four hours, missing shots of cutting the cake or tossing the garter. Try not to be locked into a specified number of hours with high overtime charges.

→ Most photographers won't sell you the film or negatives of your wedding pictures. If you come across a photographer who offers to take your pictures for a set fee and give you the film at the end of the reception be cautious. Before agreeing to do this, contact a professional lab and get the price of developing the film and having 5 x 7 or 8 x 10 prints made. You might find that with his fee, and the print costs, you'd be paying a lot more for the pictures. Another drawback is that the photographer is probably going to want to get paid when he hands over the film, before you've seen the quality of the shots. You have no guarantees of what you're going to get, and he has no incentive to take the best shots or correct problems, since you may never see him again after the reception. If you choose to go this route, don't agree to pay in full until after you've had the film developed. And state in your contract that if the pictures don't turn out, you owe nothing.

CREATIVE PHOTO IDEAS

→ On the guest book table, set around the room, or mounted on the wall, display a few photos of the bride and groom from birth to marriage. You might also include the wedding pictures of both sets of parents.

→ Have Polaroid pictures taken of each guest alone, or with the bride and groom, to give as a favor before they leave.

→ Place a disposable camera on each table. Instruct the guests to take pictures during the reception. It will not only be entertaining, but you'll get a lot of great candid shots. Don't forget to arrange for someone to collect all the cameras at the end of the reception.

→ Keep a camera with you throughout your planning and make a nice pre-wedding album. Capture the following moments: buying your rings, trying on dresses for yourself and the bridesmaids, addressing and mailing invitations, showers, a picture of getting your marriage license. Remember the fun of planning your wedding.

→ Order extra pictures for special friends.

→ Don't forget your honeymoon photo album. Be sure to pack your camera.

→ Have a friend take Polaroid pictures of your wedding day. You can take the pictures along on your honeymoon.

→ Make sure you don't have suntan lines, or that your face doesn't get sunburned. A red face won't look attractive in the pictures.

MONEY SAVING TIPS

- Some photographers who work out of their homes offer lower prices. Because their overhead is lower, they're able to pass these savings on to you.

- Don't order the fancy leather upgrade album. Either take the standard album or see if you can order the package without the album and receive a discount. You may get an album as a wedding gift.

- Opt for a less popular time. Check photographers' price structures. Some may agree to shoot your wedding for less if it's on Friday night or Saturday morning, when they're not as busy as, say, on a Saturday afternoon or evening.

- A word of caution: Be careful when trying to cut costs on photography. I recommend using a professional wedding photographer for at least the ceremony pictures. These pictures represent lasting memories you'll want to share with family and friends for years to come. Some brides have been extremely disappointed when a professional wasn't used. Don't forget — when the day is over, it's too late to do anything about bad pictures.

WHAT *to* ask YOUR *Photographer?*

Will he personally be taking the photographs of your wedding?
If not, ask to meet the person who will be.

_____

Does he work with an assistant and will he have
back-up equipment in the event of a problem?

_____

Is he familiar with your ceremony and reception location?

_____

Can you give him a list of special people with whom you want pictures?

_____

How many hours does his price include?

_____

What's the charge, if any, if the reception should last longer than planned?

_____

Will he stay through the cake cutting and garter toss?

_____

How much time will you need to allow for the formal
wedding photos taken either before or after the ceremony?

_____

What are the photo package prices?

_____

What are the individual picture prices?

_____

What about parents' albums?

_____

When will the proof pictures be ready?

_____

How long will the prints take, once they have been ordered?

_____

Will he sell the album or negatives?

_____

How many years does he keep the negatives?

_____

What does he normally wear when photographing a wedding?

_____

Will he wear a tuxedo or other specified attire?

_____

Ask if he's a member of Wedding Photographers International.
(Membership usually reflects a high level of professional
 competence and ethics.)

_____

PHOTO *and* VIDEO checklist

Before the Ceremony

- ❏ Bride alone in dress
- ❏ Bride touching up makeup or adjusting veil
- ❏ Bride with mother
- ❏ Bride with maid or matron of honor
- ❏ Bride with bridesmaids
- ❏ Bride with both parents
- ❏ Bride putting on garter or placing penny in shoe
- ❏ Everyone getting their flowers
- ❏ Bride leaving house
- ❏ Bride and father getting into the car
- ❏ Groom alone
- ❏ Groom with best man, shaking hands, looking at his watch
- ❏ Groom and ushers putting on boutonnieres
- ❏ Groom with his parents
- ❏ Groom leaving for the ceremony
- ❏ Other moments dressing

Others

- ❏ _____
- ❏ _____
- ❏ _____

At the Ceremony

- ❏ Guests arriving
- ❏ Bride and father getting out of car
- ❏ Groom's parents being seated, or in procession
- ❏ Bride's mother being seated, or in procession
- ❏ Usher escorting guests
- ❏ Groom and groomsmen at the altar
- ❏ Processional
- ❏ Bride and father starting down the aisle

- ❏ Altar and decorations
- ❏ Giving-away ceremony
- ❏ Bride and groom exchanging vows
- ❏ Ring ceremony
- ❏ The kiss
- ❏ Bride and groom coming up the aisle
- ❏ Recessional
- ❏ Bride and groom outside place of worship with guests
- ❏ Bride and groom getting into the car
- ❏ Bride and groom looking through rear car window

Others

- ❏ _____
- ❏ _____
- ❏ _____

Before the Reception

- ❏ The couple together
- ❏ Bride with her attendants
- ❏ Groom with his attendants
- ❏ Bride and groom with all the attendants
- ❏ Bride and groom with their honor attendants
- ❏ Bride and groom with child attendants
- ❏ Bride with her parents
- ❏ Groom with his parents
- ❏ Both families together
- ❏ Bride and groom with officiant
- ❏ Bride's and groom's hands

Others

- ❏ _____
- ❏ _____
- ❏ _____

PHOTO *and* VIDEO checklist

At the Reception

- ❑ Bride and groom getting out of the car
- ❑ Bride and groom making a grand entrance
- ❑ Receiving line
- ❑ Couple greeting guests in the receiving line
- ❑ Guests signing the guest book
- ❑ Bride and groom dancing
- ❑ Bride and her father dancing
- ❑ Groom dancing with his mother
- ❑ Bride dancing with her father-in-law
- ❑ Groom dancing with his mother-in-law
- ❑ Both sets of parents dancing
- ❑ Bridesmaids and ushers dancing
- ❑ Guests dancing
- ❑ Cake table
- ❑ Bride and groom cutting the cake
- ❑ Couple feeding cake to each other
- ❑ Bride and groom receiving toasts
- ❑ Buffet tables
- ❑ Bridal party's table
- ❑ Parents' table
- ❑ Guests' tables
- ❑ Musicians
- ❑ Bride tossing the bouquet
- ❑ Groom tossing the garter
- ❑ Bride and groom changing into going-away clothes
- ❑ Bride and groom saying good-bye to parents
- ❑ Guests throwing rice
- ❑ Decorated getaway car
- ❑ Bride and groom getting into the car
- ❑ Guests waving good-bye
- ❑ Couple looking out rear window as car drives off

Others

- ❑ _____
- ❑ _____
- ❑ _____

Names of guests photographer shouldn't miss.
(Have a relative or attendant responsible for
pointing these people out to the photographer.)

- ❑ _____
- ❑ _____
- ❑ _____
- ❑ _____
- ❑ _____
- ❑ _____
- ❑ _____
- ❑ _____
- ❑ _____
- ❑ _____
- ❑ _____
- ❑ _____
- ❑ _____
- ❑ _____
- ❑ _____
- ❑ _____
- ❑ _____
- ❑ _____
- ❑ _____
- ❑ _____
- ❑ _____
- ❑ _____
- ❑ _____

PHOTOGRAPHY *worksheet*

	Estimate #1		Estimate #2	
	Name _____		Name _____	
	_____		_____	
	Phone _____		Phone _____	
	Description	*Cost*	*Description*	*Cost*
PORTRAITS Engagement Wedding				
PHOTOGRAPHER FEE Number of Hours Number of Shots				
WEDDING ALBUM Number of Pictures Size of Pictures				
PARENTS' ALBUM Number of Pictures Size of Pictures				
INDIVIDUAL PICTURES 8 X 10 5 X 7 4 X 5				
MISCELLANEOUS				
TOTAL				

PHOTOGRAPHER SELECTED

Name _____

Address _____

Phone _____

Deposit _____

Arrival Time _____

Date Ready _____   Balance Due _____

Lights, camera, action*!*

WEDDING *Videography*

To tape or not to tape, that is the question.

The industry's technology is becoming more sophisticated, and so is the consumer. Consequently, videotaping has become much less obtrusive that it used to be with many talented videographers achieving a multiple camera effect with only one camera. The technology trend is toward SVHS or digital video cameras, which perform admirably in low light situations and therefore don't require additional lighting that will ruin your carefully selected mood lighting.

Capturing your wedding on videotape can allow you to enjoy the wedding in its entirety without benefit of nervous butterflies in your stomach or pressing demands on your attention as you follow a well-orchestrated schedule. It's also a lovely way to share the day with friends and family who were unable to attend. As with everything wedding related, there are a wide variety of styles and price ranges, with your wedding style and budget being the determining factors. Be sure to check rules and regulations your ceremony site may have with regard to videotaping.

It's also a good idea to have the videographer meet with the photographer at least once before the wedding day so they can coordinate their styles, strategy, and traffic patterns.

The most common video styles are:

REAL TV

This is video shot with only one camera, starting at the beginning of your ceremony and running straight through to the end of the reception with no interruptions or editing, live and uncut, warts and all. Since this eliminates the need for editing and only one camera is used, it's the least expensive option. Just be forewarned that there may be parts you'll want to fast forward through.

Always make sure the videographer brings a second camera as a backup!

As Time Goes By

This type of video can be as long and as nostalgic as you'd like to make it. It starts by showing photographs of the couple as children, then progresses to photos of romantic, fun times they have shared together, followed by scenes from the ceremony, reception, and sometimes ending with shots from the honeymoon. It can include commentary and interviews with family members or close friends.

The Docudrama

This type of video covers the entire day as if filming a documentary. The segments of the day's events tell a story similar to the way the events occurred on your special day. It may start with shots of the bride and groom getting ready, then progress through the ceremony and reception, capturing spontaneous moments and interviews with family and friends, then end as the bride and groom leave the reception. This video format is the most popular and most commonly used, and can vary in price, according to the quality of the equipment and editing. This style requires more footage, sometimes two cameras, and lots of editing time, therefore it's the most expensive.

Finding a Good Videographer

→ *Recommendations from friends is always the best source.* Review the videotapes of friends who have recently tied the knot. If you're impressed, get the name and number of that videographer and put him on your short list.

→ *Wedding Photographers.* Your wedding photographer can be one of the best sources, since photographers and videographers often work together at weddings. They should know several people in the industry, and will be able to give you names of a few they work with best. Even with this referral, be sure to set up appointments to view their sample tapes yourself before making your final decision.

→ *Bridal Fairs.* Bridal fairs or local bridal shows are a great resource for meeting videographers and seeing samples of their work. Get business cards and information from the ones that impress you most, then follow up with a more in-depth interview.

→ *Ceremony Site Coordinators.* Because many of the ceremony site coordinators go over the rules and regulations with the videographer and are present the day of the wedding to view his work, they can often be a good source. They'll also recommend someone who is familiar with your ceremony location and its regulations.

- → *Bridal Magazines.* Sometimes larger, established videography companies will run regional ads in the national bridal magazines. Still, interview them and view their sample tapes. You may even want to get a list of references.

- → *Online Local Directory Services.* Many wedding websites have local vendor searches available where brides and grooms can locate vendors in their area. This isn't necessarily a recommendation, but rather a directory, so do your research and interview the leads thoroughly.

- → *WEVA.* Contact the Wedding and Event Videographers Association for a listing of videographers in your area. Phone: 941-923-5334; www.weva.com

WHAT MAKES A HIGH-QUALITY VIDEO?

Here are a few things to look for when viewing a sample tape of a videographer you're considering.

- → Up-to-date, high-quality, professional video equipment, including the editing and dubbing machines that utilize the newest technologies.

- → Spontaneous and natural reactions captured on tape, while maintaining a formal approach to the ceremony.

- → The ability to tell a story, detailing the way the events occurred on your wedding day.

- → Good, steady use of the camera, clear sound, good color and a sharp picture.

- → Notice how the shots are framed. Does the image fill the frame nicely, without having certain things cut out, like the bride's headpiece?

- → Notice the editing techniques used. Do they use a seamless electronic method of editing? Does the video look smooth as it moves from one scene to the next?

TYPES OF EDITING AND EQUIPMENT

In-Camera Editing – done while the tape is still in the camera by simply stopping the shooting process during uninteresting moments, or rewinding the tape and shooting over unwanted footage. Leaves little room for error and is the least expensive way to go.

Post-Editing – done on editing equipment at the videographer's studio, after the ceremony and reception. The videographer reviews all the footage then edits together the most interesting moments, usually in sequence. Music, special effects, titles, and still photographs can also be dubbed or edited in to give the video the same high quality that you would see on television.

Sound and microphones can be a make or break issue for the success of your video so discuss all the ins and outs of the available options beforehand.

Wired Microphones can be clipped onto the groom, officiant, or podium, but can limit your movements and pick up outside interference.

Wireless Microphones are the most popular and are usually worn around the groom's waist. To avoid picking up any outside interference and to get good clear sound, be sure the videographer uses a high band wireless microphone.

TRENDS IN VIDEOGRAPHY

- → Obtaining quotes and interviews from close friends and family on camera.

- → Including music from your ceremony and reception in the final video edit.

- → Incorporating still photographs of the wedding couple as babies, or photos of special moments they have shared. Some are even ending the video with photos of their honeymoon.

- → High quality.

- → Spending an extra $100 or so for a lighting assistant to give the video some extra polish.

WHAT to *ask* your *Videographer*

Ask about the quality of the equipment and recording tapes they use.

_____

Is it updated, high-quality, professional video equipment,
including editing and dubbing machines?

_____

How many cameras do they use to shoot the wedding?

_____

Do they use a wireless microphone to capture the best audio?

_____

What type of editing do they do?

_____

Is it post-edited or in-camera edited?

_____

What is their fee?

_____

Is it an hourly charge or flat fee for shooting the wedding and reception?

_____

How many hours of coverage are provided?

_____

Are editing, titles and music included in the quoted price?

_____

Is the unedited master tape available to purchase?

_____

What is the cost of additional tapes?

_____

When will you receive your final tape?

_____

Are there any additional charges for mileage
between wedding and reception?

_____

Are there any other charges that might be extra?

_____

Will they have back-up equipment in the event of a problem?

_____

Do they need any special lighting or electrical outlets?

_____

Are they familiar with your ceremony and reception locations?

_____

Have they shot a wedding in the location before?

_____

Will they meet you at the ceremony site ahead of time to
go over the best shooting angles?

_____

Ask to see an actual video done by the person shooting your wedding.

_____

Sometimes large video companies show you samples done by
the owner, then send someone less experienced to shoot your wedding.

_____

Ask to get a contract detailing exactly the type of video coverage
you're expecting, number of cameras, amount and type of editing,
titles and music included in the price, name of camera persons,
the date, time, location, and appropriate dress to be worn. ✳

_____

PHOTOGRAPHER and *Videographer* information

Photocopy and provide a copy to the photographer and videographer.

Bride's Name _____ Phone _____

Wedding Date _____ Time _____

Wedding Location _____

Reception Date _____ Time _____

Reception Location _____

PHOTOGRAPHER

Photographer _____ Phone _____

Assistant _____ Phone _____

Engagement Pictures _____ Date _____ Time _____

    Location _____

Bridal Portrait _____ Date _____ Time _____

    Location _____

Wedding Day _____ Arrival Time _____ Phone _____

    Location _____

Ceremony Site Restrictions/Guidelines _____

_____

_____

Appropriate Dress _____

VIDEOGRAPHER

Videographer _____ Phone _____

Assistant _____ Phone _____

Wedding Day _____ Arrival Time _____ Phone _____

    Location _____

Ceremony Site Restrictions/Guidelines _____

_____

_____

Appropriate Dress _____

VIDEOGRAPHY *worksheet*

	Estimate #1		Estimate #2	
	Name _____		Name _____	
	_____		_____	
	Phone _____		Phone _____	
	Description	*Cost*	*Description*	*Cost*
VIDEOGRAPHER'S FEE Number of Hours Number of Cameras				
VIDEOTAPE LENGTH				
SOUND				
EDITING				
ADDITIONAL CASSETTES				
MISCELLANEOUS				
TOTAL				

VIDEOGRAPHER SELECTED

Name _____   Deposit _____

Address _____   Arrival Time _____

Phone _____   Date Ready _____   Balance Due _____

The long *and* winding *Road*

ARRANGING *your* perfect WEDDING *transportation*

*H*ere comes the bride, all dressed in... well, you know how it goes. But the thing that nobody ever tells you is, how did that bride get there! Not to mention her bridal party, and her parents, and her out-of-town guests.

While it's not required etiquette-wise, arranging for transportation to and from the ceremony and reception for your wedding party and close family members will most likely bring you peace of mind. After all, you do want your wedding party, family, and out-of-town guests to arrive at the church and reception on time.

WEDDING TRANSPORTATION — GETTING FROM POINT A TO POINT B

While at times you may feel that you're playing a game of three-dimensional chess, keep in mind that the key to this task is organization. First determine how many people need transportation, and where they need to be picked up and taken to. Depending on your budget, you may consider renting limousines for the entire wedding party, or at least one limo or sedan to take you and your father to the church, escort you and your groom to the reception, and for your final departure. If you find limousine service for the entire bridal party and out-of-town guests too expensive, then arrange for friends or relatives to help with transportation. Assign specific names to specific drivers and their vehicles so no one gets lost in the shuffle. You might also check into renting a large car or a van for your attendants use.

LIMOUSINES

Limousine service is available in most cities. A quick search through the local yellow pages will land you a list of names. Call a few companies about six to eight months before the ceremony to compare their prices. Find out the price per hour, the minimum number of hours (most require two to three hour minimums), and if there are any package rates. Most will require a credit card number or a deposit in advance to reserve the date, at which time the balance will be due.

When placing your reservation, don't forget to give them the exact pick-up time, the address, the destination, and approximate length of rental time needed. Don't forget to ask about their cancellation policies.

THE GRAND GETAWAY

As any actress knows, a girl is only as good as her exit, so make sure yours speaks volumes. Often the first trick to any graceful exit is getting away successfully. At your own wedding, this is much easier said than done. There's always one more guest to greet or thank, one more long lost relative to hug, one last old boyfriend to kiss . . . no, no. Scratch that. After much planning and deliberation, you've surrounded yourselves with the people who matter the most to you. Now that you've got them all in one room, you can't just walk away. Can you?

Yes. You can. You've fed and watered them, and made yourself available to them for the last four hours. They've petted you, and hugged you, and pinched your cheek to death. You've done your duty, so get out of there. Quick. (Here comes Aunt Martha!)

Each of your guests deserves a moment of your time during the wedding reception, or at the very least a hearty hello and thank you for coming. But, eventually, you'll have to leave. Everyone will. They're just waiting for you to make the first move.

The style you've chosen for your wedding will dictate the method of transportation you choose for your getaway. Think Cinderella and her pumpkin coach, Butch Cassidy and Etta Place on their old fashioned bicycle, Aladdin and Jasmine on their magical flying carpet, Julia Roberts and Richard Gere on their galloping horses, well, you get the idea. Your getaway can be as fanciful or practical as you'd like.

Even if you've decided to stick with the ever-popular automobile, keep in mind that many places rent all manner of exotic automobiles, expensive luxury cars, antique cars, and sleek sporty models, so consider checking these out and see if they're more in keeping with your image than a standard limo. Or better yet, if a friend or relative owns one, see if they'd be willing to let you borrow it for the occasion.

Want something truly out of the ordinary? Here are some unique exits you might want to try.

* Horse-drawn carriages are *tres* romantic.

* A hot air balloon can certainly take you away from it all.

* For a red hot exit, consider hiring a fire engine to take you from the church to the reception. Check with a local fire station.

* A horse-drawn sleigh could be a romantic touch for a winter wedding, or one at a ski resort.

* A bicycle built for two. Or two bicycles built for one.

* Pedicab — a cart for two which is pulled by a bicycle — is a unique mode of transportation, providing the distance is not too far.

* Sail away on a boat or gondola, if the ceremony or reception is near water.

However you decide to make your exit, remember it is the perfect photo-op for your first step on your lifelong journey as man and wife.

DECORATING IDEAS FOR THE CAR

This is one of those traditions that is nearly unavoidable. Just make sure it isn't damaging to the car, or hinders your driving ability. Suggest (or have someone you trust suggest) that the decorators write "Just Married" on a large poster, which can be taped to the back of the car, or suggest they use non-damaging paint. Don't let them use shaving cream, or, if they do, wash it off as soon as possible. Old shoes and tin cans along with colored streamers, ribbons, bows, bells, and colorful balloons can make the car look festive. *

Transportation *worksheet*

Option #1

Name _____   Phone _____

Type of Vehicle _____   Cost Per Hour _____

Minimum Hours _____   Overtime Rate _____

Option #2

Name _____   Phone _____

Type of Vehicle _____   Cost Per Hour _____

Minimum Hours _____   Overtime Rate _____

Option #3

Name _____   Phone _____

Type of Vehicle _____   Cost Per Hour _____

Minimum Hours _____   Overtime Rate _____

COMPANY CONTRACTED WITH: *Choice #* _____

TRANSPORTATION NEEDS

Quantity	Description	Number of Hours	Cost per Hour	Total Cost
_____ Limousines	_____	_____	_____	_____
_____ Horsedrawn Carriages	_____	_____	_____	_____
_____ Horsedrawn Sleighs	_____	_____	_____	_____
_____ Antique Cars	_____	_____	_____	_____
_____ Rental Cars	_____	_____	_____	_____
_____ Trolley Car/Bus	_____	_____	_____	_____
_____ Bus/Van	_____	_____	_____	_____
_____ Boat/gondola	_____	_____	_____	_____
_____ Plane/Helicopter	_____	_____	_____	_____
_____ Hot-air Balloon	_____	_____	_____	_____
_____ Fire Engine	_____	_____	_____	_____
_____ Other	_____	_____	_____	_____

Total Cost _____

Deposits Paid _____

Balance Due _____

WEDDING *Day* transportation

TRANSPORTATION TO CEREMONY SITE

Name	Pick-up Time	Pick-up Location	Vehicle/Driver
Bride			
Bride's Father			
Bride's Mother			
Bridal Attendants			
Groom			
Groom's Attendants			
Groom's Parents			
Grandparents			
Other Guests			

TRANSPORTATION TO RECEPTION SITE

Name	Pick-up Time		Vehicle/Driver
Bride and Groom			
Bridal Attendants			
Groom's Attendants			
Bride's Parents			
Groom's Parents			
Grandparents			
Other Guests			

TRANSPORTATION FROM RECEPTION SITE, TO HOTEL, HOME, ETC.

Name	Pick-up Time	Destination	Vehicle/Driver
Bride and Groom			
Bridal Attendants			
Groom's Attendants			
Bride's Parents			
Groom's Parents			
Grandparents			
Other Guests			

Never look *a* gift *Horse* in the *Mouth*

Your complete GUIDE to *gift* REGISTRY

As if you're not lucky enough to have found that perfect someone and to be throwing the granddaddy of all parties to celebrate it, now you're going to be deluged with all manner of gifts. And not just any gift, but gifts you get to pick out yourself! While finding the right person can feel like winning the emotional lottery, registering for all the lovely wedding gifts and goodies that will be coming your way makes it feel as if you really did just win the lottery.

At first glance, some brides balk at the whole notion of registering for gifts. After all, isn't that akin to just coming out and asking people to get you something? It seems so materialistic or demanding. Rest assured that this is not so. It is a highly respected (and necessary) solution to the age-old question, what to buy the darlings? Think of gift registry as a brilliant defense tactic against forty-seven blenders, thirty-two plastic fish singing "Old Man River," and seventy-four gifts from taste impaired relatives (from his side of the family – naturally).

The only thing you can't do is mention in your wedding invitation (or engagement announcement or any other written communication) where you have registered. That information, like the most delicious of gossip, needs to be gotten out by word-of-mouth, osmosis, or telepathy. Think of it this way. If you pretend it's a rumor, it'll spread like wildfire. Especially with a few close friends and relatives fanning the flames for you.

WHERE TO REGISTER

Pretty much anywhere you want. Seriously. Wedding registry has become big business and everyone is getting in on the act. This is great for you and your wedding guests because the sheer volume and availability of gift registries make it just that much easier.

Another recent entry into the registry game is the advent of online registration, which puts registering for gifts, and buying them, a mere mouse click away. This can be especially beneficial when your families are scattered across the nation and your guest list is culled from all parts of the country.

KITCHEN
table advice

Don't underestimate the emotional impact of integrating yours and mine into ours, a merging of two distinct tastes and value systems into one. If he sat down to a formal Sunday dinner every week of his life, he will have much different opinions as to the absolute necessity of formal china than yourself, whose family only managed to eat together during the Super Bowl, and that was on paper plates with plastic forks.

All Major Department Stores

Building Supply Stores such as *Home Base, Home Depot*

Hardware Stores, either local hardware stores or specialty hardware stores like *Renovation Hardware*

Sporting Good Stores like *Sports Mart, Sports Chalet, Big Five*

Upscale Gardening Stores like *Smith and Hawken* or local nurseries

Mortgage Lenders – registering for contributions to a down payment on a house is becoming ever more popular

Travel Agents whether for the honeymoon or another recreational trip

Home Furnishing & Accessory Stores – *Crate and Barrel, Williams Sonoma, Pottery Barn, Eddie Bauer Home Stores, Pier One, Ikea, Strouds, Linens & Things*

On-Line Registries – there are a number of websites that feature convenient registry features

TEN QUESTIONS TO ASK BEFORE YOU REGISTER

1. Do you need an appointment?

2. What is the store's return policy?

3. How easy is it to return things?

4. How do they keep track of your registry and gifts? A computer database is the preferred method as it is the most quickly updated.

5. How often to you update the registry? The more often the better so as to avoid as much duplication as possible.

6. How long does it take to get your gift registry up and running?

7. Does the store have a toll-free phone line?

8. Do they accept phone purchases?

9. Do they have a website?

10. Do they ship gifts? Any additional charge for this service?

11. How long does your registry list stay in their records? A year after the wedding date is the ideal since guests have up to one year to purchase a gift for you.

Once you're ready to register, prepare for the trip like you would for a day hike in the Swiss Alps. Wear comfy shoes, bring water, have high protein snacks close at hand (the last thing you need is to get lightheaded while selecting those wedding gifts!), and have an escape route or survival plan in your back pocket. It also doesn't hurt to remind yourself that it doesn't all have to be done in one day.

WHAT TO REGISTER FOR

Pretty much anything your want. Seriously. While many couples still stick with the tried and true china, silver, and crystal, many more are branching out and availing themselves of the huge number of choices out there, from honeymoon trips to charitable donations.

→ House Accessories and Gadgets

→ Kitchen Stuff

→ China

→ Crystal

→ Silver

→ Sporting Goods

→ Linens

→ Wines

→ Home Improvements

→ Garden Supplies

→ Mortgage Down Payments

→ Honeymoons

→ Vacation Travel

→ House Cleaning Services
  (for the practical minded couple.)

If you go with traditional items like china and silver, you'll probably need to spend a bit of time deciding on which patterns and styles both of you will be willing to live with for the rest of your lives before you actually venture out to register for it. Go window-shopping, surf the Web, look at magazine ads to get some great ideas of what's out there.

REGISTERING DO'S AND DON'TS

DO realize that just because you've registered for it doesn't mean you'll get it. In other words, don't count your china before it's packed.

DO register for enough gifts with respect to your wedding list. If you've invited 300 people, make sure and register for that many gifts.

DO register at a wide variety of locations that all your guests will have access to.

DO complete the registration process by the time you send out your invitations. It's also perfectly acceptable, if not downright recommended, to register earlier so that early shoppers or shower guests can have access to the information.

DO keep scrupulous track of every gift you receive and who gave it to you. (You will need this later for writing your thank you notes.)

DO plan for guests who bring their gifts to the reception instead of having it sent directly to you either before or after. Set aside a specific table for these gifts in an area that gets relatively little traffic if possible. Assign someone to be in charge, making sure to tape the cards to the packages and guide people to where they can leave them.

DON'T open gifts brought to the reception at the reception itself. Wait until later that day or when you return from your honeymoon.

DON'T register for things that are so expensive that few people you know can afford them.

DON'T register for "phantom" gifts, intending to trade them all in for more expensive gifts later.

DO think twice before displaying your gifts at the reception. Many people feel that the old tradition is not in good taste and may even risk embarrassing a guest or two, something you never, ever want to do. Also, while the two of you probably love staring at all your loot in one big shiny pile, don't make the mistake of assuming others will find this pastime nearly as fascinating. A more practical reason to refrain from this practice is that gifts have a discerning habit of "walking" away from reception displays.

KITCHEN
table advice

Writing
such a huge amount
of thank you notes
can be daunting.

In fact, so much so that I've
devoted an entire book to the
subject. For more ideas and
advice on how to tackle this
overwhelming task, take a
peek at *Heartfelt Thank Yous:
Perfect Ways for Brides to Say
Thank You*

THE OCCASIONAL GIFT BOO-BOO

A BROKEN OR DAMAGED GIFT

Occasionally, through no fault of the gift giver, a gift will arrive broken or damaged. Unless the gift was sent insured, the chances are the giver can do nothing about it at this point, and will most certainly feel badly about the mishap — possibly even feel obligated to send a second one — so avoid mentioning the fact that it broke. If the gift was sent directly by a department store, you can contact the store. Their customer service department will most likely see to the replacement of the gift.

RETURNING GIFTS

Even with the miracles of modern registry, duplicate gifts happen. It is not necessary to tell the gift giver that it was their particular gift you returned. This is where the painstaking research you did before you registered will come in handy as you will only have selected stores that make returns as easy as pie. (Although, anyone who's ever made a successful pie knows that they are not easy!)

THE GIFT ARRIVES WITH NO MENTION OF THE SENDER

Try calling the store to see if you can track the gift that way. If it didn't come from a store, check the package for a hint as to where it came from, geographically speaking. Hopefully that can help you narrow it down. Also check with your parents and close friends, maybe they can help you determine the mystery giver.

THE WEDDING IS CALLED OFF

When a wedding is called off or canceled, then all of the gifts need to be returned to the givers, even the monogrammed and personalized ones. Include a brief note with each gift you're returning, thanking the person for their thoughtfulness and explaining that the wedding will not be taking place.

THANKING PEOPLE FOR THEIR GIFTS — THE MUST-HAVE-ITS

You **must** send a thank you note for every wedding (shower, engagement, etc.) gift you receive. The note **must** be written by the bride or the groom. Unlike other wedding tasks, this one cannot be delegated. The thank you notes **must** be sent out in a timely fashion. This means two weeks for gifts received before the wedding. For gifts received after the wedding, one month is recommended but you have up to three months before the etiquette police begin pounding on your door.

Ten Tips to Stay on Top of Your Thank You Notes

- Buy all your thank you note stationery and supplies early on and keep it handy.

- Keep careful track of who gave you what.

- Write the note as soon as possible after receiving the gift.

- If you have several notes to get out at once, prioritize them according to which gift giver is most likely to be offended by a late note.

- For notes written before the wedding, you must use your maiden name.

- Make sure both of you do your part in writing those notes. (Grooms — this means YOU too!)

- Mention the gift in detail in the thank you note and add a line or two on how much you enjoy it or how you plan to use it.

- Add a conversational line or two to make the thank you note more personalized.

- If the gift was money, thank them for their generosity or generous gift and mention what you plan to use it for. Never mention the amount.

- Consider addressing your thank you notes at the same time you address your wedding invitations. Especially if there are people helping you. ✻

REALITY *check*

Few occasions bring about such a rousing round of good wishes as the wedding. People are so happy and supportive of you and your new life that they all feel they have to do something as a sort of send off, hence, wedding gifts. Just a reminder: Even though almost everyone sends them, wedding gifts are not mandatory! Ever. This means you are not even allowed to think a single mean thought about someone who doesn't send you one.

FORMAL DINNERWARE

	Want	Rec'd
Store:		
Phone:		
Pattern:		
Manufacturer:		
Dinner plate		
Luncheon plate		
Dessert/salad plate		
Bread/butter plate		
Buffet plate		
Cream soup bowl		
Soup/cereal bowl		
Fruit bowl		
Rim soup bowl		
Coffee cup/saucer		
Demitasse/saucer		
Teacup/saucer		
Teapot		
Coffeepot		
Sugar/creamer		
Salt/pepper		
Serving bowls		
Serving platters		
Gravy boat		
Egg cup		
Other:		

INFORMAL DINNERWARE

Store:		
Phone:		
Pattern:		
Manufacturer:		
Dinner plate		
Salad plate		
Bowls		
Cups/saucers		
Mugs		
Serving pieces		
Other:		

FORMAL FLATWARE

	Want	Rec'd
Store:		
Phone:		
Pattern:		
Manufacturer:		
Dinner fork		
Dessert/salad fork		
Cocktail fork		
Tablespoon		
Soup spoon		
Tea/dessert spoon		
Demitasse spoon		
Iced tea spoon		
Dinner knife		
Steak knife		
Butter spreader		
Serving spoon		
Gravy ladle		
Serving fork		
Cold meat fork		
Cake knife		
Pie server		
Salad set		
Carving set		
Sugar spoon/tongs		
Lemon fork		
Butter knife		
Silver chest		
Other:		

INFORMAL FLATWARE

Store:		
Phone:		
Pattern:		
Manufacturer:		
No. of place settings		
Serving pieces		
Other:		

HOLLOWWARE/SERVERS

	Want	Rec'd
Tea service		
Coffee service		
Water pitcher		
Champagne cooler		
Serving bowls		
Serving platters		
Trays		
Bread tray		
Service plates		
Salad bowl		
Compote		
Tureen		
Chafing dish		
Condiment dish		
Cream/sugar set		
Salt/pepper		
Dessert dishes		
Gravy boat		
Candlesticks		
Napkin rings		
Other:		

CRYSTAL

	Want	Rec'd
Store:		
Phone:		
Pattern:		
Manufacturer:		
Goblets		
White wine		
Claret		
Champagne		
Liqueur		
Brandy		
Cocktail		
Iced tea		
Other:		

GIFT *registry* checklist

CASUAL GLASS/BARWARE   *Want Rec'd*

Store:

Phone:

Pattern:

Manufacturer:

	Want	Rec'd
Goblets		
Wine		
Old-fashioned		
Highball		
Iced tea		
Beer mugs		
Cocktail		
Fruit juice		
Other:		

BAR NEEDS

	Want	Rec'd
Ice bucket		
Wine rack		
Ice crusher		
Coasters		
Jigger/tools		
Corkscrew/wine opener		
Punch bowl set		
Decanters		
Other:		

KITCHENWARE

	Want	Rec'd
Coffee maker		
Coffee grinder		
Juicer		
Food processor		
Blender		
Mixer		
Microwave		
Toaster/toaster oven		
Electric skillet		
Deep fryer		
Slow cooker		
Pressure cooker		
Microwave cookware		
Ovenware		

	Want	Rec'd
Cookware		
Bakeware		
Wok		
Tea kettle		
Hot tray		
Mixing bowls		
Storage containers		
Canister set		
Spice rack		
Kitchen utensils		
Cutlery		
Cutting board		
Wooden salad bowl set		
Other:		

LINENS

	Want	Rec'd
Formal cloth/napkins		
Informal cloth/napkins		
Place mats		
Cocktail napkins		
Potholders/dish towels		
Aprons		
Comforter		
Bedspread		
Mattress pad		
Pillows		
Bed sheets		
Blanket		
Electric blanket		
Beach towels		
Bath towels/face cloths		
Guest towels		
Bath mat		
Rug/lid cover set		
Accessories		
Other:		

DECORATIVE ITEMS   *Want Rec'd*

	Want	Rec'd
Vases		
Lamps		
Clocks		
Pictures		
Bookends		
Area rugs		
Baskets		
TV tables		
Accessories		
Other:		

ELECTRONICS

	Want	Rec'd
TV/video system		
Stereo		
Camera equipment		
Clock radio		
Portable TV/radio		
Calculator		
Security devices		
Telephones		
Other:		

GENERAL

	Want	Rec'd
Luggage		
Exercise/sporting equip.		
Barbecue		
Patio furniture		
Picnic basket		
Sleeping bags		
Carpet cleaner		
Tools		
Hobbies/games		
Other:		

GIFT *list*

Name	Gift	Store	Thank You Sent
1.			
2.			
3.			
4.			
5.			
6.			
7.			
8.			
9.			
10.			
11.			
12.			
13.			
14.			
15.			
16.			
17.			
18.			
19.			
20.			
21.			
22.			
23.			
24.			
25.			
26.			
27.			
28.			
29.			
30.			
31.			
32.			
33.			

GIFT *list*

Name	Gift	Store	Thank You Sent
34.			
35.			
36.			
37.			
38.			
39.			
40.			
41.			
42.			
43.			
44.			
45.			
46.			
47.			
48.			
49.			
50.			
51.			
52.			
53.			
54.			
55.			
56.			
57.			
58.			
59.			
60.			
61.			
62.			
63.			
64.			
65.			
66.			

Never Look a Gift Horse in the Mouth

GIFT *list*

Name	Gift	Store	Thank You Sent
67.			
68.			
69.			
70.			
71.			
72.			
73.			
74.			
75.			
76.			
77.			
78.			
79.			
80.			
81.			
82.			
83.			
84.			
85.			
86.			
87.			
88.			
89.			
90.			
91.			
92.			
93.			
94.			
95.			
96.			
97.			
98.			
99.			

Party On!

A Guide to Pre-Wedding Parties

The months before the wedding are always great fun. Besides the excitement of being newly engaged and all the planning and shopping, you can trust your friends and relatives to come through with rollicking celebrations in your honor. It's a time of good will, good cheer, and good friendships. The more time you've spent planning your own wedding, the more you'll be aware of how much time and effort goes into planning a party of any kind. Take extra care in showing your appreciation to your shower host or hostess with thank you notes, or maybe a little gift or flowers.

BRIDAL SHOWERS

The traditional bridal shower was a girls-only affair and a way to help outfit the couple's new home, or assemble the bride's trousseau. Tradition dictates that a close friend, maid of honor, relative, or bridesmaid may give a shower. It's not considered proper for the shower to be hosted by the bride or groom's mother or immediate family. The concern is that it will seem as though they are fishing for presents on the bride's behalf. This particular rule of etiquette, however, is often ignored, especially if the maid or matron of honor, or other bridesmaids, live in another town, are the bride's sisters, or are party planning impaired.

Showers take place anywhere from six months to two weeks before the wedding. It would be a Really Bad Idea to have a shower the week before the wedding since that week is almost always jam-packed with last minute pre-wedding activities and details.

To keep the shower from being too big a financial weight, it's nice if two or three people host one together. Often, there will be several different showers; one for your family friends, one for your girlfriends, and another thrown by your coworkers or friends from school. If that's the case, try not to invite the same people to every shower. Wedding expenses can add up, especially for your bridal party, so don't take the fun out of it by sending them to the poor house.

PLANNING THE SHOWER

Generally, the hostess and the bride get together to determine a date, a guest list, and what kind of shower it will be. Sometimes the hostess will want to surprise the bride. In that case, she would get the information from the fiancé or the bride's mother. The traditional all-female shower is usually an afternoon luncheon or tea, with anywhere from ten to thirty guests. Written invitations are usually sent, but are not mandatory. Guests are usually close friends or relatives, or perhaps you may have one shower for each group.

While not everyone who is invited to the wedding needs to be invited to the shower, everyone who is invited to the shower should be invited to the wedding, or there will be hurt feelings. The exception to this would be coworkers or school chums who wanted to throw the bride-to-be a shower of their own.

IDEAS FOR GIRLS-ONLY SHOWER THEMES

LINGERIE OR PERSONAL SHOWERS

These showers are fun. Gifts can include all the beautiful things most people don't buy for themselves: sexy nightgowns, camisoles, luxurious underwear, bras, robes, you get the idea. Other fun ideas would be indulgent pampering gifts such as perfume, bath accessories, jewelry, or perhaps even a fun, lacy garter for the bride-to-be to wear under her wedding gown. Consider buying a special frame and sneaking a baby picture of the bride's fiancé from his mother. It will not only surprise the bride, but will be a unique gift she'll be sure to adore.

LINEN SHOWERS

Thick lush, towels, warm toasty blankets, crisp linen sheets, fluffy pillows, elegant tablecloths, sunny placemats, and napkins — all the linens needed to outfit a new home. It helps if you have your color and decorating scheme set. Better yet, make sure you've registered for the type of things you want.

KITCHEN SHOWERS

Kitchen gift ideas are endless, with new gadgets and timesaving devices appearing on the shelves with delightful frequency. Things for the kitchen have the added benefit of ranging in cost from inexpensive to more expensive appliances. Again, it's helpful if you take the time to register for items before the shower.

One fun idea is to have each guest bring a favorite recipe along with one item needed for its preparation. Some examples: chocolate chip cookies with the cookie sheets, quiche Lorraine with a quiche dish. The hostess may provide a recipe box to put the recipes in, or write them in a book designed for this. Entitle it "The Private Cookbook."

COUPLES SHOWERS

Watch out girls, here come the boys!

Traditional girls-only showers are making way for the growing popularity of couples showers. This is a wonderful way to include men in the whole wedding process and celebration. These showers usually turn out to be one big party (and there's certainly nothing wrong with that!) but with gifts and, possibly, games. The men always end up having a great time and wondering why we've been keeping these types of parties to ourselves all these years.

IDEAS FOR COUPLES SHOWERS

BARBECUE OR GRILLING SHOWER

The guests can all pitch in and get the couple a super-duper deluxe barbecue, if they don't already have one. Barbecues and grills come in all sizes and price ranges. There are also some great accessories for today's grilling trends: tongs, spatulas, grilling sauces, barbecue cookbooks, seasonings, and other outdoor dining items.

TECHNO SHOWER

Chances are that one or both of the marrying couple will have a home office of some kind. This shower has the guests bringing all sorts of gizmos and gadgets for the techno savvy couple, from desk accessories to computer aids and everything in between. How about going in on matching Palm Pilots so the busy couple can coordinate their schedules?

THE MICROBREWERY SHOWER

Never before has beer attained such lofty heights as it has with the recent trends toward microbreweries. Consider pilsner glasses, mugs, books, uncommon or limited edition beers, books on microbreweries, or beginning beer brewing kits.

THE COFFEE BAR SHOWER

What new couple isn't looking forward to sharing the perfect cup of espresso in bed? Espresso machines, special kinds of coffee beans, latte cups, espresso cups, sturdy coffee mugs, tasty syrups, and delightful dippers such as cookies, biscotti, and flavored candy sticks make great gifts for the coffee-loving couple.

THIS OLD HOUSE SHOWER

It's a fact of married life that we often turn to the task of feathering our nests once we've become a couple. This shower is a great way to help out with that daunting task. You can supply gift certificates to home renovation places, hardware stores, books, or even contribute your own manual labor.

THE HEALTH AND FITNESS SHOWER

Staying fit is a high priority in all of our lives. This type of shower helps the new couple stay motivated and well. Consider fitness equipment, supplies, gadgets, pedometers, health club memberships, and gift certificates.

OPENING THE GIFTS

With all the excitement and passing of gifts, it's easy to misplace the cards. Have someone, usually the honor attendant or other bridesmaid, write down what the gift was and who gave it as it's being opened. She may want to jot down the first words out of the bride's mouth. A traditional shower game is reading back the bride's comments at the end of the gift opening — it can be quite entertaining.

Show your appreciation by sending a thank you note immediately. (This is not an option. This is a must.)

For more great ideas on shower themes, games, decorations, recipes, and party favors, my book, *Bridal Showers*, is an in-depth look at hosting a bridal shower that will be fun and memorable.

BRIDESMAID'S PARTY

Bridesmaids' parties are held by the bride as an extra thank you to all her attendants for standing by her side throughout these tumultuous months and for wearing those darling dresses she picked out. What better way to tell your bridesmaids how much you appreciate their unwavering help and support than by throwing a special party just for them? Besides being a great way to thank them, it's a nice opportunity for them to meet each other if they aren't already acquainted, and take care of final dressing issues and makeup and hair coordination. You may also decide to give them their attendant gifts at that time.

Traditionally, the bridesmaid's party has been a luncheon, afternoon tea, or even a dinner party including spouses or dates. Other great ideas for a bridesmaid's party are:

Movie Night – A perfect chance to go out for a quick dinner and catch that chick flick none of you could convince the men in your life to see.

Elegant Luncheon – Hosted at your place or held at an indulgent restaurant.

Tea – Even for women who never have tea, bridesmaids' parties are the sort of occasion that calls for an elegant high tea at a posh restaurant.

Pajama Party – Less formal than the other choices, but no less fun. Get all the girls together for a sleepover. Wear your silliest pajamas and have everyone bring their favorite beauty products to share and try out.

Day at the Spa – Treat the girls to an indulgent day at a local spa featuring massages, facials, the works.

Camping Trip – An all girls camping trip, complete with ghost stories and s'mores.

THE BACHELOR/ BACHELORETTE PARTY

The bachelor/bachelorette party can be a night to remember or one you can't wait to forget. Since it's being thrown in your honor, make it clear to the hosts what your level of comfort is. While very much a part of the wedding tradition, the bachelor party doesn't have to equate with raunchy bad taste. If you're much more comfortable with a PG-13 rating, or even a PG, than the traditional NC-17, communicate that. Firmly.

This party is the groom's last night out with the boys as a single man and may be hosted by the groom himself, his best man, or the ushers. If you keep the activities toned down, the groom's father and the father of the bride may also attend. It also presents a good opportunity for the groom to pass out his attendants' gifts.

The bachelorette party is the modernized version of what's sauce for the gander is sauce for the goose. Girls feel less left out if they're out having a blast of their own. Besides, political correctness decrees that if he gets a last fling, so does she.

Never have the party right before the wedding. The weekend before is a good choice, unless most of the invitees are coming from out of town. Then consider daytime events — hosting a ball game, a day at the beach, or a barbecue on the day of the rehearsal or on the day of the wedding itself if it's scheduled for the late afternoon or evening.

The bachelor/bachelorette's party traditionally begins with a dinner where the groom makes a toast to his bride. After drinking to the toast, each of the men would smash his glass so that it could never be used for a less worthy purpose. The tradition is rarely carried to this extreme, but the groom may still toast his bride if he chooses.

Some bachelor party ideas that are more in keeping with today's sensibilities could be a concert, sporting events, or real-life adventures such as rough water kayaking or river rafting, bungee jumping, parachuting, or parasailing.

A WEDDING BRUNCH OR BREAKFAST

Hosting a light breakfast or early lunch the day after the wedding is a wonderful way for a friend or relative to participate in the wedding festivities. It's a great chance to say goodbye to out-of-town guests the morning after your wedding, and many brides and grooms postpone leaving for their honeymoon until after this event, although it's certainly not required. It is usually casual, with relaxed seating and buffet or open house style refreshments.

If SOMEONE is *throwing a* morning-after *breakfast* or *brunch*, keep in mind the bride and groom don't have to attend. It is perfectly acceptable (expected even) for them to head on out of town on their honeymoon. If the newly married couple wants to attend, that's fine also. ✳

twenty-three

The BUSINESS *side* of *Marriage*

MAKING it ALL *Legal*

*I*nto every fantasy a little reality must fall. While weddings are about creating the ultimate fantasy celebration, the act of marriage also requires the two of you to take care of a few legal and business affairs. These include getting your marriage license, changing your name if you plan to, and preparing a prenuptial agreement if you and your fiancé have decided on one.

YOUR MARRIAGE LICENSE

No matter how many guests witnessed your marriage, you'll need a marriage license to make it truly legal. Marriage license requirements are determined by each state. To find out the requirements in your state, call or write the county clerk's office. The requirements vary from state to state, but generally they are laws concerned with the age of consent, residence, citizenship requirements, and freedom of couples from venereal disease. For the most case, the licenses are good only in those states in which they are issued. The license may also only be good for a set number of days, say thirty days or sixty days, before expiring.

Questions to ask

- → Do you need to apply in person and together?
- → What is the waiting time before and after the license is issued?
- → Who needs to sign it?
- → What age requirements apply to the bride and groom?
- → What are the residence requirements?
- → Is a blood test or doctor's certificate needed?

- → What is the fee?
- → What identification or proof of age is required?
- → Is proof of divorce needed?
- → What medical tests are required? Many states require blood tests in order to detect venereal disease.
- → Are AIDS tests required? If so, have the test done about three months in advance. It can take six to eight weeks to get back the results.

RELIGIOUS OR CEREMONIAL REQUIREMENTS

It's important to double-check your house of worship or officiant to be sure you have met any requirements they have before they will perform your marriage ceremony. These may include, but aren't limited to:

→ Pre-marital counseling

→ Church membership

→ Becoming baptized in the house of worship's particular denomination

→ Banns (for Catholic ceremonies)

→ Special procedures for people who have been divorced

LEGALITIES FOR REMARRIAGE

If you or your fiancé is getting married for the second time, the following is a list of what you'll need to provide in order to obtain a new marriage certificate.

→ Copy of Divorce Decree or Dissolution of Marriage – original or a certified copy

→ Date of final divorce

→ County and state where divorce was granted

→ Grounds for divorce

→ Whether or not former spouse is living

TO CHANGE YOUR NAME, OR NOT?

While the practice of keeping or hyphenating your name is more accepted than ever, as many as 85 to 90 percent of brides are sticking with tradition and taking their husband's name. Consider your particular situation and discuss your needs and preferences. Your options are:

→ Keep your maiden name

→ Take your husband's last name

→ Use your husband's last name socially, and use your maiden name professionally

→ The bride hyphenates both names and the groom keeps his own

→ Both the bride and groom hyphenate their last names

→ Use your maiden name as a middle name

→ The groom takes the bride's last name

Your decision will be based on a variety of factors, among them: professional status, ease of spelling and pronunciation, desire to keep your family name, feeling of commitment and tradition. Your ultimate decision will also take into account the children's needs (if any are involved) and social considerations.

You must determine which name you will use legally and then which name you will use socially. The following are a few options and what is required to exercise them.

Keep Your Maiden Name. Should you choose to keep your maiden name, in most states you don't have to notify any official agencies. Check your state for any special requirements. Sign your maiden name on the marriage certificate and on all legal documents just as you did before.

Use Your Maiden Name Professionally, and Your Husband's Name Socially. Many women are choosing this option, especially when they are already established and known professionally by their maiden names. Problems can arise when you intermix the two names on legal documents. To avoid this, use only your maiden name on all legal documents and when filing your joint tax return. The IRS may require proof of your marriage and request a notarized copy of your marriage license.

Hyphenate Your Names. This is a popular option when you want to retain both last names. The woman's last name appears first, followed by the husband's last name. The woman may decide to use the full-hyphenated name on legal documents, and use only her husband's last name socially.

Be sure to record your name change with all the agencies listed on the "Name and Address Change Worksheet," and sign your marriage certificate the same way.

Taking Your Husband's Name. If you are planning to change your name by taking, or adding, your husband's last name, start by signing that name on the marriage certificate and all future documents. Get the necessary paper work or requirements to record your name change on all legal and official records.

Have Your Husband Take Your Name. It's not a common practice, but today some grooms are changing to their wife's last name. This is a viable alternative when the wife, for professional reasons, can't change her last name, and the couple wants to use just one name for family and social ease. Another reason might be if the groom's name is difficult to spell or pronounce. He should make the same changes on legal and official records that are listed on the "Name and Address Change Worksheet" and contact the local county clerk's office to see if there are any further requirements in your state.

PRENUPTIAL AGREEMENTS

Today, more and more couples are marrying later in life and have accumulated assets or established careers before getting married. Others are marrying for the second or third time and have assets from previous marriages, child support, or inheritance to consider. Many of these couples are turning to the use of prenuptial agreements to clarify what each person brings into the marriage, and how the assets will be divided in the event of a divorce or death.

THE PRENUPTIAL AGREEMENT

The prenuptial agreement is a legal contract entered into before the marriage (a postnuptial agreement is entered into after the marriage). Don't make the mistake of assuming that any discussion of a prenuptial agreement is unromantic or a sign of lack of commitment. This contract is merely designed to anticipate and resolve areas that could become a matter of dispute between the two parties at a later date. Prenuptial agreements are most commonly used in prearranging financial matters and protecting future inheritances. But they may also be used to specify rights and privileges within a marriage, or to provide for the division of property, or the custody of children in the case of divorce. The terms of the agreement become legally enforceable only when the parties are seeking a divorce or when one of them dies.

If you'll be marrying in a state other than the one in which you live, you'll need to check that state's marriage license requirements as well.

CHANGING *Your* NAME AND *address*

If you are planning on changing your name, you may want to take care of some changes before the wedding. Some may require a copy of your marriage license with notification, so check ahead of time.

→ Social Security card – local office of the Federal Social Security Administration

→ Driver's license

→ Car registration

→ Voter's registration

→ Passport

→ Employer or school records

→ Bank accounts – changing or opening joint accounts

→ Stocks or bonds

→ Wills – drawing up a will or changing the beneficiary

→ Insurance policies – automobiles, home, health

→ Pension plans

→ Property titles or leases

→ Charge accounts

→ Subscriptions

→ Club memberships

→ Post Office – new name and new address

WHO NEEDS A PRENUPTIAL AGREEMENT?

If you are both young, have not accumulated any real assets, and are not likely to inherit a sizable amount, you probably don't need a prenuptial agreement. Each state has laws that automatically establish certain contractual regulations on how property is divided. Once you are husband and wife, these existing laws may fit your needs perfectly well and no other contract would be necessary.

A prenuptial agreement should be considered by any individual, regardless of age or previous marital status, who is coming into the marriage with considerable assets, including stocks, real estate investments, cars, jewelry, art, or right of inheritance. Today, most couples in this situation find nothing unromantic about planning their lives together in a practical way, especially when they both have such assets. Couples find that the discussion and resolution of these issues will give them added security and more confidence in their decision to marry and build a life together.

The signing of a prenuptial agreement, or not, finally comes down to a decision you both will have to make. Discuss it openly and determine what's right for you. Some couples feel that discussing these matters and requesting a prenuptial agreement from your fiancé hinders the romance and shows a lack of commitment toward the marriage. Others feel the communication strengthens the trust and starts the marriage off on the right foot. The issue of prenuptial agreements deserves some serious consideration; you may find it helpful to consult a financial planner or an attorney to get some advice.

WHAT TO DO FIRST

→ Discuss important marital issues that you might want included in an agreement, especially assets, finances, children from previous marriages, and rights of inheritance.

→ Consult a financial planner or attorney for advice. Have your agreements written in a legal contract drawn up by one or both of your attorneys.

→ In your contract specify a certain time or date by which you will review or revise your contract, if needed — every two to five years, for example. The contracts need not be cast in concrete.

WHAT TO INCLUDE

→ All assets and property owned separately or jointly.

→ How assets and liabilities will be handled in the event of a divorce.

→ List, specifically, checking and savings accounts, credit cards, loans, cars, jewelry, art, real estate, and other property.

→ How right of inheritance will be handled (optional).

→ How new assets will be divided.

→ Who keeps the house or leased apartment, and how equity or deposits are divided.

→ How future income will be shared. (If one spouse has put the other through law school, for example, that person will want a share of the law practice, even after a divorce.) *

MARRIAGE *license* CHECKLIST

COUNTY CLERK'S OFFICE _____ Phone _____

Address _____

Appointment Date _____ Time _____

State's minimum age to marry _____

Waiting period after application _____

License is valid for days _____

License fee _____

BRIDE'S DOCTOR _____ Phone _____

Address _____

Appointment Date _____ Exam Fee _____

GROOM'S DOCTOR _____ Phone _____

Address _____

Appointment Date _____ Exam Fee _____

DOCUMENTS AND TESTS REQUIRED BY THE COUNTY CLERK IN YOUR STATE:

Required Item	Have	Need to Get Bride	Groom
❏ Proof of age (driver's license)	❏	❏	❏
❏ Proof of citizenship (birth certificate)	❏	❏	❏
❏ Doctor's certificate	❏	❏	❏
❏ Venereal disease blood test	❏	❏	❏
❏ Rubella, sickle cell anemia blood test	❏	❏	❏
❏ AIDS or other blood test	❏	❏	❏
❏ AIDS counseling	❏	❏	❏
❏ Proof of divorce	❏	❏	❏
❏ Parental consent for marriage of minors	❏	❏	❏

Bride's *Name* and *Address* CHANGE WORKSHEET

Items to Be Changed	Change Name	Change Address	Account or Policy Number, Other Information	Phone or Address to Notify Company	Done
Social Security	❏	❏			❏
Driver's License	❏	❏			❏
Car Registration	❏	❏			❏
Voter's Registration	❏	❏			❏
Passport	❏	❏			❏
Employee Records	❏	❏			❏
School Records	❏	❏			❏
Checking Accounts	❏	❏			❏
Savings Accounts	❏	❏			❏
Ira Accounts	❏	❏			❏
Safety Deposit Box	❏	❏			❏
Stocks And Bonds	❏	❏			❏
Loans	❏	❏			❏
Wills/Trusts	❏	❏			❏
Pensions	❏	❏			❏
Property Titles	❏	❏			❏
Leases	❏	❏			❏
Subscriptions	❏	❏			❏
Club Memberships	❏	❏			❏
Post Office	❏	❏			❏
Auto Insurance	❏	❏			❏
Property Insurance	❏	❏			❏
Medical Insurance	❏	❏			❏
Life Insurance	❏	❏			❏
Doctors/Dentist	❏	❏			❏
Business Cards	❏	❏			❏
Business Stationery	❏	❏			❏
Utilities	❏	❏			❏
Taxes	❏	❏			❏
Credit Cards:					
	❏	❏			❏
	❏	❏			❏
	❏	❏			❏

The Business Side of Marriage

GROOM'S *Name* and *Address* CHANGE WORKSHEET

Items to Be Changed	Change Name	Change Address	Account or Policy Number, Other Information	Phone or Address to Notify Company	Done
Social Security	❏	❏			❏
Driver's License	❏	❏			❏
Car Registration	❏	❏			❏
Voter's Registration	❏	❏			❏
Passport	❏	❏			❏
Employee Records	❏	❏			❏
School Records	❏	❏			❏
Checking Accounts	❏	❏			❏
Savings Accounts	❏	❏			❏
Ira Accounts	❏	❏			❏
Safety Deposit Box	❏	❏			❏
Stocks And Bonds	❏	❏			❏
Loans	❏	❏			❏
Wills/Trusts	❏	❏			❏
Pensions	❏	❏			❏
Property Titles	❏	❏			❏
Leases	❏	❏			❏
Subscriptions	❏	❏			❏
Club Memberships	❏	❏			❏
Post Office	❏	❏			❏
Auto Insurance	❏	❏			❏
Property Insurance	❏	❏			❏
Medical Insurance	❏	❏			❏
Life Insurance	❏	❏			❏
Doctors/Dentist	❏	❏			❏
Business Cards	❏	❏			❏
Business Stationery	❏	❏			❏
Utilities	❏	❏			❏
Taxes	❏	❏			❏
Credit Cards:					
	❏	❏			❏
	❏	❏			❏
	❏	❏			❏

The Business Side of Marriage

NAME and *Address* CHANGE *Form* LETTER

To Whom It May Concern:

    This letter is to inform you of our recent marriage and our change of address.

The account/policy number to be changed is: _____

Currently under the name of: _____

Social Security Number *(where applicable)* _____

PREVIOUS INFORMATION

Husband's Name

_____

Husband's Previous Address

_____

City   State   Zip

Phone

Wife's Name

_____

Wife's Previous Address

_____

City   State   Zip

Phone

NEW INFORMATION

Husband's Name

_____

Husband's New Address

_____

City   State   Zip

Phone

Social Security # *(when applicable)*

_____

Wife's Name

_____

Wife's New Address

_____

City   State   Zip

Phone

Social Security # *(when applicable)*

_____

As of this date _____ please change the following:

❏ Change Name   ❏ Change Address and Phone   ❏ Add Spouse's Name

Special Instructions:

_____

_____

Please send any additional forms or requirements to facilitate these changes.

If you have any questions, please contact us!

    Sincerely,

_____   _____

Husband's signature   *Wife's signature*

twenty-four

The SECOND time *Around*

IF *this* Wedding ISN'T *your* FIRST

Thirty percent of all marriages today are second marriages and so many of the old traditions are changing. There are a number of alternatives and choices that may fit your individual situation. Your decisions may be determined by you and your fiancé's age, whether children are involved, and/or if this is a second marriage for both of you or just one of you.

ANNOUNCING YOUR ENGAGEMENT

When children from previous marriages are involved, you should tell them first. Chances are they already have an idea, but they still need to hear the news from you. It needs to be handled carefully and with love. You want them to feel they are gaining another caring adult in their lives. You don't want them to feel as if they're losing a parent or having an existing parent replaced. You also need to notify a former spouse when children are involved, preferably before the children spill the news.

Afterwards, let your parents know the good news; then, of course, tell your friends and relatives. Traditionally, if it's the bride's second marriage, a formal announcement is not made. If it is the bride's first, and the groom's second marriage, a formal engagement announcement is customary.

PLANNING YOUR CEREMONY

If the bride is getting married for the first time, then everything remains traditional. The wedding may be as formal and religious as you would like, depending on your particular denomination.

One of the first things you should do when planning a second wedding is to find out all regulations or restrictions on the remarriage of a divorced person. Your house of worship or officiant is a good place to start.

If the bride has been married before, a semi-formal or informal wedding is usually chosen, rather than a large, very formal wedding. The exception to this would be if the bride never had a large, formal first wedding, or has no children. Another exception could be when it is the bride's second, but the groom's first marriage. In this case the groom's parents may want to host the wedding or the couple may choose to pay for it themselves. In any case, it is not right to expect the bride's family to pay for a second large wedding.

When it is both the bride's and the groom's second marriage, it is best to have a tasteful semi-formal or informal wedding. It may still be in a church, chapel, home, hotel, or club. There should be a maid or matron of honor in the ceremony but no bridesmaids. Similarly, the groom should have a best man but should only have ushers if they are needed, and they would not stand at the altar. When there are children from previous marriages, the couple may want to involve them in some way, depending on their ages.

THE WEDDING DRESS

With the increase of second marriages, designers in the bridal industry are making a great number of beautiful dresses for the encore bride-to-be. You may select a romantically feminine, lacy dress of mid-calf or ankle length in white or ivory, or a traditionally elegant knee length dress or suit in white or pastel. What you choose to wear will depend on the formality of the ceremony, the time of day and, most important, what you feel good wearing.

Yes, you may wear white. However, a veil, the symbol of virginity, should not be worn. Instead, wear a hat or a wreath of fresh flowers. You may also want to carry a bouquet or a flower-trimmed prayer book.

INVITATIONS AND ANNOUNCEMENTS

When the ceremony is larger than just a few close friends and relatives, including, say, thirty or more guests, you should send printed invitations.

Usually the person who is hosting the ceremony and reception issues the invitations. Again the wording of them will depend on your individual situation (examples are given in the chapter on invitations).

Gifts are not expected for a second wedding, though many guests may choose to send one. Accept any gifts graciously and acknowledge them with thank you notes. It is not correct to indicate "no gifts" on the invitation.

When a large reception follows a small ceremony, a formal reception invitation should be sent to all the guests; simply insert a ceremony card for guests who are invited to both.

THE RECEPTION

The reception may be any size or style you wish. Neither the bride's nor the groom's previous marriages have any effect on this. Having a large reception is a nice way to include friends who couldn't be a part of the ceremony.

You may still toast with champagne, cut the wedding cake, and have a "first dance." You might want to consider omitting first wedding customs like tossing the bride's bouquet and garter.

REAFFIRMING YOUR WEDDING VOWS

You've hit the jackpot. You're living the romantic life we all aspire to and have been married for ten or even fifty years. What better way to celebrate your good fortune and dedication to each other than by reaffirming your vows.

Reaffirming the wedding vows has become more popular in recent years, especially with couples who had civil ceremonies or eloped, due to convenience or lack of finances. The renewal of vows occasionally takes place shortly after the wedding day, but more commonly takes place years after the couple was originally married.

The couple may choose to repeat the same vows

they once said, or they may want to write new ones that express the way their love for one another has grown over the years. The ceremony possibilities for a reaffirmation are varied. You may choose a small ceremony with close friends and family, or larger one that includes new friends you have acquired over the years. You may want to have it in a church, or plan it at your home, or in your garden, a perfect symbol of the life you have nurtured together. It's a nice idea to make children, if there are any, a part of the ceremony. Many choose to combine it with a special anniversary, such as the tenth or twenty-fifth. Then they have the ceremony first, followed by a festive party.

WAYS TO INCLUDE CHILDREN

Whenever children are involved in a wedding, the engaged couple has to make a decision as to the extent of that involvement. The choices will be determined by the couple's own preferences and the needs and desires of the children. Merging two separate families is not always easy. Depending on how it is handled, it can either be unifying for the couple or it can add increased tension to an already difficult task. It is important to realize that the way the issue of children is dealt with now can influence how successful you may be in merging the two families later.

The most important thing is for you and your fiancé to communicate and discuss with each other your feelings and thoughts on the children's role in the wedding. The remarriage of a parent is difficult for most children to accept. To make it as easy as possible for children to adjust to the new situation, you should include them in the wedding plans from the very beginning. They should not merely be told you're getting married, but should be made to feel they are actively involved as participants in the planning, shopping and decision-making. Of course, every situation is different. Some children may choose not to become involved, and that's

okay. But what's important is to make them feel very special during this hectic time, when they could easily feel neglected.

If you and your fiancé decide you don't want the children involved in the actual ceremony, there are a number of other ways to include them in the wedding festivities. Finding some way for each child to participate will minimize their fear of being excluded.

TIPS FOR HANDLING CHILDREN
The following are some ideas.

→ They should be the first to be told the exciting engagement news. It's best they hear it from you, and not someone else.

→ You and your fiancé should discuss ahead of time the type and degree of the children's participation with which you're comfortable. Avoid disagreements and hurt feelings.

→ Consider including them in the bridal party — as bridesmaids, best man, usher, flower girl, or ring bearer.

→ Ask for their help in specific areas. Take them shopping and ask their opinions.

→ Include the children in a "special ceremony" within the wedding ceremony.

SPECIAL CEREMONIES TO INCORPORATE CHILDREN

CIRCLE OF ACCEPTANCE
This ceremony is a nice way to incorporate children into the ceremony. The children are called up to the altar. With their parent, the officiant, and new stepparent, they hold hands to form a circle. The officiant says that he realizes the children have had the undivided love and attention of their parent, and that it may be difficult to accept someone else into the family circle. They are reminded that now they have the love and support of both their parent and the new stepparent. He

suggests that, in the future, they should reflect back on this moment to help them overcome any difficult times. The officiant then states, "Your parents wish to seek your blessing and support..."; at that moment the children are asked to express their acceptance.

THE FAMILY MEDALLION CEREMONY

The Family Medallion is a symbol demonstrating that parents and stepparents intend to be faithful to the children brought together by remarriage. It was created by the Rev. Roger Coleman out of his experience as a clergy person performing wedding ceremonies, often with children present.

The Family Medallion is an attractive necklace given to children during the wedding. This unique symbol has three raised circles on its face. Two circles represent the marriage union, while the third symbolizes the importance of children within the marriage. Because the Family Medallion represents family love in the same way the wedding ring signifies conjugal love, it has become a universal symbol for family relationships.

After the newlyweds exchange vows, the children of both spouses are invited to the altar. During a brief ceremony, the couple places a Family Medallion around the neck of each child, as they pledge to love and support all the children either spouse brings to the marriage. This ceremony, "Celebrating the New Family," is easily adapted to any wedding tradition. ✳

Practice makes *Perfect*

YOUR *rehearsal* and REHEARSAL *Dinner*

There is an awful lot of stuff to remember for your wedding ceremony. Not only that, but you're relying on quite a number of different people to remember it. It would be easy to feel as if the execution of the details is completely out of your control. Not necessarily so. That is why there is the rehearsal.

The rehearsal is of critical importance. Only when you rehearse (and rehearse, and rehearse) can you be sure that you and everyone else involved has a good command and understanding of the parts they'll play and when to play them. Besides, everyone feels more comfortable if they've practiced a time or two.

Generally, the rehearsal takes place the night before the wedding, or at the most, two to three days before. Any earlier and it's too easy for people to forget what they've spent so much time practicing. Traditionally, there is a dinner party that follows the rehearsal, which is often a fun, intimate way to spend the night before your wedding with those closest to you.

Try to have as many of the details of the wedding in place for the rehearsal. Confirm that your ceremony site is available. (It is because you had the foresight to reserve it for the rehearsal far, far in advance, back when you booked the site for your wedding.) It's great if any musicians, soloists, or organists can attend, but the cost might be prohibitive. If that's the case, try to have recorded music from a small boom box or such available. Being able to rehearse to the actual music will help the attendants to measure their steps on the way down the aisle.

Mark out where the flowers and candles will be, and allow for any extra space you will need to accommodate them.

Your officiant or clergyman will be of big help here, they'll be able to direct you in the finer points of ceremony logistics. If you are uncertain or have any questions, now is the time to ask.

You will most likely run through the ceremony, without vows, but will be able to understand the order of the different elements.

It is a good idea to have a time schedule for the wedding day to hand out to everyone, as well as a list of each attendant's personal duties. For example, if all the bridesmaids are to dress together, let them know where and at what time they should be there. The ushers need to know you expect them there at least thirty minutes before the ceremony is to begin, and that they are to seat the brides' family on the left, and the groom's family on the right.

The Rehearsal Dinner

Traditionally hosted by the groom's parents, this is a chance for everyone to get together after the rigors of practicing the ceremony. In an effort to keep it from becoming too expensive or, worse yet, overshadowing the reception, you will want to keep it somewhat casual and informal. Choose a place that is conducive to good food, a relaxed atmosphere, heartfelt toasts, and the occasional emotional outburst.

At the very least, your entire wedding party is invited, along with their significant others. You will also include your immediate families, the parents of any children in the wedding party, and your officiant and their spouse. More and more, if couples have a number of out of town guests, they are including them in this event. It's a great opportunity to connect prior to the giddy busyness of the wedding day.

The dinner should be scheduled immediately after the rehearsal. Keep in mind that it doesn't have to be a dinner. If you're intent on making an early night of it (and you should be!) you can have a rehearsal brunch, lunch, or afternoon picnic or barbecue.

The rehearsal dinner is a great opportunity to thank your parents and your attendants, and give them any gifts that you may have for them. *

REHEARSAL *party* guest *list*

Date of Party _____

Location _____

Time _____

Phone _____

Name	Address	City	State	Zip	Phone
1.					
2.					
3.					
4.					
5.					
6.					
7.					
8.					
9.					
10.					
11.					
12.					
13.					
14.					
15.					
16.					
17.					
18.					
19.					
20.					
21.					
22.					
23.					
24.					
25.					
26.					
27.					
28.					
29.					
30.					

Practice Makes Perfect

REHEARSAL *checklist*

REHEARSAL SITE _____ *Date* _____ *Time* _____

   Address _____

   Contact Person _____ *Phone* _____

REHEARSAL DINNER SITE _____ *Phone* _____

   Address _____ *Time* _____

DON'T FORGET:

	Packed	Note
"Planning a Wedding to Remember"	❏	
Attendants' Checklist and Information	❏	
Parents' and Helpers' Duties and Information	❏	
Coordinator's Checklist	❏	
Wedding Programs	❏	
Maps or Written Directions	❏	
Wedding Day Transportation Information	❏	
Practice Bouquet	❏	
Shoes to Be Worn	❏	
Unity Candles	❏	
Wine Goblets, Wine, Opener for Ceremony	❏	
Toasting Goblets for Reception	❏	
Cake Knife and Server for Reception	❏	
Guest Book and Pen	❏	
Marriage License	❏	
Fee for Site Rental	❏	
Fees for Musicians	❏	
Fee for Officiant	❏	
Gifts for Helpers	❏	
Gifts for Attendants	❏	
Activities, Announcements, Comments	❏	

Practice Makes Perfect

Your HONEYMOON

PLANNING THE *Trip* of a *Lifetime*

*T*here is probably no other trip you will take that is as fraught with as much emotional significance and high expectations as your honeymoon. It's no surprise that many couples choose to spend the first night at an elegant hotel suite nearby in order to save the frazzle dazzle of jet travel until they have gotten at least a little rest.

When you study travel brochures a good nine to twelve months before the wedding, rock climbing, scuba diving, parasailing, and spelunking will all probably sound like wonderful adventures. But, if you've never done anything like it before, it might be best if you don't attempt it on your honeymoon. Too many new things, in too short a space of time, do not a relaxing and rejuvenating trip make. An exception to this would be if you are an Xtreme Adventure Couple for whom a trip without at least one blood pounding adventure (other than getting to spend time with each other — which is perfectly heart stopping enough for some) wouldn't be any fun. It's easy to underestimate just how drained and fatigued you might be after your wedding. Think about it. Twelve plus months of planning, saving, researching, partying, and anticipating have just come to an end. Don't you think you deserve a little down time?

Don't be surprised if you encounter the After Wedding Let Down Syndrome. You've been focusing on and planning the Big Day for months now, with it sometimes reaching almost obsessive proportions. Any day with that big a build up is bound to have a serious drop off when it is over. It's perfectly normal, expected even, and is not a sign that you've made a horrible mistake. Which is why it is best to avoid planning too much on your honeymoon. The two of you need this time to reconnect, reflect, and rejuvenate.

PLANNING YOUR HONEYMOON

Great, romantic honeymoons can be had in all price ranges, from less than $1,000 all the way up to $10,000 or more. As with weddings, it's important to set a realistic budget for this once-in-a-lifetime getaway. Once you have a budget in mind, begin exploring all the possibilities. Often travel agents will know about great deals that aren't advertised to the general public, and other ways to help you stretch that honeymoon dollar.

Begin your planning and saving as soon as possible, preferably right after you become engaged. The further in advance you plan, the better position you'll be in for taking advantage of off-season pricing and other early bird discounts. If you don't have a good travel agent, find one. A good travel agent can provide first-hand knowledge that can make final decision-making a lot easier. He/she can recommend the best places to stay. Travel agents are up on the latest and cheapest air fares, and give you tips on things to do, and what to take with you. Be sure to ask about:

- → Airline travel (or other preferred transportation)
- → Car rental
- → Cruises
- → Lodging
- → Promotions
- → Special rates
- → Tour packages
- → All-inclusive resorts

Don't forget to find out what documentation you'll need for visiting your location(s), especially if it's out of the country. Also check to see if there have been any travel advisories issued by the U.S. government, declaring certain areas to be unsafe for American travel.

CHOICES, CHOICES

It can be difficult trying to select the perfect honeymoon when the whole world awaits. The following questions are designed to get you talking and help narrow your focus as to what you are looking for in a honeymoon so you can decide on what is right for YOU.

HONEYMOON QUESTIONS

❋ ❋ Do you want to be with a lot of other people, partying, socializing, and enjoying activities together? Or do you want to spend as much time alone together as possible, savoring your new couple-dom?

_____

❋ Do you want a honeymoon resort that caters to and specializes in newly married couples? Or would that be too much of a good thing?

_____

❋ Are you interested in dressing up every night, indulging in cocktails and candlelight? Or do you want to spend the entire time in your bathing suits?

_____

❋ Do you like the idea of individual cabins or bungalows? Or a large hotel complex?

_____

❋ Do you want to wander off the beaten path and explore the native surroundings? Or opt for a pampering, all-inclusive hotel?

_____

❋ Are newer adventures on the menu? (Other than being newly married.) Do you want to try scuba diving, mountain climbing, or some other physical challenge? Or do you just want to kick back after the wedding and enjoy some uninterrupted time alone, resting and rejuvenating?

_____

❋ Do you want to explore the mysteries of a fabulous romantic city together? Or commune with nature's beauty?

_____

❋ Does the idea of Travel with a capital T appeal to your nomadic soul? Or does closer to home sound better?

_____

❋ Is your honeymoon budget tight? Or do you have lots of money to spend?

_____

Once you've decided on a destination, find out everything you can about it so that you'll be in the know when you arrive. Find out some of its local history, the best restaurants, must-see landmarks, and one-of-a-kind experiences. You may end up choosing to do none of them, but at least you will have made an informed decision.

PASSPORT _to_ anywhere

You'll need to apply for a passport at least six weeks in advance of your trip. You can't apply for a passport in your married name until after you've legally done the deed, so make international reservations in your maiden name. Photocopy your passport and keep the copy separate from your original, just in case.

SPREAD the _Word_

True love is hard for people to resist, even if they aren't the ones in love. While traveling or making traveling arrangements, it doesn't hurt to let people know you're on your honeymoon. Often service providers, especially those whose business isn't solely derived from honeymooning couples, will offer up all sorts of upgrades or complimentary services; flight and room upgrades, champagne in the room, or a complimentary dinner or drinks at the hotel's restaurant.

Now that you've narrowed down your wants and needs, here are some ideas to get you started.

Great Bargains
Aruba
Bahamas
California
Canada
Dominican Republic
Florida
Hawaii
Jamaica
Las Vegas
Mexico

Most Popular Honeymoon Sports
Snorkeling
Diving
Golf
Bicycling
Hiking
Tennis
Skiing
River Rafting
All Terrain Vehicles

Top Ten Beaches
Hawaii
Tahiti
Jamaica
Mexico
Cayman Islands
U.S. Virgin Islands
St. Lucia
British Virgin Islands
Aruba

Reclusive Hideaways
Antigua
Bali
British Virgin Islands
Fiji
Hawaii
St. Lucia
Tahiti

Winter Honeymoons
Alaska
Aspen, Colorado
Austria
Canada
Lake Tahoe
New England
Switzerland

Scuba Duba-Doo
Australia
Bahamas
British Virgin Islands
Cancun
Cayman Islands
Hawaii
Tahiti
U. S. Virgin Islands

Casinos
Atlantic City
Bahamas
Las Vegas
Monaco
Puerto Rico
Tahoe

Driving the Distance
California Coast
Napa Wine Country
French Riviera
Miami and Florida Keys
New England
Four Corners
British Columbia

Great Honeymoon Cities
Paris
Venice
San Francisco
New York
Rio de Janeiro
Athens
New Orleans
Sydney
London
Barcelona
Montreal
Miami

SOME HELPFUL HINTS

→ Take most of your money in traveler's checks for security.

→ Take national credit cards, if any, for things like car rentals.

→ Make a list of all traveler's checks, credit cards, and checking account numbers. Take it with you, but keep it in a separate location.

→ Label luggage with names, address, and phone number on the inside, as well as the outside.

→ Make a list of luggage contents. The list will be helpful if needed for claiming any losses.

→ Don't forget a camera; have it well labeled.

→ Carry with you the names, addresses, and phone numbers of your family in the event of an emergency.

→ Leave your destination and hotel plans with both families in case they need to reach you.

→ Make sure you have homeowner's or renter's insurance that covers your belongings, including all your new gifts. If not, increase your coverage.

→ Take your driver's license, marriage certificate, and passport or visa, if needed. ✳

HONEYMOON *Itinerary*

TRAVEL AGENCY

Address _____

Agent _____ Phone _____

Number of Days _____ Estimated Cost _____

Honeymoon Dates: From _____ To _____

Honeymoon Destination(s): _____

WEDDING NIGHT

Hotel _____ Phone _____

Address _____

Room Accommodations _____ Room # _____

Rate _____ Includes _____ Reservations ❑ Made ❑ Confirmed

TRAVEL RESERVATIONS *(airline, ship, train, rental car)*:

Departure/Pickup Date:	Time:	Carrier/Number:	Phone:	Arrival/Return Rate:	Date:	Time:	Confirmed
_____	_____	_____	_____	_____	_____	_____	❑
_____	_____	_____	_____	_____	_____	_____	❑
_____	_____	_____	_____	_____	_____	_____	❑
_____	_____	_____	_____	_____	_____	_____	❑
_____	_____	_____	_____	_____	_____	_____	❑
_____	_____	_____	_____	_____	_____	_____	❑

HOTEL RESERVATIONS

Arrival Date _____ Departure Date _____ ❑ Confirmed

Hotel _____ Phone _____

Address _____

Arrival Date _____ Departure Date _____ ❑ Confirmed

Hotel _____ Phone _____

Address _____

Arrival Date _____ Departure Date _____ ❑ Confirmed

Hotel _____ Phone _____

Address _____

Honeymoon *checklist*

Papers and Documents

Items needed, depending on travel destination	Packed/Have		Need to Get	
	Bride	Groom	Bride	Groom
Driver's License	❑	❑	❑	❑
Marriage License	❑	❑	❑	❑
Passports	❑	❑	❑	❑
Visas	❑	❑	❑	❑
Copy of Birth Certificate	❑	❑	❑	❑
Inoculations Needed	❑	❑	❑	❑
Copies of Prescriptions	❑	❑	❑	❑
Airline Tickets	❑	❑	❑	❑
Other	❑	❑	❑	❑

Traveler's Checks

Have ❑

_____   _____

Bank   Phone

Numbers: _____

Numbers: _____

Credit Cards *(Information to be used in the event cards are lost or stolen):*

Card Name	Company/Bank	Account Number	Phone	Bride's	Groom's
_____	_____	_____	_____	❑	❑
_____	_____	_____	_____	❑	❑
_____	_____	_____	_____	❑	❑
_____	_____	_____	_____	❑	❑
_____	_____	_____	_____	❑	❑
_____	_____	_____	_____	❑	❑
_____	_____	_____	_____	❑	❑
_____	_____	_____	_____	❑	❑

Checking Account Numbers *(In the event checks are lost or stolen):*

Name on Account	Bank	Account Number	Phone	Last Check #
_____	_____	_____	_____	_____
_____	_____	_____	_____	_____
_____	_____	_____	_____	_____

Doctors *(In case of emergency):*

Doctor's Name	Phone	Allergies, Medical Condition
Bride _____	_____	_____
Groom _____	_____	_____

Your Wedding *Day*

IT'S HERE . . . NOW *What?*

After months of planning, obsessing, and paying close attention to detail, it's here. Your wedding day. Quite possibly the single most important and remembered day of your life. Also, quite possibly, one of the biggest contradictions. It is supposed to be a day you spend in an ethereal cloud of romance and emotion. But, unless you've enlisted the services of an official bridal consultant or planner, or have an awful lot of help from family and friends, YOU are in charge of orchestrating one of the most complex and detail-oriented days of your life. Unless you have nerves of steel, the two of you will most likely be a wee bit nervous.

The good news is, the more you plan and check and double-check now, the better you can kick back and enjoy your wedding day. Savor it. Live in the moment. One of the best ways to live in the moment is to have planned every one of them so everybody involved knows which exact moment they're supposed to be living in. In a word, Wedding Day Schedule. Make one, a very detailed one, and give it to everybody involved, from the bridesmaids to the officiant to the caterer. Leave no person uninformed and leave no part of the day to chance.

YOUR WEDDING DAY SCHEDULE SHOULD INCLUDE:

- → A detailed, blow by blow, estimated schedule for the entire day
- → Names and expected times of arrival of all the players
- → Phone numbers of everyone involved, including cell phones and pagers
- → Directions
- → Transportation assignments and schedule

GETTING READY FOR THE CEREMONY

The first priority here is to have gotten a good night's sleep. Generally, the bride and her bridesmaids and close female relatives enjoy dressing together. It's part of the fun, so try to make time for that. Of course, you've given everyone in your bridal party a copy of the schedule so they know what time to arrive at your house or the church. Toward the very end of the dressing period, you may want to have the photographer join you for some fun, "getting dressed" shots.

259

The groom, best man, and ushers are all getting ready as well, and they know where to be when because you've given them a copy of the master schedule as well.

Make sure the bouquets and boutonnieres have arrived and that the ushers know their duties and have their list for special seating.

AT THE RECEPTION

Congratulations! Your hands and knees can stop shaking. You've made it through the ceremony, so relax, greet your guests, and enjoy the celebration. The reception usually starts with a receiving line, a nice way to greet guests and thank them for sharing your special day. If the number of guests is small, you may want to greet them immediately after the ceremony.

PLANNING YOUR TIME

As with the ceremony, the time goes by quickly, and it's a good idea to make a timetable for yourselves, your caterer, musicians, and photographer. Of course, this will be just a guideline to help maintain a smooth flow of events, but is especially necessary when you have a time limit on the location.

Most receptions last from three to five hours. Adjust your schedule accordingly. Below is a sample schedule.

FIRST HALF-HOUR

_____ Wedding pictures are taken, if they weren't before the ceremony. Guests start arriving, mingling, and getting something to drink. Music has begun.

SECOND HALF-HOUR TO HOUR-AND-A-HALF

_____ Receiving line is formed, guests pass through. Guest book is signed, and table cards picked up, if any. Hors d'oeuvres or finger food are passed.

SECOND HOUR

_____ Buffet is announced or guests seated, if you are having a sit-down meal. Wedding party is seated and served. Food is served to guests. Best man proposes the first toast.

THIRD HOUR

_____ Any speeches are made by the bride, groom, or family. First course is cleared from head table. Bride and groom have the first dance. Guests may follow on the dance floor.

THREE-AND-A-HALF HOURS

_____ Tables are cleared. Guests may mingle or dance. Musicians announce cake-cutting ceremony. Cake is cut and served. Dance music resumes.

LAST HALF-HOUR

_____ Bride throws bouquet.

_____ Groom throws the garter.

_____ Bride and groom change into going away clothes. Rice, birdseed, or dried rose petals are given to guests, if not placed on the table earlier, then tossed on the bride and groom as they run to their car. The bar closes, music stops, and guests start to leave. Parents gather personal belongings and gifts before leaving.

EVER AFTER

Settle into your getaway vehicle, then turn and look deep into each other's eyes. Now smile. Laugh even. You can be giddy with relief, or heady with joy, both are perfectly fitting. Congratulations. You've found the one you love and designed a celebration to match — truly "A Wedding to Remember." ✳

Bride's WEDDING Day checklist

Items	Packed
Written Vows or Poem to Be Presented	❑
Wedding Gown	❑
Veil and Headpiece	❑
Additional Headpiece for Reception	❑
Special Bra, Panties	❑
Special Slip	❑
Extra Hosiery	❑
Shoes	❑
Gloves	❑
Jewelry	❑
Make-up, Perfume	❑
Nail Polish and File	❑
Curling Iron, Curlers	❑
Comb, Brush	❑
Hairspray, Extra Bobby Pins	❑
Mirror	❑
Toothbrush, Toothpaste, Breath Mints	❑
Iron or Steamer	❑
Garter	❑
Penny or Sixpence	❑
Bible, Hanky, Etc.	❑
Ring Pillow	❑
Flower Basket (If not being delivered by florist)	❑
Going-away Outfit	❑
Going-away Undergarments	❑
Going-away Shoes and Hosiery	❑
Accessories, Etc.	❑
Wedding Night Bag (Placed in getaway car)	❑
Honeymoon Suitcases (Placed in getaway car)	❑

Groom's WEDDING Day checklist

Items   *Packed*

Written Vows or Poem to Be Read .... ❏

Coat .... ❏

Trousers .... ❏

Shirt .... ❏

Vest or Cummerbund .... ❏

Shoes .... ❏

Socks .... ❏

Suspenders .... ❏

Tie .... ❏

Ascot .... ❏

Studs and Cuff Links .... ❏

Handkerchief .... ❏

Underwear .... ❏

Hat .... ❏

Gloves .... ❏

Toiletries .... ❏

Money .... ❏

Credit Cards .... ❏

Other .... ❏

GOING-AWAY CLOTHES:

    Jacket .... ❏

    Slacks .... ❏

    Shirt .... ❏

    Belt .... ❏

    Tie .... ❏

    Shoes, Socks .... ❏

    Accessories .... ❏

Honeymoon Itinerary, Tickets, Etc. .... ❏

Wedding Night Bag (Placed in getaway car) .... ❏

Honeymoon Suitcases (Placed in getaway car) .... ❏

BEVERLY CLARK

c o l l e c t i o n

Turn your celebrations into something extraordinary

Here at the Beverly Clark Collection, we feel that each wedding is as unique and individual as the bride who plans it. Our goal is to provide you with as many choices as possible so you can design your perfect wedding. From practical planning tools such as our #1 best-selling "Planning A Wedding To Remember", to exquisitely designed bridal accessories that will capture your heart, we strive to offer a wide selection of exclusive keepsakes that will help make your special day even more memorable. The following is a sampling of our products. To see our complete line we invite you to browse our website www.beverlyclark.com or visit one of our retailers near you. Whether your wedding style is traditional, elegant, tailored, understated, glamorous, adventurous or whimsical, we have the perfect accessories to help you in creating a celebration that is uniquely your own.

The finest quality materials and workmanship, combined with unique design elements and exceptional customer service, make the Beverly Clark Collection the perfect choice for today's discerning bride. We invite you to browse this catalog, take a personal tour and experience...

17Q

Silver Heart Penholder

Ornate silverplated heart-shaped penholder
makes a cherished keepsake. 3" - 17Q

With black ink.

Love Knot

*An elegant band
of matte satin is
fashioned into a
dramatic knot.
White or Ivory.*

Guest Book - 92AI
Ring Pillow - 92BI
Penholder - 92CI
Memory Book Embossed - 92DI
Pillar Candle - 92PI
Flower Girl Basket - 92VI
Garter - 92GI

Lucky Sixpence for Your Shoe

*"Something old, something new,
Something borrowed, something blue,
With a sixpence in your shoe."*

— ANCIENT NUPTIAL RHYME

Keepsake booklet recounts tradition of the coin on your wedding
day and provides a place for your own family to record their
traditions with this Lucky Sixpence. To be handed down generation
to generation. Gift envelope, coin and booklet - 17H

English Garden

A cheerful burst of colorful flowers decorate this ensemble, making it look as if it had just been hand-picked from an English garden. The silk flower cluster is in hues of mauve, peach, yellow, lilac and lavender. Ensemble is available in ivory only. Guest Book, Penholder, Ring Pillow, and Memory Book come accented in your choice of dusky mauve or moss green sheer organza ribbon. The flowergirl basket, servers, flutes, pillar candle, and garter are accented with both colors.

Guest Book
  Mauve Ribbon - 90AM
  Moss Green Ribbon- 90AG
Ring Pillow
  Mauve Ribbon - 90BM
  Moss Green Ribbon- 90BG

Penholder
  Mauve Ribbon - 90CM
  Moss Green Ribbon- 90CG
Memory Book Embossed
  Mauve Ribbon - 90DM
  Moss Green Ribbon- 90DG

Flutes - 90L
Server Set - 90N
Pillar Candle - 90P
Flower Girl Basket - 90V
Garter - 90G

4

Simplicity Collection

Luminous, satin edged organza ribbon coupled with silken cord embellish peau de soie for a simple, graceful style. White and Ivory. White penholder comes with silver pen, ivory with gold.

Guest Book - 76A
Ring Pillow - 76B
Penholder - 76C
Memory Book -
 Embossed - 76D
Flutes - 76L
Pillar Candle - 76P
Flower Girl Basket - 76V

Also available but not shown:
Simplicity Tapers – 76T
Silverplated
 Cakeknife & Server Set - 76N

76P   76D

76A

76V   76C

76L

76B

76LI

76BI

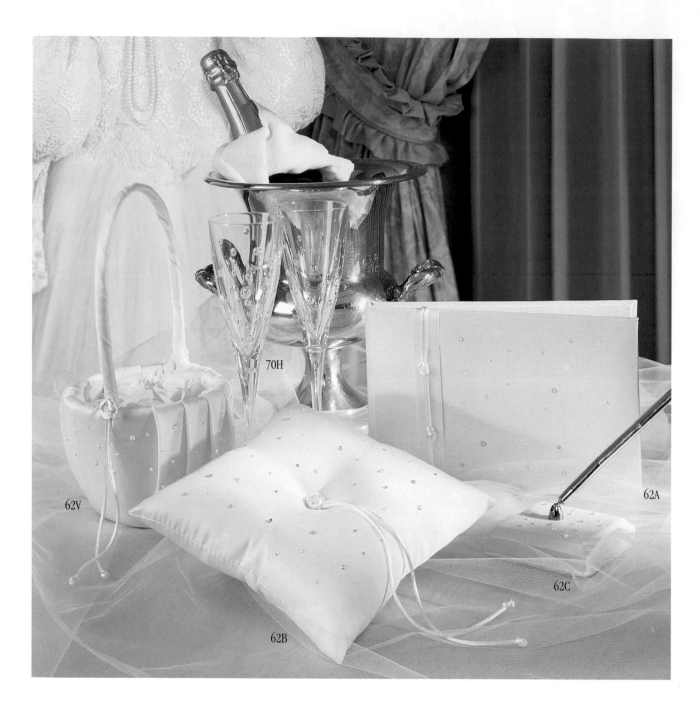

Celebrity Collection

Every bride is a star with the sophisticated glamour of white peau de soie
adorned with pearls and Swarovski™ crystals. White only.

Guest Book - 62A   Flower Girl Basket - 62V
Ring Pillow - 62B   Available but not shown: Memory Book Embossed - 62D
Penholder - 62C   Also shown: Celebration Flutes - 70H

93A

93C

93B

93D

93P

93V

93B

Birds of a Feather

Feathers, both delicate and flirty, add high fashion and drama to this white peau de soie collection.

Nestled deep in the feathers are three small pearl accents. White Only.

Guest Book - 93A	Pillar Candle - 93P	Available but not shown:
Pillow - 93B	Flower Girl Basket - 93V	Flutes - 93L
Penholder - 93C	Pillar Candle - 93P	Server Set - 93N
Memory Book Embossed - 93D	Flower Girl Basket - 93V	

Organza Bow Collection

Delicate Organza bow wrapped over Moiré, highlighted by a Satin rose. White or Ivory. Both white and ivory penholders available with gold or silver pen.

Guest Book - 35A
Ring Pillow 7" square with
4" pearled edge Organza ruffle - 35B
Penholder - 35C
Penholder with Silver Pen - 35CX
Video Box - 35D
Flutes - 35L
Drawstring Purse -35E
Money Bag -35K
Flower Girl Basket - 4R
Memory Book:
Color Illustrated Pages - 35G
Embossed Pages - 35H

Also avaialble but not shown:
Organza Bow Flutes - 35L
Pillar Candle - 35P Matching Tapers - 35T
Pearl Edged Purse - 35Y
Crystal Cakeknife & Server Set - 35N
Silver Cakeknife & Server Set - 35S

The Springtime Collection

Gossamer thin, layers of blush pink or lilac tulle enfold an elegant scattering of delicate hydrangea petals to create a look that is as fresh as early spring. White peau de soie with lilac, ivory peau de soie with blush pink. White penholder comes with silver pen, ivory with gold.

Guest Book - 58A
Ring Pillow - 58B
Penholder - 58C
Memory Book -
   Embossed - 58D
Flutes - 58L
Pillar Candle - 58P
Flower Girl Basket - 58V

Also available but not shown: Springtime Tapers — 58T
Crystal Cakeknife & Server Set - 58N

Whisper

The sheerest whisper of chiffon cascades into four flower-like petals, accented with a pearl cluster in the center. A row of satin-covered buttons adorn the flowergirl basket. White or Ivory.

Guest Book - 94A
Ring Pillow - 94B
Penholder - 94C
Memory Book
 Embossed - 94D
Pillar Candle - 94P
Flower Girl Basket - 94V

Amour Collection

This sophisticated collection shown in ivory peau de soie accented with beautifully sculpted rum pink roses. White rose detail available on white satin.

Guest Book - 41AI
Ring Pillow - 41BI
Penholder - 41CI
Memory Book:
Color Illustrated Pages - 41DI
Embossed Pages - 41EI
Pillar Candle - 41P
Flower Girl Basket - 41VI

Also available but not shown:
Tapers - 41T
Flutes - 20Q
Purse - 41Y
Money Bag - 41M
Garter - 19T
Crystal Cakeknife & Server Set - 20R
Silver Cakeknife & Server Set - 41S

Trés Beau Collection

Rich Moiré fabric enhanced with satin and organza ribbon bows. White or Ivory. Both white and ivory penholders available with gold or silver pen.

Guest Book - 38AI
Ring Pillow - 38BI
Penholder - 38CI
Memory Book:
Color Illustrated Pages - 38DI
Embossed Pages - 38FI
Flower Girl Basket - 4UI

Also available but not shown:
Penholder with
   Silver Pen - 38CXI
Pillar Candle - 38PI
Matching Tapers - 38TI
Crystal Flutes - 38LI
Crystal Cakeknife & Server Set - 38NI
Silver Server Set - 38S
Money Bag - 38MI
Purse - 38YI

Radiance Collection

*White peau de soie is accented
with silver edged organza ribbon,
white ribbon and
rosette, and rhinestone sparkle.
White only.*

Guest Book - 68A
Ring Pillow - 68B
Penholder - 68C
Memory Book - Embossed - 68D
Crystal Cakeknife &
 Server Set - 68N
Pillar Candle - 68P
Flower Girl Basket - 68V

Also available but not shown:
Flutes - 68L

Classique Collection

*A classic tailored bow enhances
this sophisticated, matte satin
ensemble. White or Ivory.*

Guest Book - 47A
Ring Pillow - 47B
Penholder - 47C
Memory Book with
Embossed Pages - 47D
Flower Girl Basket - 47V

Also available
but not shown:
Money Bag - 47M
Pillar Candle - 47P
Purse - 47Y

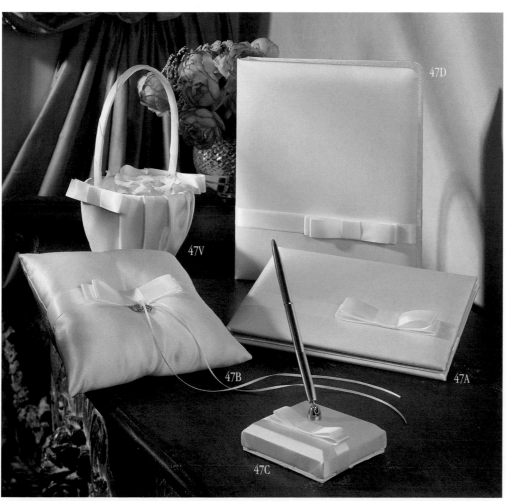

Vintage Collection

Delicate applique adorned with handmade satin ribbon roses and
miniature hand sewn pearls. White peau de soie with white applique
and silver pen, ivory peau de soie with ivory and blush applique and
gold pen. Flutes, servers and pillar candle are decorated with
coordinating rose clusters and organza ribbon. White or Ivory.

Guest Book - 55A
Ring Pillow - 55B
Penholder - 55C
Memory Book - Embossed - 55G
Flower Girl Basket - 55V
Pillar Candle - 55P
Baroque Pillar Stand - 29B
  and
Baroque Taper Holder Set - 29C

Also available but not shown:
Flutes - 55L
Silverplated Cakeknife &
  Server Set - 55N

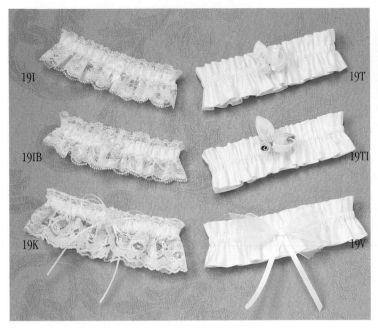

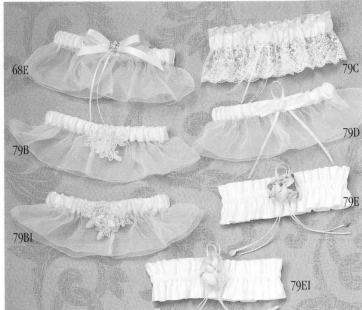

LEFT: 19I Angel
         19IB Angel with blue ribbon
         19K Queen Ann, also available as Throwing Set - 19KT

RIGHT: 19T Amour, also available as Throwing Set, - 19TT
         19TI Amour Ivory, also available as Throwing Set, - 19TTI
         19V Trés Beau, also available as Throwing Set - 19VT

LEFT: 68E Radiance
         79B Vintage White, also available as Throwing Set - 79BT
         79BI Vintage Ivory, also available as Throwing Set - 79BIT

RIGHT: 79C Petite Fleur, also available as Throwing Set - 79C
         79D Elegance, also available as Throwing Set - 79DT
         79E Springtime Lilac
         79EI Springtime Pink

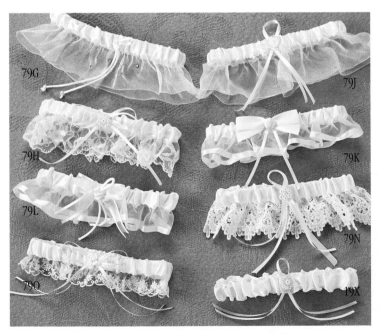

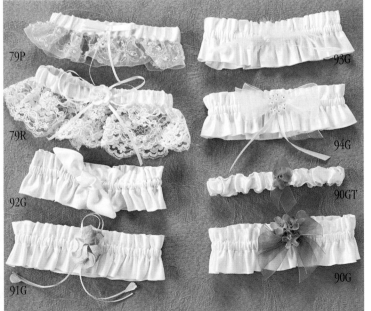

LEFT: 79G Celebrity, white only, also available as Throwing Set - 79GT
         79H Bridal Tapestry, also available as Throwing Set - 79HT
         79L Simplicity, also available as Throwing Set - 79LT
         79O Emily

RIGHT: 79J Primrose, also available as a Throwing Set – 79JT
         79K Sheer Romance, also available as a Throwing Set – 79KT
         79N Victoria
         19X Simplicity Throwing Garter

LEFT: 79P Silver Shimmer, White Only
         79R Charisma, also available as a Throwing Set – 79RT
         92G Love Knot, also available as a Throwing Set – 92GT
         91G Something Blue

RIGHT: 93G Birds of a Feather, White Only,
            also available as a Throwing Set- 93GT
         94G Whisper, also available as a Throwing Set – 94GT
         90G English Garden, Ivory Only,
            also available as a Throwing Set (shown) – 90GT

All of our garters come in white and ivory unless otherwise indicated.

Silver Goblets

Silver Vine Goblets

Silverplated goblets recreate a vintage style. 7.5" 7oz. - 17L

Victorian Goblet

Loving Cup reproduction of Queen Victoria's original goblet created by Charles Fox, whose work is recognized as some of the finest of the early Victorian period. Handcrafted, silverplated 6.5" 8oz. Sold individually. - 17E

17L

17E

20Z

Silver Cakeknife & Servers

Kings Crown

Ornate faux ivory handles with silverplate accent. Sold as set — 20Z

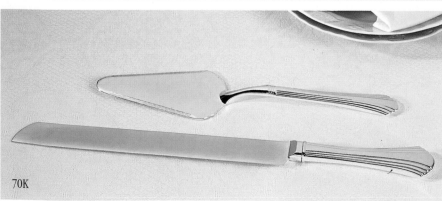

70K

Harmony Cakeknife & Servers

Understated, elegant silverplated cakeknife and server set— 70K

Flutes

70H

RIGHT:
Palatial Flutes

Exquisitely cut lead crystal flutes add romance to any occasion. Made in France 10" holds 6.25 oz. - 70I

TOP RIGHT:
Celebration Flutes

The effervescence of champagne is captured in these elegant cut crystal flutes. 10" 6.25 oz. - 70H

70I

BOTTOM RIGHT:
Pompidou Flutes

A contemporary style flute with gold accent. 9" 5 oz. - 20V

20V

20G

Mazel Tov Keepsake™

Celebrate old customs. Elegant 9" lace bag is trimmed with ribbons, complete with easy-to-break wine glass. White or ivory. 6.5"- 20G

80D

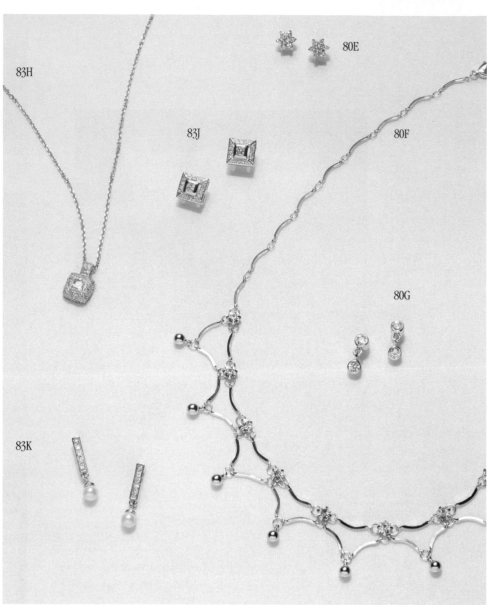

83H

80E

83J

80F

80G

83K

83F

83G

Jewelry Collection

Star Shine

Five dainty cubic zirconia stars hang from a 16" sterling silver chain. - 80D
Star shine earrings for pierced ears. - 80E

Interfusion

Platinum toned rhodium is fused into a delicate, 16" beaded chain, then accented with rhinestones for a look that is refined and graceful. - 83F

Moonlit Branch

Sterling silver and cubic zirconia capture the beauty of moonlight cast down upon a delicate branch. 16" - 83G

Stardust Pendant

One perfect cubic zirconia is set in a vintage, sterling silver setting then suspended from a dainty, 16" silver chain. - 83H

Stardust Earrings

Center cubic zirconia set in sterling silver and surrounded by glittering pave crystal. Pierced - 83J

Star Shine Earrings

For pierced ears. - 80E

Haley's Comet

One lustrous pearl suspended from a glittering "tail" of cubic zirconia. Pierced. - 83K

Northern Lights Earrings

Two sparkling rhinestone drops for pierced ears. - 80G

Northern Lights

Sparkling rhinestones and beads of silver suspend from this 16" necklace, capturing the beauty and brilliance of the Northern Lights. - 80F

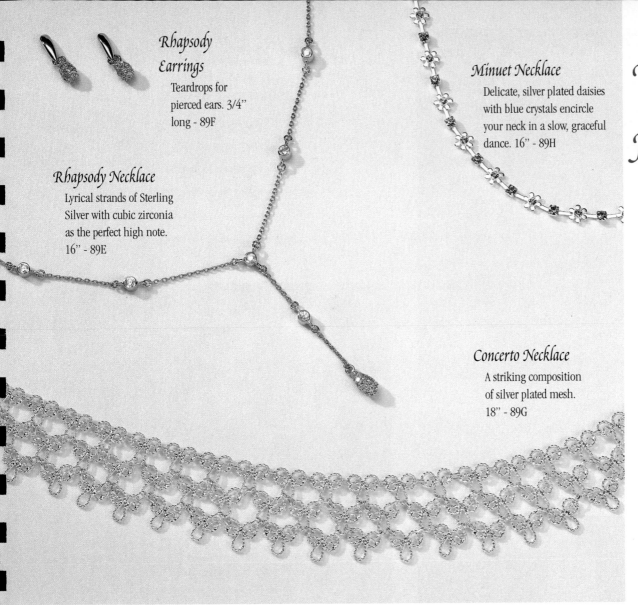

Rhapsody Earrings

Teardrops for pierced ears. 3/4" long - 89F

Rhapsody Necklace

Lyrical strands of Sterling Silver with cubic zirconia as the perfect high note. 16" - 89E

Minuet Necklace

Delicate, silver plated daisies with blue crystals encircle your neck in a slow, graceful dance. 16" - 89H

Concerto Necklace

A striking composition of silver plated mesh. 18" - 89G

Wedding Melodies Jewelry Collection

BELOW:

Grey Mist

Floating simulated grey pearls on a slender silver strand, 16" - 86B Coordinating earrings - 86D

Mist

Floating simulated white pearls on a slender silver strand, 16" - 86A Coordinating earrings - 86C

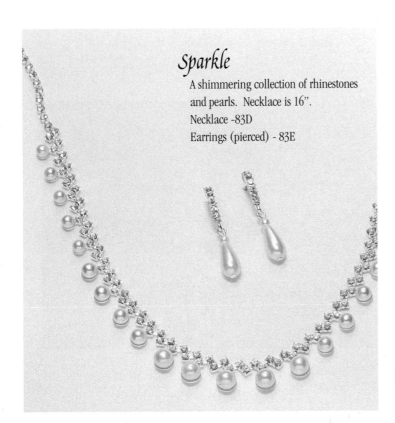

Sparkle

A shimmering collection of rhinestones and pearls. Necklace is 16".
Necklace -83D
Earrings (pierced) - 83E

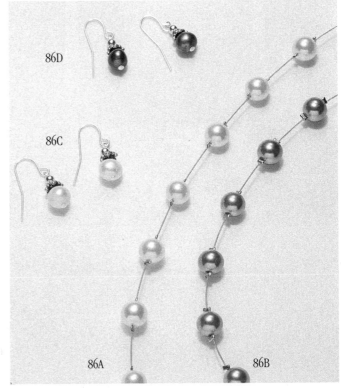

86D

86C

86A

86B

Unity Candle Collection

The lighting of a Unity Candle to symbolize marriage as "two becoming one" has become an integral part of today's wedding service for many couples. Each of our Unity Candles includes a 20 page booklet with information regarding this wedding tradition. The booklet includes poems, prayers, blessings and ceremony suggestions for incorporating this popular custom.

Ornate Silver Candelabra

Easily converts to a three taper candelabra (attachment included). Silverplated. 12.75" h - 29U

Framed Floral Portrait Pillar Candle - 27P
Framed Floral Taper - 28P

Small Brass Unity Candle Holder

Holds 3" Unity Candle and 2 Tapers, 3.75"h X 11"w - 29E
Trés Beau Pillar Candle - 38PI and Matching Tapers - 38TI

Ruffled Gold Unity Stand

This unity stand easily converts to a three taper candelabra with the included attachment kit. 9" h - 29R

Ruffled Gold and Silver Unity Stand

Conversion attachment included. 9" h - 29T

Silver Unity Candle Holder

Holds 3" Unity Candle and 2 Tapers, 3.75"h X 11"w - 29X
Organza Bow Pillar Candle - 35P   Matching Tapers - 35T

Crystalline Unity Candle Holders

Made in France of 24% lead crystal. Pillar stand can
also be used as a candy dish or floating candle holder.
Pillar Stand 4.75" tall – 29V   Taper Holders 8.5" tall – 29Z

Framed Floral Portrait Candle

White or Ivory. 9" high - 27P

Framed Floral Tapers

White or Ivory, 10" high - 28P

Brass Contemporary Unity Set

Sold in a set for pillar and taper candles - 29W

Loving Sentiment Candle

"On this day, I marry my friend ..."
9" x 2.75"   White only - 27M

Sculptured Heart Candle

Dramatically sculpted with romantic heart center.
8.25" h x 3.5" w. White only - 27N
Sculptured Heart Tapers 10" h. White only - 28K

Large Brass Unity Holder

Holds 4" Unity Candle and 2 Tapers,
6" h x 11" w - 29D

Picture Frame Placecards™

Not just for weddings, but perfect for showers, teas, dinner parties, holidays, fundraisers or corporate events. Mini frames advise guests of their seats and make wonderful favors. All frames on this page include calligraphy insert cards. Can be used horizontally or vertically. 3" X 4" Sold in packs of 10. Frame opening 2" x 3". Decorations not included.

FRONT TO BACK:

18S - Ivory Moiré	18B - White Brocade
18Q - White Moiré	18N - Ivory Brocade
13M - Brushed Silver	18R - Matte Gold

FRONT TO BACK:

13N - Spring Green	13Q - Loden	18U - Black Moiré
13O - Lilac	13L - Wine	18K - Assortment (14)
13P - Sapphire Blue	18C - Gold Moiré	

Picture Frames

These beautiful silverplated frames are an elegant way to advise guests of their seating arrangements and provide them with a keepsake of your wedding. All frames listed below include calligraphy insert cards. Opening size noted below. Cobalt blue or black velvet linings.

LEFT:

Large Silver Arch Frame
4.625" x 6.75",
Opening 3.25" x 4.625" - 60J

Large Triple Banded Frame
4.75" x 6.125",
Opening 3.125" x 4.625" - 60K

60K

60J

Baroque Silver Rectangle Frame
4.625" x 3.625", Opening 3" x 2.25" - 60F

Silver Celebration Frame
3.125" x 1.5", Opening 2.125" x 1.5" - 17ZA

Matte Wave Silver Frame
4" x 3", Opening 2.75" x 1.75" - 60U

Petite Simply Silver
2" x 1.5", Opening 1.5" x 1" - 60A

Simply Silver Frame
2.5" x 2", Opening 1.75" x 1.25" - 60W

60F

17ZA

60W

60A

60U

FRAMES SOLD IN PACKS OF 10.

Gold Frames
Detailed wooden frames
with gold finish. 2 x 3.5"
Regency, pack of 10,
Opening 2.125"x 2.25"- 60R
Versailles, pack of 10,
Opening 2.125"x 2.625"- 60S

60R

60S

21

Favors

Organza Bags

Little bags of shimmering organza in a fresh palette of colors offer wonderful ways to thank your guests. Fill with candy, birdseed, rose petals, potpourri. Perfect for decorating, can also be used as gift bags. Sold in sets of 20. 3.25" w x 5.25" h

61M - White 61R - Sapphire
61N - Ivory 61S - Loden
61O - Pale Lilac 61T - Ruby
61P - Shell Pink 61U - Silver
61Q - Sky Blue 61V - Black

61W - Assortment Pack
(2 each of all ten colors)

Wedding Bubbles

What could be more romantic than sending the newlyweds off in a shower of bubbles! These tiny bottles hold a bubble wand and 0.6 oz. solution.

Undecorated, pack of 24 - 17ZI
Champagne Bottle, pack of 24 - 17ZL
Dove Bubbles, pack of 24 - 17ZM
Wedding Cake Bubbles – 17ZN

CANDY AND DECORATIONS NOT INCLUDED.

Gift Favor Box

A present for your guests that needs no wrapping!
White porcelain is accented in gold or platinum.
Sold in sets of 10.
White and Gold. 2"x 2"x 2.5" h - 66A
White and Platinum 2"x 2"x 2.5" h - 66F

Porcelain Shopping Bag

A dainty little porcelain bag just waiting to be
filled with treats for your guests. White porcelain
can be written on with liquid paint pens or
decorated as you wish. Sold in sets of 10.
2.5"w x 2.5" h x 1.5"d
White Porcelain Shopping Bag - 67S

Placecard Holders

Porcelain Bow Placecard Holder,
White only. Sold in sets of 20. 2" x 3" - 66V
Silver Star Placecard Holder , 1" x 1" - 66T
Silver Shell Placecard Holder, 1" x 1" - 67T
Silver Sphere Placecard Holder, 1" x 1" - 67U
Placecard Sample Pack
(1 each of four styles) - 60Z6

Silver Coaster

Silver Coaster with an ornate
edge makes a perfect dish in
which to put truffles, petit
fours, and other confections.
Lends itself to a wonderful
variety of decorating
possibilities. 3.825"
Silverplate Coaster
(set of six) - 17ZB

Silver Basket

This charming silver basket
makes a memorable keepsake
that your guests will love to take
home. Use as is or let your
imagination be your guide as
you decorate and fill this
appealing wedding keepsake.
3.5"w x 4" h
Silverplate Favor Basket
(pack of 10) - 65H

Silver Bell

Use alone or personalize
this bell with your own
decorations for a
wonderful wedding
keepsake that your guests
will treasure. 4" h
Silverplate Bell - 65B

67A

67C

61G

67B

Favor Boxes

Floral Favor Boxes

White high-gloss boxes are topped with a silk flower. Now available in two styles

Sold in sets of 20. 2" x 2" x 2.5"

67A - Periwinkle Zinnia
67B - Buttercup Zinnia
67C - Cranberry Zinnia
61G - Crème Zinnia
61I - Zinnia Floral Assortment (5 each of four colors)

61E - Red Rose
61F - Yellow Rose
66D - Ivory Rose
67D - Peach Rose
61H - Rose Floral Assortment (5 each of four colors)

61E

61F

66D

67D

Cake Top Collection

Silhouette Caketop

This bridal couple makes a sophisticated, elegant caketop and will serve as a wonderful keepsake afterwards.
5.5" h x 3.5" w x 6.4 oz. Ivory - 6W
White - made especially for the Beverly Clark Collection - 6X

Love Doves

Musical. Love birds rest upon book of inspiration, accented with tiny pink roses against white bisque finish. Porcelain 5.5" h x 4" w 9.2 oz. plays "Speak Softly Love" - 6R

Wedding Cake Charm Bracelet

Our popular Victorian tradition wedding cake charms are now available as a charm bracelet. Perfect shower or bridesmaid gift. 7.5" – 89I

17ZCH

Wedding Cake Charms

Revive a romantic, Victorian tradition with these Wedding Cake Charms. Attached to white pulling ribbon, each of six silverplated charms brings a loving spell to your bridesmaids and foretells their future. - 17ZCH

Set includes:
Engagement Ring - *Next To Marry*
Heart - *Love will come*
Bouquet - *A Blossoming Relationship*
Horseshoe - *Lucky in Life*
Anchor - *Hope and Adventure*
Key - *The key to Happiness Awaits You*

Simply Elegant Money Bag

Sheer organza ribbon and pearl somethings adorn this peau de soie money bag. White or Ivory - 4A

Simply Elegant Money Box

Rich Moiré covered money trunk allows guests an elegant place to deposit their cards or envelopes. May be used later as a keepsake jewelry trunk. Accented with ribbon rose and cording. White or Ivory. 8.5" x 12.5" x 7.75" - 3K

Invitation Tray

Display your wedding invitation for all to see in this gold invitation tray. Opening 6.5" x 4.5" - 65P

Crystal Symmetry Penholder

is made of 24 % lead crystal 2.5" h x 2.5" w 1.5"h - 65Z

Silver Reflections Penholder

3" h x 2.5" w 1.25"h - 65X

Masquerade Crystal Penholder

This intricately cut crystal penholder holds a tarnish resistant gold pen. 2.25" h x 2.5" w - 3V
Also available in silver - 3VS

Baroque Pen

An elegant writing instrument of intricately sculpted silverplate. Silverplated - 17V

Faux Mother Of Pearl Pen

The luster of faux mother of pearl makes a striking presentation next to your guest book. - 65S

Family Medallions

*"With its three merged circles,
the Family Medallion™ celebrates love
as a relationship of more than two people,
it is a symbol of family.
As the Family Medallion™
is placed around the neck of each child,
it provides a unique opportunity
for those being married
to pledge their love
to all the children
either spouse brings to the marriage."*

— Roger Coleman

For second marriages involving children,
the Family Medallion brings them into
the ceremony, signifying the creation of a
new family. Pendants come with 18"
chain, keepsake booklet, poem and
numerous ceremony examples.

Silver Family Medallion - 23E
Family Medallion - 23A

Flowergirl Necklace

Delight one of the youngest
members of your bridal party
with this charming keepsake.
Sterling Silver. .75" x .5", 15"
chainComes gift boxed. - 23F

Flowergirl Gifts

Angelique Garter

A miniature lace garter
that is perfect for little
flower girls who want to
feel all grown up. — 23G
Removable Angel Pin
can be used as jewelry.

Tussy Mussies

Intricately designed bouquet holders

Trumpet Blossom
Goldplated or Silverplated
4.75" - 17TQG

Rose Garden Goldplate and
Silverplate - 17TR

Pearlescent Scepter. 7.25" - 17TS

Trumpet Blossom
Silverplated 4.75" - 17TQS

Wedding Party T-shirts & Hats

This is a special time in your life — announce it to the world with these highest quality, 100% luxurious cotton T-Shirts with beautifully embroidered lettering.

Bride - 21A
Groom - Black -21B
Ring Bearer with Bear detail - 21C
Flower Girl with bouquet detail - 21D
Mother of the Bride - 21E
Mother of the Groom - 21F
Bride Hat - 21H
Groom Hat - Black - 21J
Father of the Bride Hat - 21M
Father of the Groom Hat - 21N

Handkerchief Collection

16H

All the handkerchiefs include a four page booklet with poem and instructions to convert bridal handkerchief to a baby bonnet. A true heirloom keepsake. Handkerchiefs available in white only unless otherwise noted.

LEFT:

"Mother's Tears" Handkerchief

Our popular Venise handkerchief embroidered with touching sentiment.
White only 11" - 16H

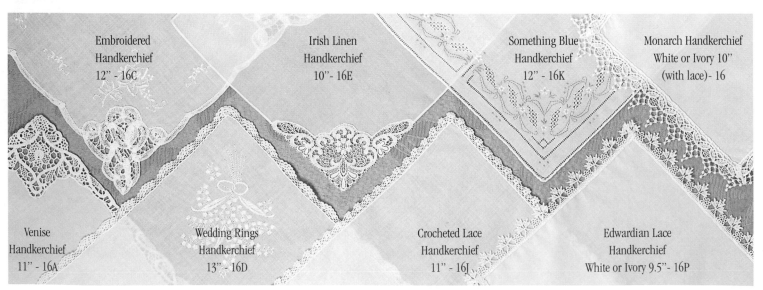

Embroidered Handkerchief 12" - 16C

Irish Linen Handkerchief 10"- 16E

Something Blue Handkerchief 12" - 16K

Monarch Handkerchief White or Ivory 10" (with lace)- 16

Venise Handkerchief 11" - 16A

Wedding Rings Handkerchief 13" - 16D

Crocheted Lace Handkerchief 11" - 16J

Edwardian Lace Handkerchief White or Ivory 9.5"- 16P

Congratulations!

You're engaged and your feet haven't touched the ground since. Well, soon you'll have to come back down to earth and begin planning the most romantic, exciting, and demanding day of your life.

Weddings carry an enormous weight in that they are a celebration that reflects the full emotional intensity of our decision on whom to marry. Toss in the fairy tale dreams of your youth, parent's dreams of a family reunion, and friends' expectation of an extravaganza on par with a Hollywood production, and it's no wonder planning them can cause some people to question their sanity, or at the very least, their grasp on reality. Rest assured, it can be done, gracefully no less.

In this new and completely updated and revised edition of "Planning a Wedding to Remember", America's #1 best-selling wedding planner, we've included planning tools and ideas that will help engaged couples remember to have fun and enjoy the planning process.

- Engaging new tips and ideas
- Quizzes to help you identify your own personal wedding style
- How to delegate and compromise
- A chapter on the wedding planning tools available on the World Wide Web
- Planning and etiquette advice
- Checklists
- Planning calendars
- Worksheets

Favorable Occasions
Favors for Weddings, Parties and Other Special Occasions
by Beverly Clark

Brides want to "give something back" to their guests and a "handmade" touch is often just what they're looking for to make their wedding uniquely their own. *Favorable Occasions* features a number of beautiful favors for all occasions, weddings, showers, dinner parties, Christmas parties as well as instructions on how to make them yourself. Filled with beautiful color photographs and simple, black and white instructional drawings, this book shows readers a wide variety of favors to make for all occasions. Each favor design includes a materials list, estimated time required, estimated price range of the project and whether it is designed for the beginning craftsperson or those more experienced. Each section will include favors that are simple and quick, as well as more elaborate, complex projects that are meant to be enjoyed by the craft enthusiast.

220 pages. 7" x 10" - 15V

Heartfelt Thank Yous
Perfect Ways for Brides to Say Thank You
by Beverly Clark

Being showered with wedding gifts is a wonderful experience, but making sure to thank all the generous gift givers can be overwhelming. This book provides information on how to write thank you notes that will make every gift giver feel special, as well as practical advice, checklists, index of phrases to use in the writing of your thank you notes, and a section on how to personalize the thank you note process.

7" x 7" 96 pages. - 15Y

Weddings
A Celebration

This magnificent coffee table book is a pictorial excursion through the world's most exquisite weddings. More than 500 luxurious color photographs feature romantic events from the traditional to the uncommon.

Featuring chapters on:

* Wedding Style
* Invitations and Favors
* Flowers
* Cakes
* Receptions
* The Wedding Party

This book is certain to spark the imagination of every bride. - 15R

15R

15C

15H

15E

Wedding Music Collection CD

22 of the most romantic, classical, popular, and original songs that are perfect for the wedding day. Also includes a place for notes on music selections that serves as a keepsake. - 15C

Wedding Memories

Record moments from courtship through 1st anniversary. Color illustrated, space for 26 shower and 242 wedding guest signatures and thoughts. - 15H

Bridal Showers

Includes special touches and unique ideas for throwing a fabulous shower! Full of planning and organization ideas, menu suggestions, recipes, fun themes, and Beverly Clark's special timesaver tips. 166 pages. - 15E

BEVERLY CLARK

c o l l e c t i o n

Turn your celebrations into something extraordinary

1705 S. Waukegan Road
Waukegan, IL 60085   877.862.3933
www.beverlyclark.com
email: info@beverlyclark.com
Price $2.00

WeddingLocation.com

Dear Brides and Grooms,

After years of helping millions of brides and grooms plan the wedding of their dreams using my books and bridal accessories, I have made it even easier to review and select a world of choices for your perfect wedding and reception location. Your dream location is now closer than you think... visit my Web site www.WeddingLocation.com and see where it takes you.

Beverly Clark

- ## quick, easy, direct site
  focusing on locations that host weddings and receptions

- ## preview all the features of the locations at home...
  no more wasted visits and telephone calls

- ## customize match your style, size, financial and
  geographic needs to fit your search

- ## contact locations instantly from the Web site

- ## save your favorite locations to review later and
  share wtih family and friends

- ## Looking for a *Romantic Getaway?*
  Enter our monthly contest to win a trip for 2 to a Romantic Destination

WeddingLocation.com

Fairmont Vancouver
Vancouver, Canada

Wilson Creek Winery
Temecula, California

Celebration Hotel
Celebration, Florida

Wyndham Rose Hall Resort,
Montego Bay, Jamaica

a world of possibilities.
Over 10,000 locations to choose from.